A FORCE FOR GOOD

ALSO BY DANIEL GOLEMAN

A FORCE FOR GOOD

The Dalai Lama's Vision

for Our World

Daniel Goleman

BLOOMSBURY

LONDON · OXFORD · NEW YORK · NEW DELHI · SYDNEY

Bloomsbury Publishing
An imprint of Bloomsbury Publishing Plc

50 Bedford Square
London
WC1B 3DP
UK

1385 Broadway
New York
NY 10018
USA

www.bloomsbury.com

First published in Great Britain 2015

Book design by Dana Leigh Blanchette
Title-page, part-title and chapter-title images © iStockphoto.com

British Library Cataloguing-in-Publication Data
A catalogue record for this book is available from the British Library.

ISBN: HB: 978-1-4088-6349-7
TPB: 978-1-4088-6343-5
ePub: 978-1-4088-6348-0

2 4 6 8 10 9 7 5 3 1

Printed and bound in Great Britain by CPI Group (UK) Ltd, Croydon CR0 4YY

To find out more about our authors and books visit www.bloomsbury.com.
Here you will find extracts, author interviews, details of forthcoming
events and the option to sign up for our newsletters.

Contents

Introduction

by the Dalai Lama

The fifty-six years since I left Tibet as a refugee for freedom in India have been hard for Tibetans including myself. One instruction from our tradition that has helped sustain us is to try to transform even the most adverse circumstances into opportunities. In my own case, life as a refugee has broadened my horizons. If I had remained in Tibet, I would most likely have been insulated from the outside world, shut off from the challenge of different points of view. As it is, I have been fortunate to have been able to travel to many different countries, to meet many, many different people, to learn from their experiences and share some of my own with them. This suited my own temperament that dislikes formality, which only serves to create distance between people.

As a human being I acknowledge that my well-being depends on others and caring for others' well-being is a moral responsibility I take seriously. It's unrealistic to think that the future of humanity can be achieved on the basis of prayer or good wishes alone; what we need is to take action. Therefore, my first commitment is to contribute to human happiness as best I can. I am also a Buddhist monk, and according to my experience, all religious traditions have the potential to convey the message of love and compassion. So my second commitment is to foster harmony and friendly relations between them. Thirdly, I am a Tibetan, and although I have retired from political responsibility, I remain concerned to do what I can to help the Tibetan people, and to preserve our Buddhist culture and the natural environment of Tibet—both of which are under threat of destruction.

I am very happy to see that my old friend Dan Goleman has written this book exploring and describing how these basic commitments have unfolded over the past several decades. An experienced writer and someone with an active interest in the science of our inner and outer worlds, he has been very helpful to me and is well qualified to express these things clearly as he has done here.

The goal of happier human beings living together and supporting each other more fully in a more peaceful world is, I believe, something we can achieve. But we have to look at it taking a broad view and a long-term perspective. Change in ourselves and in the world in which we live may not take place in a hurry; it will take time. But if we don't make the effort nothing will happen at all. The most important thing I hope readers will come to understand is that such change will not take place because of decisions taken by governments or at the UN. Real change will take place when individuals transform themselves guided by the values that lie at the core of all human ethical systems, scientific findings, and common sense. While reading this book, please keep in mind that as human beings, equipped with marvelous intelligence and the potential for developing a warm heart, each and every one of us can become a force for good.

February 8, 2015

PART ONE

A World Citizen

CHAPTER ONE

Reinvent the Future

The British Broadcasting Corporation transmits its world-news report globally, the shortwave signals reaching even the remote Himalayan hill district of Dharamsala and its ridge-hugging town McLeod Ganj, where Tenzin Gyatso, the fourteenth Dalai Lama, lives.

He numbers among the BBC's most devoted listeners, having started in his youth back in Tibet. He sets great store in its reliability as a news source, tuning in whenever he is home at 5:30 A.M., about the time he has breakfast.

"Every day I listen to BBC," the Dalai Lama told me, "and I hear news of killing, corruption, abuse, mad people."

The BBC's daily litany of human injustices and suffering has led him to the insight that most tragedies are the result of a single deficiency: a lack of compassionate moral responsibility. Our morals should tell us our obligations to others, he says, as opposed to what we want for ourselves.

Reflect for a moment on any morning's news as a barometer of humanity's lack of that moral rudder. The reports flow as a sea of negativity that washes over us: children bombed in their homes; governments brutally suppressing dissent; the devastation of yet another corner of nature. There are bloody executions, invasions, hells on earth, slave labor, countless refugees, even the working poor unable to feed and house themselves. The litany of human failings seems endless.

There's a curious sense of déjà vu about this. Today's news echoes last year's, last decade's, last century's. These tales of woe and tragedy are but current tellings of very old stories, the latest missteps in the march of history.

While we can also take pride in the progress made during that long march, we can only be troubled by the persistence of destruction and injustice, corruption and grinding inequality.

Where are the counterforces that can build the world we want?

That's what the Dalai Lama calls us to create. His unique perspective gives him a clear sense of where the human family goes wrong and what we can do to get on track to a better story—one that no longer incessantly repeats the tragedies of the past but faces the challenges of our time with the inner resources to alter the narrative.

He envisions a much-needed antidote: a force for good.

More than anyone I've ever known, the Dalai Lama embodies and speaks for that better force. We first met in the 1980s, and over the decades I've seen him in action dozens of times, always expressing some aspect of this message. And for this book he has spent hours detailing the force for good he envisions.

That force begins by countering the energies within the human mind that drive our negativity. To change the future from a sorry retread of the past, the Dalai Lama tells us, we need to transform our own minds—weaken the pull of our destructive emotions and so strengthen our better natures.

Without that inner shift, we stay vulnerable to knee-jerk reactions like rage, frustration, and hopelessness. Those only lead us down the same old forlorn paths.

But with this positive inner shift, we can more naturally embody a concern for others—and so act with compassion, the core of moral responsibility. This, the Dalai Lama says, prepares us to enact a larger mission with a new clarity, calm, and caring. We can tackle intractable problems, like corrupt decision-makers and tuned-out elites, greed and self-interest as guiding motives, the indifference of the powerful to the powerless.

By beginning this social revolution inside our own minds, the Dalai Lama's vision aims to avoid the blind alleys of past movements for the better. Think, for instance, of the message of George Orwell's cautionary parable *Animal Farm:* how greed and lust for power corrupted the "utopias" which were supposed to overthrow despots and help everyone equally but in the end re-created the power imbalances and injustices of the very past they were supposed to have eradicated.

The Dalai Lama sees our dilemmas through the lens of interdependence. As Martin Luther King Jr. put it, "We are caught in an inescapable network of mutuality, tied in a single garment of destiny. Whatever affects one directly, affects all indirectly."

Since we are all enmeshed in the problems, some of the needed solutions are within our reach—and so each one of us potentially numbers in this force for good. We can begin now, he tells us, to move in the right direction—to any degree we can, and in whatever ways are available to us. All of us together can create a movement, a more visible force in history that shapes the future to break free of the chains of the past.

The seeds we plant today, he sees, can change the course of our shared tomorrow. Some may bring immediate fruits; others may only be harvested by generations yet to come. But our united efforts, if based on this inner shift, can make an enormous difference.

The life journey that led the Dalai Lama to this vision has followed a complex course. But we can pick up the final trajectory to this book from the moment he attained a sustained global spotlight.

A Prize for Peacemaking

The place is Newport Beach, California; the date, October 5, 1989.

The Dalai Lama enters the press conference for his just-announced Nobel Peace Prize, to a chorus of clicking cameras and a strobe-like staccato of flashbulbs.

The Dalai Lama had heard he won the prize only hours before and was still on a learning curve. A reporter asked him what he would do with the prize money, at the time around a quarter of a million dollars.

Surprised to find that money went with the prize, he answered, "Wonderful. There's a leper colony in India I've wanted to give some money to." His immediate thought, he told me the next day, was how to give the money away—perhaps also to the starving.

As he often reminds people, he does not think of himself as the exalted "Dalai Lama" but rather as a simple monk. As such, he had no personal need of the money that came to him with the Nobel. Whenever the Dalai Lama receives a gift of money, he gives it away.

I remember, for example, a conference with social activists in San Francisco; at the sessions' end, the finances were announced (itself an unexpected gesture at such an event). There was around $15,000 left over from ticket sales after paying expenses, and on the spot the Dalai Lama announced—to everyone's pleasant surprise—he was donating it to a participating group for disadvantaged youth in Oakland, which had been inspired by the event to hold similar ones on their own. That was years ago, and I've seen him repeat this generous gesture of instant donation in the years since (as he has done with his share of the proceeds from this book).

The call from Norway saying its ambassador was on his way to deliver the 1989 Nobel Peace Prize declaration in person had come the night before, at 10:00 P.M., long after the Dalai Lama's 7:00 P.M. bedtime.

The next morning the Dalai Lama was doing his spiritual practices, which start at around 3:00 A.M. and last until 7:00 A.M. or so (with a break for breakfast and the BBC). No one dared intrude to inform him of the prize, so the public announcement went out before anyone could tell him the news.

Meanwhile, his private secretary was turning down a tsunami of interview requests from the top media around the world—a contrast with previous years, when reporters had often been reluctant to cover him. Suddenly the global press was clamoring for him; it seemed every major TV network and newspaper in the world was calling for an interview.

Though the phones were ringing constantly, that morning the Dalai Lama calmly instructed his secretary to continue with his scheduled event for the day, a meeting with neuroscientists. Because he would not cancel this meeting, the requests were turned down or delayed. A press conference could be added to his schedule at the end of the afternoon.

By that hour, close to a hundred reporters and photographers had reached a local hotel ballroom for the impromptu press conference. As they gathered, the photographers jockeyed in something like a rugby scrum for the best front-of-the-room camera angles.

Many reporters there had been hastily recruited from the nearby Hollywood pool that covered the film industry and were accustomed to an entirely different breed of celebrity. Here they confronted one who was neither thrilled by fame and money nor overly eager for exposure in the world press.

In the age of the selfie, when so many of us feel obligated to broadcast our every move and meal, these are radical positions. You are not the center of the universe, his very being seems to tell us—relax your anxieties, drop your self-obsession, and dial down those me-first ambitions so you can think about others too.

Consider his reaction to winning the Nobel. I happened to be present for his press conference, because I had just finished moderating a three-day dialogue between the Dalai Lama and a handful of psychotherapists and social activists on compassionate action.

Interviewing him for *The New York Times* the day after he heard about the prize, I asked him once again how he felt about it. In what he calls his "broken" English, he said, "I, myself—not much feeling." He was pleased instead with the happiness of those who had worked to get him the prize—a reaction signifying what his tradition would call *mudita,* taking joy in the joy of others.

Consider his playful streak. Archbishop Desmond Tutu, his dear friend, particularly seems to trigger this joyous, impish face of the Dalai Lama. When the two are together, they banter and joke around like small boys.

But no matter the decorum an event calls for, the Dalai Lama seems always ready to laugh. I remember a moment during a meeting with scientists when he told a joke at his own expense (as is often the case). He had been to many such meetings with scientists before, and, he told me, it reminded him of an old Tibetan story about a yeti who was catching marmots.

This yeti had stationed himself at the entry hole to a nest of marmots, and when one popped out, the yeti would lunge to grab it and capture it by putting the marmot under him as he sat down. But every time the yeti reached for another marmot, he would have to stand up—and the marmot previously captured would run off.

That, he said with a laugh, was just like his memory for all the scientific lessons he'd learned!

Then there was the time he was waiting in the wings at a college where he and a group of scientists were about to have a panel discussion. The prelude to that meeting was an a cappella choir of high school students entertaining the audience. But as they started, the Dalai Lama, intrigued, walked out alone on the bare stage, hovering near the choir as they sang, rapt.

It was an off-script moment—the rest of the panel and the university officials who were prepared to formally greet him remained backstage, befuddled. The Dalai Lama, self-contained, stood there beaming at the singers—oblivious to the members of the audience, who were beaming at him.

At an invitation-only meeting, two dozen CEOs were seated at a long conference table, with the Dalai Lama at the head. As they talked, a photographer who had been hired to document the session ended up on the floor next to the Dalai Lama's chair, clicking away with a huge telephoto lens.

The Dalai Lama stopped in mid-sentence, looked down at the photographer with bemusement, and suggested he just lie down for a quick nap. At the end of the session the same photographer snapped a rather formal group photo of the Dalai Lama with the business honchos.

As that group pose was breaking up, the Dalai Lama motioned the photographer over and, hugging him close, posed for a photo with him.

Such small moments seem unremarkable taken alone. But they number among myriad data points telling me the Dalai Lama lives by unique emotional settings and social algorithms: an empathic attunement to those around him, humor and spontaneity, and a level-ing sense of the oneness of the human family—as well as remarkable generosity, to name a few.

His refusal to be sanctimonious about himself—and readiness to laugh at his foibles—strikes me as one of his most endearing quali-ties. He flavors compassion with joy, not dour and empty platitudes.

These traits are no doubt grounded in the study and practices the Dalai Lama has immersed himself in since childhood and still de-votes himself to for five hours each day (those four in the morning and another hour at night). These daily practices surely shape his moral sense and his public persona.

His self-discipline in cultivating qualities like an investigative curiosity, equanimity, and compassion undergirds a unique hierar-chy of values that gives the Dalai Lama the radically different per-spective on the world from which his vision flows.

We first met in the early 1980s when he visited Amherst College; his old friend Robert Thurman, then a professor there, introduced us. At that meeting, I remember, the Dalai Lama let it be known that he sought serious discussions with scientists. This resonated with both my own background as a psychologist and my occupation as a science journalist for *The New York Times*.

In the ensuing years I arranged or took part in a handful of meet-ings for him with scientists in my own field, and for several years I sent him articles about scientific discoveries from the *Times*. My wife and I have made it a habit to attend his talks and teachings whenever we can. And so when I was asked to write this book, I jumped at the chance.

While most of my books explore new scientific trends and go into some detail, and though the Dalai Lama bases his vision on sci-ence rather than religion, this is not a science book. I bring in scien-tific evidence as it supports the vision or to illustrate a point, not as a primer. Those readers who want more can go to the sources I cite (and reader be warned: The endnotes here are "blind," without numbers in the text—but are there in the back nonetheless).

The vision that has emerged from my interviews with the Dalai Lama is, I'm sure, flavored by my own interests and passions, as is the telling. Even so, I strive to be true to his basic insights and the essence of the call he makes to each one of us.

The Man

Tenzin Gyatso came to this worldwide role through accidents of history. For more than four hundred years, since the institution began, no Dalai Lama—Tibet's religious and political head—had resided outside the territories of Tibetan Buddhism. As a child, this fourteenth Dalai Lama roamed the massive Potala Palace in Lhasa, where he was groomed, like those before him, in topics like philosophy, debate, and epistemology, and in how to fill his ritual role.

But with the invasion of Tibet by Communist China in the 1950s, he was thrust into the wider world, finally escaping to India in 1959. There he has resided since, never to return to his homeland.

"At sixteen," he says, "I lost my freedom," when he stepped into the role of Tibet's religious and political head of state. Then, when he left, he says, "I lost my country."

The moment of this transition was captured in the film *Kundun,* which tracks the Dalai Lama's early years. As he crosses into India from Tibet, the young Dalai Lama gets off his horse and looks back at the Tibetan guards who have escorted him this far. The tone is a bit wistful—partly because they have left him there in this alien new land, partly that he will likely never see them again; they are riding back to a country in danger, for which they may risk their lives.

As those familiar faces recede into the distance, the Dalai Lama turns, realizing he is now among strangers: his Indian hosts, who are welcoming him to his new home. But these days, as the actor—and his longtime friend—Richard Gere put it in introducing him at a public event, "Wherever he goes, he is among friends."

No previous generation of people living outside Tibet has had the chance that we have today to see a Dalai Lama. He travels incessantly, making himself available around the globe—speaking in Russia with devout Buddhist Buryats one day, scientists in Japan the next week, hopscotching from classrooms to overflowing auditoriums.

Perhaps the only force that hinders him from reaching more people is his inability to obtain visas from the many nations throughout the world that, pressured by China, fear economic consequences if they allow him on their soil. In recent years, hard-liners within the Chinese Communist leadership apparently see every activity of the Dalai Lama as somehow political, aimed at undermining China's grip on Tibet.

Even so, a sampling of one itinerary has him speak to students in New Delhi on "secular ethics," then journey to Mexico City where, among many other engagements, he addresses a thousand Catholic priests on religious harmony, has dialogues with a bishop, and gives a public talk at a stadium on compassion in action—and then is off to New York City for two days of teaching, before hopscotching to a peace summit in Warsaw, a quick stopover on his way back to New Delhi.

With this global immersion, he has stepped into a larger role as global statesman. It was slow going at first.

In the years before his Nobel, the Dalai Lama's press conferences drew just a handful of reporters. I remember the dismay his official representative in the United States expressed to me in 1988 when he made a major concession to the Chinese, saying his goal for Tibet was autonomy, not independence.

Though of momentous import to those supporting the Tibetan

cause (and likely one trigger for his Nobel Peace Prize the next year), the statement ended up as a one-paragraph story in *The New York Times,* picked up from a wire service and buried deep in the inside pages.

Since the Nobel, though, his movements have attracted more and more people and press, and he has become an icon even in pop culture: His face was once featured in an ad for Apple (with the phrase "Think Different"), and a seemingly endless (though sometimes spurious) series of inspirational quotes has been attributed to him.

His attitude here is spacious: While one senses he would just as soon be doing his predawn practices, the publicity, the celebrity, and the media storm can all be used for the good. Now his compassionate message, as his longtime English-language interpreter Thupten Jinpa puts it, has "a bigger microphone."

The Dalai Lama numbers among the small handful of widely admired public figures today who embody an inner depth and gravitas. Few if any "boldface names" match his moral stature or the power of his presence, let alone his breadth of appeal. His appearances worldwide draw huge audiences, often filling stadiums.

The Dalai Lama has traveled the world for decades, meeting with people of every background, social level, and outlook—all contributing to his perspective. The people he routinely engages range from denizens of shantytowns—from São Paulo to Soweto—to heads of state and Nobel-winning scientists. To his vast range of encounters he brings his own unflagging motivation: compassion.

He sees the oneness of humanity—the we—rather than getting lost in the us-and-them differences. The issues faced by "our human family," as he calls it, are global, transcending boundaries, like the growing gap between rich and poor and the inexorable decay from human activities of the planetary systems that support life.

From this rich mix, the Dalai Lama has fashioned a plan that can bring hope, drive, and focus to us all—a map we can turn to in orienting our own lives, in understanding the world, assessing what to do, and how to shape our shared future.

His vision for humanity, like the man himself, embodies a way of being and perceiving that upends many values rampant today. He envisions a world more caring and compassionate, one wiser in dealing with our collective challenges—a world more suited to the demands of an interconnected planet. And this vision of what could be goes beyond wishful thinking to offer the seeds of the pragmatic antidotes we need more urgently than ever.

A Transformative Voice

There was a child born to illiterate villagers in an isolated village. He had to flee his homeland and has been a man without a country for more than half a century.

He has never owned a home or a car or had a salary, let alone investments of any kind. He never had a family of his own.

He never attended an ordinary school; his education was a series of tutorials in arcane philosophical methods, rituals, and a curriculum developed some six hundred years ago.

And yet he has met regularly for deep discussions with some of the most advanced scientists in the world. He frequently visits with high-powered leaders, schoolchildren, and ordinary citizens of every kind, including those who live in slums, around the world. He travels ceaselessly, always ready to learn.

This, of course, describes the Dalai Lama, a person utterly rare on the planet, free from the many obligations that delimit the concerns of most of us to our own lives, our family and friends, our community, our country.

While he has none of the training of a specialist, his expertise speaks to other dimensions of life. He has accumulated wisdom rather than mere knowledge.

His is a special expertise. He is an expert on reflection and stillness, on selflessness and compassion. Almost none of us would even consider meditating five hours a day as does the Dalai Lama. Yet there is much we can learn from his deep practice and the resulting insight and caring that applies to how to live a good and fulfilled life.

When it comes to investing, we consult a financial expert; to our health, a doctor. And when it comes to our inner life, to how to be a force for good in this world, we can trust the Dalai Lama as an expert whose guidance can benefit us all.

Begin with looking inward and managing our own minds and hearts, he tells us. Then look outward from a more balanced place in ourselves, and consider the good we can do.

Don't be discouraged by the terrible news we hear; in reality, that reflects a small portion of the human story. Beneath the ugly tip of that glacier lies a vast reservoir of sensitivity and kindness—and each of us can enlarge that goodness.

Leadership happens to be an area I've written about often in recent years, and I find in the Dalai Lama several lessons for any leader. As we'll see, his vision for a better world excludes no one but rather reaches to every stratum of society and to people everywhere. There are no in-group biases in his message; he offers guidance to us all.

Nor does he dictate what action we should take. While he has several explicit goals in mind, he leaves up to each of us whether we follow his lead or not and, if so, how we choose to act.

He has no interest in our money, our "likes," our e-mail addresses to add to some list, or collecting us as "followers." He offers his perspective on life freely. It is simply there for our taking.

Refreshingly, rather than having some hidden selfish agenda, his leadership message revolves around a central organizing principle: genuine compassion. And his appreciation of the web of human interconnection gives him a genuine concern for all of us.

In talking with leaders from Davos to D.C., I hear the same plaints: Our guiding values have the very rich leaving the poor in the dust, planetary systems on course to meltdown, and governments paralyzed in the face of such urgent challenges. We need, they tell me, a new brand of leadership, one that excludes the mix of cynicism and self-interest that has left us facing a dystopian future.

The wider our sphere of influence, the more people we guide. In this sense the Dalai Lama has a global role, touching millions. He has become a de facto world citizen, wandering incessantly for more than a half century, spending months each year in far corners, meeting people of all kinds. The world's concerns are his.

Leaders guide attention, directing our efforts toward what matters. Typically this has meant addressing what's urgent in the short term: this quarter's targets, the next new thing, the coming election.

The business press tells us the best leaders are those whose wily strategies win market share and profit growth for their companies and spotlights executives who have shepherded their companies to exceptional fiscal performance. And while government leaders may sometimes try to fulfill a vision that rises above the gravitational pull of petty politics, the inertia of that system all too often prevents them.

While so many leaders today operate within the limits of things as they are and for the benefit of a single group, none of these concerns or limitations confines the Dalai Lama. This lets him expand our thinking to see how our systems can morph to benefit the widest range of people.

This makes the Dalai Lama a transformative leader, one who looks beyond the givens of today's reality to offer a map to a better future worldwide. Such leaders have grander horizons and so can tackle our largest challenges, thinking far into our future, paying attention to the issues that matter in the long run and for everyone.

They act not just for themselves or their own groups or organizations but rather for us all, on behalf of humanity itself. These are not by and large the leaders we have but are the voices we need. The world yearns for this kind of leadership.

The more altruistic the guiding values, the longer the time horizon, and the broader the human needs a leader addresses, the greater that leader's vision can be. Transformative leaders serve a transcendent purpose, pointing the way to a new reality. That's what draws me to the Dalai Lama's vision.

He may seem a surprising source for such guidance. People around the world admire his wisdom and compassion and are drawn by his charisma. But few realize his value as a futurist who ponders our problems and their solutions globally and over centuries, a visionary who senses what we will need to meet the demands of our coming reality.

There have always been two sets of audiences as the Dalai Lama toured the world: those interested in Buddhism, who attend his religious teachings, and the large throngs at his public talks. As the years have passed, his personal mission leaves him less interested in addressing the same crowds of Buddhists over and over; his religious appearances have dropped in number as his public talks have increased.

In articulating his vision, he speaks to each of us, not from his religious role but by wearing the hat of a global leader who genuinely cares about the well-being of every person on the planet.

As I write these words, this global leader is about to turn eighty years old. The time is ripe for a written message, a map into the future, from the Dalai Lama to the world's people.

The Vision

A while back a provocative article, "The Death of Environmentalism," argued that the movement had become overly negative in its doom-and-gloom messages. Martin Luther King Jr., it pointed out, captured the hearts of millions with a speech declaring, "I have a dream," not a nightmare.

Our course of action will be more compelling if guided by a positive vision, a guiding image of what things could be like one day. Considering what life *could* be like invites originality, new ideas, innovations.

To survive, of course, we need to recognize what's going wrong. But to thrive we need a North Star to follow to better alternatives—a rebooted GPS toward a more optimistic tomorrow. In formulating his transformative vision for our shared future, the Dalai Lama does not dwell on what's amiss but guides our focus to what could be right in our world.

"Vision," Jonathan Swift wrote, "is the art of seeing things invisible" to other people. The Dalai Lama's vision urges us to consider promising possibilities beyond the dark and dismal media messages we get daily.

On his travels worldwide, the Dalai Lama has articulated bits and pieces of this map toward a better future, but the totality has never before been consolidated in a single volume. With his guidance, I've sketched that vision here as a set of interlocking scenarios that combine his articulation with living examples, people and projects that are already making his vision a reality.

Our journey here starts with taking responsibility for better managing our own minds and emotions, which the Dalai Lama calls *"emotional hygiene"*: lessening the power of destructive emotions and fostering more-positive modes of being.

Such self-mastery lets us better target, cultivate, and act on the human values that he sees as forming a *"universal ethic"* based on the oneness of humanity and best expressed as *compassion toward all.*

The platform for this compassion-driven ethic and the self-mastery that enables it may seem surprising. The Dalai Lama does not look to any religion or ideology but rather grounds this world-view in empirical findings. *A science of compassion* can help humanity, he argues, by putting human values on a firmer footing.

A *muscular compassion* powers forceful action to expose and hold accountable toxic social forces like corruption, collusion, and bias. Compassion unleashed gives us a new orienting pole for upgrading systems like economics, politics, and science. In action, this means transparency, fairness, and accountability—whether in the stock market, financing an election, or reporting data.

In the realm of economics, an ethic of compassion leads to focusing on how goods are distributed, not just on how to accumulate them. A *compassionate economy* reflects concern, not greed. And businesses can find ways to do good even as they do well.

Understandably, from compassionate values flows an imperative to *"care for those in need"*—the poor, the powerless, and the disenfranchised. But this means going beyond simple charity to, wherever possible, help those in need rise to the task of caring for themselves with dignity.

Our planet is our home, and our home is burning, he cautions. Human activity of all kinds degrades the global systems that support life on this planet—and all of us together should make every effort to *"heal the planet."*

In a time when conflicts spawned by ethnic hatreds seem rampant, the Dalai Lama has the audacity to envision a long-term peacekeeping strategy, a day when disputes will be resolved *"by dialogue, not by war"*—an end to the us-versus-them mindset at every level, from small groups to entire peoples and nations.

And to carry the vision into the future, an *"education of the heart"* should help students cultivate tools for self-mastery and caring and for lives in keeping with these human values. If such education became a universal standard, coming generations would naturally act with compassion.

Finally, he urges us all to *take a long view of history,* but *"act now,"* moving toward the fulfillment of this vision in any way we can, using whatever means we have at hand. These changes will take generations; even if we will not live to see the fulfillment, the Dalai Lama urges, we can start this evolution toward compassion. Everyone can do something; each of us has a role to play. Our efforts writ large can reinvent the future.

Taken together, these elements are synergistic, the whole being greater than any single part. The Dalai Lama's vision can be seen as a set of interlocking decision rules for navigating our lives and our society to a better tomorrow.

The alternatives to business-as-usual outlined in this view have particular appeal in a day when more people are recognizing the false hope for fulfillment through power, money, or fame; the pointlessness of rushing ourselves into a frazzle; and the gift of a life lived with generosity, discernment, and joy.

The vision applies beyond our personal lives, offering a set of design principles for a society that enables the best in human nature. Its basis lies not in unfounded belief but in science and basic human values, and it speaks to us all.

In offering this map to a better tomorrow, the Dalai Lama transcends his roots. His message is not just for Buddhists or Tibetans but also for the whole of humanity, as well as those yet to come.

These possibilities for humanity transcend the drumbeat of negativity delivered by the daily news. These are not mere utopian whimsies but are even now embodied in practical strategies, some explicitly guided by his words, others independently arisen yet aligned. The goals are lofty, but, as we will see, results already in are encouraging.

To transform the Dalai Lama's vision into aligned action, this book has an accompanying Web platform, where all of us are invited to join together: www.joinaforce4good.org. This Web companion to the book you are reading will lead you to more resources as you go along, guiding you to actions you can take (or on which you can model your own) if you wish to join the Dalai Lama's Force for Good.

As we explore the contours of these possibilities, we will encounter people and projects already signaling how what might sound like mere noble dreams has become reality. The Dalai Lama directly inspired some; others simply align with his vision. To some extent he articulates what many feel already and are acting on. The Dalai Lama serves as an unofficial spokesperson for these exemplars of compassion in action, who all too often toil below our collective radar.

The Dalai Lama makes no claim to authority on the specifics for solving the crises of our day, be they social, political, economic, or environmental. But his own makeup, training, and life give him a deep assurance about the qualities of being we need to develop in order to be most effective in taking up these issues.

There's a Tibetan expression, he says, that translates roughly as "Make sure your brain is not too stuck, too rigid." Our human problems are increasing rapidly. Instead of taking for granted the world we have been given, we should constantly be questioning received wisdom and hidden assumptions. We must stay flexible and improve our minds, he tells us, as we act in the world.

We can each help, beginning wherever we are. The solutions will come in one form or another to each of us as we face our own corner of this vast vision. There is not one magical answer for all these questions but rather myriad ways small and large to change things for the better.

It is not enough merely to espouse a noble plan, the Dalai Lama tells us—we need to move toward it. The Dalai Lama's vision beckons us all.

Every one of us can be a force for good.

PART TWO

Looking Inward

CHAPTER TWO

Emotional Hygiene

Psychologist Paul Ekman may be the world's leading connoisseur of emotions, an avid explorer of the universe of feelings over his lengthy scientific career. Among Ekman's unique skills: reading a person's fleeting emotions via subtle changes in the movements of muscles in the face.

Not long before my initial encounter with Ekman back in the 1970s, he had spent a year—on a federally funded grant—staring into a mirror, as he struggled to master and map the movements of every single facial muscle. There are more than one hundred, and though some had been thought to be beyond conscious control, Ekman managed to tackle them all.

With that basic skill in hand, Ekman then mapped the movement of each muscle involved in expressing the basic palette of human emotion. His earlier research in the remote jungles of New Guinea with tribes that had virtually zero contact with modern life led Ekman to establish that six emotions are universal in human experience and in their expression: fear, anger, disgust, joy, surprise, and sadness.

His algorithms for the face's movements as we express each of these basic feelings—the Facial Action Coding System (or FACS)—have become a staple of emotions research. FACS has found applications ranging from helping police detect when a suspect might be lying to software that powers the animation of cartoon characters' faces. And designs for a new generation of "emotionally intelligent" programs, loosely derivative of Ekman's original research, might, for instance, help people with autism read other people's emotions.

The first time he and the Dalai Lama met, Ekman told me, the Dalai Lama's face struck him as unusual. For one, it expresses the full range of feeling; most people suppress open expression of at least some range of emotion (particularly those we may have learned to feel shame or fear about as children).

For another, when he meets someone who is in the grip of a strong emotion like intense sadness, the Dalai Lama's face spontaneously mirrors that feeling—and then quickly returns to his usual state of equanimity combined with enjoyment.

His demeanor suggests the Dalai Lama has an inner balance combined with empathic attunement. But he has not always been such an emotional paragon.

Take the time in 1959 when he fled to India. The Dalai Lama was in his mid-twenties and nervous about what was ahead as he readied for that escape in the Potala Palace. He found consoling advice on being confident in a chapter from a favorite text, which he read just before fleeing, disguised as a guard. That flight on horseback over the Himalayas was fraught with risk: not just the freezing cold and the uncharted paths over treacherous slopes, not just having to travel by night to stay hidden, but the constant threat of discovery by Chinese soldiers.

In the intervening half century, as a head-of-state-in-exile (a post from which he fully retired in 2011), he has had to struggle with helping other Tibetans survive as refugees and has tried, with little success, to negotiate with the Chinese—difficult, even futile, tasks. As he admits, "For sixty years I've faced a lot of problems."

While the Dalai Lama seems a model of virtue, he too has known anger, grief, and disappointment. I find it encouraging that even for him, who so naturally embodies compassion and equanimity, this was not always the case.

"When I was young, fifteen or twenty," he confides, "I had a very short temper." But the Dalai Lama knows that any of us can develop greater inner strengths with the right effort, because he has followed his own path to self-mastery.

"After sixty years of practice, I find significant change at the emotional level. Today, compared with twenty or thirty years ago, my mental stability is much better. Of course, irritation will arise sometimes, but it disappears quickly. When the worst news comes, I feel uncomfortable for a few minutes, but afterward I don't feel much disturbance."

While anger comes to him in short bursts, it does not fester or lead to enduring hostility, let alone hatred. He has become slower to anger and quicker to recover. Psychologists see such rapid recovery from a disturbing state as signifying resilience, one hallmark of well-being. It also may signify a well-toned vagal nerve, one conduit through which the brain manages much of our body, such as heart rate. But there are further advantages.

"If we hear disturbing news but do not have a calm and clear mind," the Dalai Lama explains, "then our initial reaction may be, 'Oh, I must do something, this is very bad.' But if at a deeper level we stay calm and lucid, then we will make a better response."

He urges each of us to follow a path to self-mastery in our own way. Bottom line: "As a result of training, my mental state remains comparatively calm. Through training we can change. We can improve ourselves."

Of course, it is rare (to say the least) for anyone to be inclined, as the Dalai Lama is, to commit five hours a day to inner practices. But we can take some small steps.

For that it helps to become aware of what the Dalai Lama calls "the enemies of our well-being": negative feelings that either lead us to harm ourselves or others or undermine us through inner turbulence, constricting mental freedom. These he calls "destructive" or "afflictive" emotions.

While every emotion has its healthy place in the ecology of the mind, each has its destructive side. When they are too strong, last too long, or are out of place, our emotions can enter the afflictive zone. For instance, desire for a meaningful goal is all to the good—while desire run rampant can turn into craving for, say, addictive drugs.

"If someone has a certain virus, we need to use the appropriate hygiene. Similarly, there's a hygiene of emotions," he says. When a destructive impulse "comes, but we show restraint—that's emotional hygiene."

Just as physical hygiene dictates we should stay clean and avoid exposure to dangerous viruses, he argues, in emotional hygiene our destructive feelings are like mental pathogens.

"In school we teach physical hygiene. So why not emotional hygiene?"

Reasoning About Feelings

In March 2008, Tibetans in Lhasa and other cities protested against the Communist government; the Chinese army shot demonstrators and arrested many protesters, particularly monks. How did the Dalai Lama react to this news?

"I visualized the Chinese officials and took their anger, suspicion, and negative feelings and offered in their place my love, my compassion, and my forgiveness. It won't solve the problem necessarily, but it was an immense help in keeping my mind calm."

By maintaining a positive feeling toward the Chinese officials while opposing their wrongdoing, he explains, "I could stay calm. With a calm mind you can be more effective with solutions or countermeasures. If you lose your peace of mind, your solutions could go the wrong way."

How could he react with composure to such upsetting news?

"Like anyone else, I too have anger in me," the Dalai Lama admits. "However, I try to recall that anger is a destructive emotion. I remind myself that scientists now say that anger is bad for our health; it eats into our immune system. So, anger destroys our peace of mind and our physical health. We shouldn't welcome it or think of it as natural or as a friend."

The Dalai Lama relies on such reasoning about events as a way to relate to the world rather than merely letting his emotions determine his reactions. Reflecting on his life this way has become part of his daily morning practice; the resulting attitudinal shift lets him better withstand the crises of his life.

He says one of the most useful kinds of realistic fear—"distaste" might be a better word—is toward our own destructive emotions. When we cultivate distaste for destructive emotions, we are better prepared when they come our way. "So when some destructive emotion seems about to come, you're ready—you know what to do."

The Dalai Lama also urges preventive tactics to minimize our destructive impulses, not so much by avoiding people and situations that trigger us but rather through a more fundamental prevention: Many such problems are due to our attitudes.

When the Dalai Lama applies reasoning, he reminds himself of an alternate understanding, one that helps him resist the pull of a destructive emotion. If we, too, cultivate methods like these regularly, then they are more effective when we really need them—when life sends us a jolt that leaves us too upset or angry.

This is not just some head-in-the-clouds wisdom from the East. The Dalai Lama found a kindred spirit with this mental strategy when he met Dr. Aaron Beck, the founder of cognitive therapy. They had an immediate rapport and talked with gusto about how to analyze what in our thinking might be distorted, what was realistic—and what the negative or positive outcomes of our own responses might be.

Though that dialogue occurred many years ago, the Dalai Lama still vividly recalls—and often repeats—an example Beck gave. When we are in the grip of anger, most of the negatives we perceive are wrong: "Ninety percent are mental projections."

Cognitive therapy seems remarkably similar to the Dalai Lama's own analytic method. Both approaches use the power of reasoning to understand and heal the mind; both encourage attitudes of acceptance and compassion. The cognitive-therapy technique of talking back to self-defeating thoughts (rather than believing them and acting accordingly) seems straight out of the Dalai Lama's playbook.

But let's face it: Coming up with the mental energy to apply such antidotes demands we be motivated in the first place. To that end, the Dalai Lama, as we've seen, urges reflecting on the damage that destructive emotions cause in our own lives (a moment of intense hostility can lead us to rashly act on impulses that end a marriage, say) and in the world at large: wars, poverty, ecological chaos.

The corrosive impacts are also internal, destroying our sense of peace, capturing our attention and so diminishing our mental freedom, crushing empathy. "An unruly, agitated human mind, given to fits of rage, malice, obsessive craving, jealousy, or arrogance," says the Dalai Lama, "can ruin lives.

"The real troublemaker is within us. Our true enemies are our own destructive tendencies."

So, he says, first cultivate the conviction that we can, with effort, overcome these tendencies in our own minds. Then find methods that we can apply as needed—particularly during our meltdowns.

The solution lies not in bottling up our negative feelings—which can intensify until they build to an outburst—but in being aware of them. By minding our feelings we can face them head-on, a first step to managing them well.

Minding Our Feelings

While we can't control when we feel anger or fear—or how strongly—we *can* gain some control over what we do while in their grip. If we can develop inner radar for emotional danger, we gain a choice point the Dalai Lama urges us to master.

When I asked the Dalai Lama how to find this inner choice point, he suggested one method: questioning destructive mental habits. Even though there may be a bit of legitimacy to our griev-ances, are the disturbing emotions we feel way out of proportion? Are such feelings familiar, recurring again and again? If so, we would do well to gain more control over those self-defeating habits of mind.

This approach takes advantage of an effect studied by Kevin Ochsner, a neuroscientist at Columbia University. While volunteers' brains were being scanned, they saw photos of people's faces show-ing emotions ranging from a woman in tears to a baby laughing. Their emotional centers immediately activated the circuitry for whichever feeling those faces expressed.

But then Ochsner asked the volunteers to rethink what might be going on in the more disturbing photos in a less alarming way: Perhaps that woman was crying at a wedding, not a funeral. With that rethink, there was a striking shift in the brain: The emotional centers lost energy, as circuits higher in the prefrontal cortex—those for pondering—activated.

As the Columbia research showed, this strategy seems to arouse circuitry in the prefrontal areas that can resist more primal limbic signals for strong negative emotions. That circuitry appears to be at play in a wide variety of methods, including the Dalai Lama's preferred strategy of reasoning with himself about his negative impulses and feelings.

Not everyone takes to reasoning to handle rocky feelings as readily as the Dalai Lama does. But there is a vast range of approaches we might try—ranging from mindfulness to various psychotherapies. Whatever method we find is fine, he says, so long as it helps us lessen the power of our destructive emotions.

One method the Dalai Lama suggests can be particularly helpful: noticing the emotional stirrings that signal destructive emotions, then thinking about what those stirrings might indicate—particularly fresh perspectives on our feelings rather than the same old rote thoughts that usually go with them.

This approach combines mindfulness of our feelings with reasoning about their causes—a method popularized in the West by "mindfulness-based cognitive therapy."

When handling our turbulent feelings, the Dalai Lama says, it helps to understand what happens in the buildup to them. This occurs in split seconds and typically goes by unnoticed. But if we can bring the buildup into our awareness, we gain a mental foothold that allows us to short-circuit what otherwise would become a destructive emotional hijack.

At the least we can notice how we feel during the hijack itself and note the negative consequences of our impulses. And with luck (or practice), we can catch ourselves in the future and change what we say or do for the better.

For this it helps to become aware of the gap between the provocation of an emotion, like anger, and our response. The same goes for our more mundane tensions, the ones we all face when whim and impulse contend with obligation and responsibility. A pause can help us sort out when those impulses and whims are just fine to act on and when obligation and responsibility matter more.

"Some people," Paul Ekman notes, "have a large gap, some small." Widening that gap makes us better able to manage our destructive emotions, as well as to make better life choices.

"This is not easy," he adds, "because emotions evolved to make us respond immediately, without conscious thought."

It can help to tune in to the ways our destructive emotions feel as they build in the body: When we're getting annoyed, for instance, do we get a queasy feeling in the stomach? Do we have certain familiar thoughts? Whatever the signals might be, we can use them in a kind of mental radar.

As we get more familiarity with bringing our attention to the chain that leads to emotional hijacks, we should gradually get better at catching ourselves. And quite often the simple act of noting them and naming them lets them subside.

If our mindfulness has become very strong, the emotion gets nipped in the bud the moment we become aware of what's stirring— we halt the impulse even before it takes hold. One test of this progression, the Dalai Lama says, comes when you confront someone who is hostile but remain calm yourself, able to use your discernment to understand why they might feel that way—rather than launching an angry rebuttal.

Getting There

A Native American story has a father telling his son, "There are two wolves battling in my heart. One wolf is violent and dangerous, the other full of warmth and compassion."

The son asks, "Which wolf will win?"

The answer: "The one I feed."

Hearing the story, the Dalai Lama noted that surrounding even viciously aggressive dogs with dogs that are peaceful brings out their own peaceable side. Something akin happens in the human mind, he added, pointing to methods that make us increasingly familiar with healthy emotions.

We can all cultivate more-constructive emotions, the Dalai Lama tells us. And, he adds, "We become much happier. This is what the scientific research finds."

Our emotions are to some extent hardwired, etched into our brain circuitry as essentials of human nature. While natural selection has endowed us with two sides, the job of culture, of families, and of ourselves is to support the altruistic side against the selfish one.

At a meeting with scientists the Dalai Lama heard about one mapping of our two sides from Phillip Shaver, a psychologist at the University of California. Shaver explained that when a child's parents tune in, empathize with her, and let her know they will nurture, guide, and protect her, she very likely will grow into a secure, loving person who trusts others and feels concern, even compassion, for them.

The Dalai Lama was intrigued to hear how such childhood shapers of emotional patterns flavor close adult relationships. He felt that his mother particularly, along with his older siblings, gave him such emotional security and the lifelong outlook that goes with it.

Shaver's colleague Israeli psychologist Mario Mikulincer had been doing a series of experiments on how to evoke secure base feelings—and so more kindness—even in people who tended to lodge in insecure patterns. People who are stuck in insecure ways of being, this research found, are less tolerant of other groups, less likely to act altruistically, and generally less compassionate.

So Mikulincer and Shaver searched for ways to shift people into a more secure sense of themselves and the world. In a series of studies, they managed to induce that shift—at least temporarily—using such simple methods as showing people words like "love" or having them recall happy memories of being with loved ones.

Such mental primes worked even when they were so rapid that people did not register them consciously. Once moved into those positive states, people suddenly expressed more tolerance and greater willingness to help someone in need—in short, more compassion.

As Shaver told the Dalai Lama, "It has something to do with love. Attachment words trigger a kind of comfort that makes tolerance for others more available mentally, even in insecure people, whose natural inclination is intolerance and lack of compassion."

When we stray toward our insecure side, we are more susceptible to a sea of negative feelings. A secure state, in contrast, diminishes our destructive emotions and amplifies our positive ones.

The Dalai Lama has long been in dialogue with brain scientists who study how the circuitry that manages our emotional reactions can be strengthened through practice. Neuroplasticity, the way experience rewires our brain, means we can retrain our emotional habits through conscious effort, altering neural patterns.

"Cultivating greater control over our inner world remains a potential for anyone, lessening destructive emotions like anger, fear, and suspicion," the Dalai Lama said. "Being able, for instance, to be

mindful of negative thoughts, whether about oneself or harsh judgments toward the people in our lives, defuses them."

Yet simple confusion about our turmoil—amplified by the mud-
died thinking of that turmoil itself—can render any of us clueless
about where we are and where we want to go in our internal world.
We could use a map.

A Map of the Emotions

The Dalai Lama envisions that this inner journey might be guided
one day by a map—one as well grounded and clear as the airline
maps that tell us that a flight from New York to Frankfurt connects
with one that continues on to New Delhi. The endpoint of that
inner journey: compassion.

"Just as you can find the way from New Delhi to New York," the
Dalai Lama says, "the map should show obstacles to compassion
and what supports its growth."

The Dalai Lama encourages each of us to take more active charge
of our own minds. For the use of those so inclined, he envisions an
internal "map of the mind," giving us the lay of the land in our mental terrain—particularly the turbulent seas of emotions—so we can
chart the way toward self-mastery.

To map that route, he adds, we first "should have sufficient
knowledge about what emotions are helpful, which can become destructive, how they develop, the connections between them.

"The more knowledge we have about that," he adds, "then the
easier it is to handle destructive emotions. That's why a map of emotions can help."

No emotion on this map is intrinsically bad or good; they all have
their uses in life. Fears can be valid signals to mobilize us to face an

actual threat, on the one hand, or, on the other, paralyzing distortions of reality, wildly exaggerated misperceptions of threats (as is fear of going outside, in agoraphobia).

The spectrum running from emotions that build our well-being to those that destroy it offers the main coordinates for this inner terrain. "It's important to know both sides," he says, "the downsides and the upsides."

When destructive emotions rule, our better nature goes dormant. So does our mental sharpness. As the Dalai Lama told a student audience, "When you have anxiety, your studies are more difficult. But if you are happy and joyful, your studies are more easily absorbed; you can go deeper."

Trust-versus-fear represents another basic contrast in this emotional map. In animals and humans alike, he adds, when there is a feeling of fear, there will be some tension and nervousness, even suspicion—which can set the stage for anger and aggression. There are two types of fear, the Dalai Lama points out: unrealistic fear, which needlessly propels us into an agitated state of fruitless ruminations, and the useful kind, which makes us cautious or mobilizes us to prepare for an expected threat.

Affection acts as an antidote to fear. "If you show me genuine affection," the Dalai Lama notes, "then automatically I feel, Oh, this person is very kind to me, so I can trust them. If you have no fear, you relax, you feel safe."

When we are gripped by destructive emotions, we fixate on what's upsetting us—we have little or no remaining bandwidth to notice others, let alone empathize with them. As we get free from agitation, we open to the world around us and so are more able to empathize and care.

"Often in our lives, we have a naïve attitude; we don't see where our moods are coming from," the Dalai Lama cautions. "We have to

delve in more detail into the real causes and conditions of our destructive emotions—the interrelationships in the ways our emotional world works."

The byways on this map can be tricky. When I asked if calmness
was a prerequisite for caring about others, his reply took me aback:
"Not necessarily—calmness can make us indifferent, like a vegeta-
ble."

There are different kinds of calmness, the Dalai Lama clarifies,
some helpful, others not. The Tibetan and original Sanskrit mean-
ings are much more precise than is English when it comes to sorting
out the differing senses of the word "calm." He sees the need for a
more developed English vocabulary for the subtleties of mind.

And, he adds, while our destructive emotions agitate us and distort our perceptions, calmness alone is not a sufficient antidote—we
need also to nurture a caring heart, lest we simply withdraw into a
self-satisfied cocoon.

Moreover, developing genuine concern takes some thinking—
not just a blank state of mind. There is a thin line between utter
calmness and torpor. The type of "calm" he sees in compassion
mixes with a lucid mind and warm heart.

Although Paul Ekman was initially skeptical of the usefulness of
a dialogue on science with the Dalai Lama, their first encounter
proved earthshaking for Ekman. As a child, Ekman had toxic relationships with his parents, and for the rest of his life he felt, as the
Dalai Lama put it, "always a little anger, anger, anger."

For instance, Ekman told the Dalai Lama, once when his wife
was away at a professional meeting in Washington, D.C., and he
was at home in San Francisco, she neglected to call at the time he
expected. That led him to be worried and then very angry.

As his anger burned, Ekman was unable to access information
that might reassure him, such as the fact that there were endless
reasons his wife might have been unable to call. And, as he told the

Dalai Lama, "Having been abandoned by my mother when I was fourteen, that anger when I'm abandoned by a woman is an emotional script in my life."

Remembering that fact might have cooled his anger too—but he couldn't bring it to mind, because he was in anger's grip. Later, after cooling down, he recalled these—and phoned his wife.

When at that first meeting Ekman introduced his daughter, Eve, to the Dalai Lama—who held Ekman's hand as they all talked during a tea break—the psychologist had a transformative experience. "For the next several months he never lost his temper," the Dalai Lama says, adding that he verified this with Ekman's wife and daughter.

Now, the Dalai Lama says, Ekman has become "very nice," and he finds him "a really wonderful, genuine scientist."

Despite how packed the Dalai Lama's schedule has become, he and Ekman have spent an unprecedented sixty hours in private conversation, generating two books.

At their first meeting, Paul Ekman found himself promising to follow through on an idea that the Dalai Lama had proposed. It became a program co-developed with meditation teacher and scholar Alan Wallace: Cultivating Emotional Balance, or CEB, integrates methods taken in equal parts from Tibetan contemplative traditions and modern psychology.

By now the Dalai Lama considers Ekman a virtual brother. For his part, Ekman tells me, "The Dalai Lama is the most exceptional person I've ever met."

Among the reasons Ekman gives: "I have never met anyone who is having such a good time, continually seeing the humorous side of nearly every situation, without sarcasm or ridicule, never humor that diminishes another person."

Ekman adds, "It feels good to be in his presence. Why? I *believe,* and I deliberately italicize that word, that he exudes goodness, perhaps not all the time, but much of the time. I suspect the goodness he exudes is related to the compassion he so strongly feels."

Ekman says the Dalai Lama once told him, "I want you to make a map of the emotions so we can navigate through hatred and resentment to get to a calm mind. We need a map so as not to get marooned. Only with a calm mind can you open your heart and use your mind well."

The metaphor of a map for our states of mind appealed to Ekman, who has set out on this inner cartography. Working with a state-of-the-art digital-mapping group, Ekman has been creating a game-like format that can run on a computer. "The idea is that you are the navigator" through the land of emotions, Ekman says.

Ekman's version of the map of emotions converts the notion of "states" of mind into spaces representing our mental landscape. There are five universal emotions (or continents) on this map: anger, fear, disgust, enjoyment, and sadness.

Each of these represents the hub of an emotions "family"— within the varieties of anger, for example, exasperation and indignation are distinctly different. Among the many other flavors in the anger cluster are enmity, hatred, and malice, all of which exaggerate the repulsive sides of someone or something.

Whether guided by such a map or any other useful method, we are each capable of making at least some small improvement—if just "ten percent happier," as a recent book on meditation put it. We can begin by dealing with our own inner confusion in finding a path to greater happiness.

This possibility partly underlies the Dalai Lama's opposition to the death penalty: Potentially, people can reform at any point in their lives. The Dalai Lama contends that even a murderer can have a deep change of heart. It's not a matter of leniency, he says. "But to kill other human beings in retribution, no matter what they have done . . . forecloses the possibility that they may change."

Cultivating Emotional Balance

Soledad State Prison, with its rows of ominous, featureless buildings surrounded by thick razor wire, seems out of place among the verdant farms of a pleasant valley near California's Monterey Bay. The tensions can flare into riots; many inmates, and even guards, have been stabbed with makeshift blades.

Eve Ekman, a medical social worker, went there one day to share the CEB program with sixty inmates.

Ron, already in prison for forty years, told of having recently heard that he would finally be paroled. He described the waves of joy, excitement, and gratitude, which spread to his friends in prison and family on the outside as he shared the good news.

Then, two weeks later, Ron heard that his parole had been repealed. Crushed, he collapsed into a deep sense of powerlessness, followed by waves of sadness, then anger. He became edgy, agitated, and withdrawn, sullenly avoiding everyone.

When Eve asked Ron to map his emotions along a timeline, he saw that after dropping his anger he turned to his fellow inmates for emotional succor. Long seen as a mentor by them, he now found them supportive. Even as he told the story, some among the sixty there called out what a "stand-up guy" he was and praised Ron.

As the session unfolded, a common inmate life story started with never having felt loved, cared for, or connected, then finding solace in drugs, and living a life filled with fear, anger, and hurt. "Anger," Eve observed, "was safer to explore than sadness—anger was their way out of sadness."

Making an emotions timeline let the inmates step back from their emotional turmoil and see that they need not be trapped forever by overwhelming feelings. The map of emotions also helped to sort this out, as did some scientific basics about emotion families.

But a powerful eye-opener for many inmates was the very idea that, while emotions can be destructive if they lead to harm, any feeling can become constructive. Eve gave the example of how anger channeled in a skillful way can fuel protests of injustice or intolerable conditions. This idea, one said, would spread like wildfire through the whole prison.

Eve and a training partner were surprised on this first encounter to find these hardened inmates—most over the age of fifty—were willing to open up about their emotional issues and that, like Ron, many had spent much time reflecting on their lives.

Guided contemplation practices offered the inmates tools for managing their inner worlds better. In one, they asked themselves four questions:

What would it be like for me to attain genuine happiness?

What would I need from the world to achieve this?

What would I need from myself—what habits would I need to learn?

Finally, how could I bring this to the world and be of service?

In another practice, the inmates learned to calm down through focus on the sensations of their breathing—and to rest in an inner refuge, without dwelling on the past or worrying about the future.

This orientation to the present was liberating for many, especially after uncovering their difficult past regrets. "You can't change what has happened," said Eve, "but you can use every moment to set a new motivation, a new aspiration."

The session closed with inmates silently wishing each person there—and themselves—well in their lives.

Life provides both our barometer of progress and our final exam.

When we spoke, Eve Ekman was planning to return to Soledad to train three of the inmates from that day to teach CEB to anyone else interested.

CEB draws on some points the Dalai Lama emphasizes for taming our destructive emotional impulses: a scientific understanding of emotions as well as contemplative methods that provide tools for a cooler reaction to heated events. "One of our goals is allowing people to realize that we can cultivate the sense of ease," said Eve.

But equally important are the reflections on, and cultivation of, a concern for others. While becoming cool and clear helps our well-being enormously, that alone is no guarantee that we will use these abilities in the service of a force for good.

For that, something more is needed: a moral compass.

CHAPTER THREE

The Kindness Revolution

Every one of the eight thousand seats in Gwinnett Arena at Emory University was filled as the Dalai Lama took the stage. As usual, he walked to the front rim and looked around, waving to everyone and greeting the occasional old friend.

Then his gaze suddenly fixed on two figures making their way toward their seats near the front. He tried to beckon them to the edge of the stage, but the crowd was too thick.

So the Dalai Lama, to the consternation of the State Department security detail guarding him, found his way off the stage and onto the floor, where he made a beeline to his dear friend Richard Moore, embracing him in a warm hug, touching foreheads in the Tibetan gesture of mutual respect.

Once back onstage, the Dalai Lama explained: "Love, love, love—he practiced that as a young boy. I call him my hero."

One day when ten-year-old Richard Moore was walking home

from school, he was blinded by a rubber bullet fired by a British soldier during the "Troubles" in Northern Ireland, his home. Remarkably, Moore quickly got over pity for himself and any hard feelings toward the soldier who had fired that bullet, forgiving whoever that might be.

Years later, the Dalai Lama visited Northern Ireland and met Moore, who told him his story. And five years after that, Moore was in the audience on the Dalai Lama's second visit to Northern Ireland—and was shocked to hear that the high point of his earlier trip had been meeting a young man who was blinded by a British rubber bullet but forgave the soldier who fired it.

Moore's attitude was to focus on his remaining abilities, not his disabilities. He got a university education and had some success in business. Eventually Moore went on to found Children in Crossfire, an organization that seeks to better the lives of poor children in countries like Tanzania, Ethiopia, and the Gambia—some having been caught up in the midst of war. The organization's chief patron is the Dalai Lama, who has become Richard Moore's close friend.

As the Dalai Lama told Moore in tribute, "Your sight can be taken away, but not your vision."

What strikes me is that the Dalai Lama—someone millions of people idealize—sees Richard Moore as a personal hero, living the life of compassion and forgiveness that the Dalai Lama espouses.

There are, of course, many forms and levels of compassion. Take, for example, a quick moment during a weeklong meeting of the Dalai Lama and a group of scientists. As he was speaking, the Dalai Lama noticed a bug that had wandered into the room, and he motioned urgently for a monk to come over.

Without missing a beat in the meeting, he asked the monk to gently carry that bug outside, lest it inadvertently get squished.

The day before the Dalai Lama won the Nobel Peace Prize, as it happens, my wife and I had taken a friend to have tea with him. A tray of fresh pastries was set on the table, and the Dalai Lama kept eyeing a particularly luscious-looking fruit tart as we spoke.

Then, just when he seemed about to reach for it, he said to my wife, "Here, you take that one."

And the next day, when the hubbub quieted at that boisterous press conference for the Nobel, the first question came from a reporter for the Associated Press, who asked, "How does it feel to win the Nobel Prize?"

The Dalai Lama thought for a moment, then replied, "I'm happy . . ." and he paused for a few beats before adding, ". . . for those who wanted me to win this prize." And when he learned about the money that accompanies the prize, his immediate concern was to whom he would give it.

A compassionate instinct and altruistic acts large and small come naturally to the Dalai Lama. Compassion should be the North Star, our final destination in this ethical GPS, the Dalai Lama tells us.

He reasons that if we were to embrace a genuine concern for others, then in our daily lives we would not only be kinder but would also be freed from reactivity based on cynicism. And our society would be more compassionate toward the powerless and voiceless.

On the other hand, the Dalai Lama is not just asking us to be kinder because he says so. Instead, he makes the case that a deeper awareness of how our emotional world affects the people around us leads to a more compassionate outlook.

Then "you have the conviction," the Dalai Lama says, "that that's what I need for me, for my well-being."

As he often says, "The moment you think of others, your mind widens."

Beyond Religion

A European clergyman once told the Dalai Lama that compassion can come only through faith and God's blessing, but the Dalai Lama had heard how animals like dolphins and elephants can show altruism.

Telling me about this conversation, he said, laughing, "I felt, Oh, even dogs and cats can be compassionate, and I don't think that's through faith!"

In taking this approach, the Dalai Lama no doubt challenges the easy assumptions of those who see him as solely a religious figure. To be sure, the Dalai Lama's understanding of the power of compassion comes from his deep spiritual reflections on human suffering and relief from that suffering.

But as a world leader, the Dalai Lama puts aside religion, ideology, or any faith-based belief system in seeking a foundation for this compassionate ethic.

He notes that, for centuries, religion provided an ethical base— but with the spin-off of philosophy from theology, postmodernism, and the "death of God," many people have been left with no absolute foundation for ethics.

Further, so often the talk about ethics polarizes people who get hijacked by extreme voices, particularly when the discussion revolves around religious belief.

Those who cause the troubles we hear about in the daily news all too often invoke as justification one or another religion—whether Buddhism, Islam, Judaism, Christianity, Hinduism, or any other.

Then there are those narrow-minded believers, says the Dalai Lama, putting his hands by the side of his eyes like blinders, "who say all creatures are the same but emphasize their own faith, forgetting the larger perspective."

Their actions show, he observes, that "deep inside" they do not take their own religion's moral values seriously and so distort or carefully select some textual sources while ignoring others, to serve their own ends. "If we lack basic conviction in the value of compassion, then the effect of religion will be quite limited."

Religions have had thousands of years to promote ethics—and have often failed, he adds. Besides, while selflessness and kindness are ideals found in most faith-based teachings, these virtues also exist in nonreligious ethical systems.

There are countless people in the world, the Dalai Lama says, "who are concerned for all humanity and yet who do not have religion. I think of all the doctors and aid workers volunteering in such places as Darfur or Haiti or wherever there is conflict or natural disaster. Some of them may be people of faith, but many are not."

And, he adds, "Their concern is not for this group or that group but simply for human beings. What drives them is genuine compassion—the determination to alleviate the suffering of others."

Enumerating the many routes to compassion, the Dalai Lama gives the example of "genuine Marxists," who "feel this for the entire working class on the planet." He praises too the dedication of many Christian groups to helping the poor.

But despite finding in compassion a theme common among all the world's great religions, he favors a more universal approach—what he sometimes refers to as "secular," not just in the sense of nonreligious but also implying inclusive. He seeks a morality of compassion that all agree upon: "My concern is the seven billion human beings alive now, including one billion nonbelievers."

The Dalai Lama sees the possibility of finding common agreement among varying ideologies and religions—and among those who hold to no faith—by emphasizing values they share. Even those who cling to ideologies that divide us, he says, can find basic agreement on a set of core human ethical values, promoting qualities like self-discipline and contentment, compassion, and forgiveness.

Few, if any, dispute the worth of these—particularly of compassion. But the basis for this ethic boils down to, he says, "the foundation for a happy life."

Genuine happiness and compassion go hand in hand.

The Case for Compassion

"My mother was uneducated, illiterate—a farmer," the Dalai Lama recalls. "But she was really kind. My brothers and sisters say they never saw her with an angry expression."

One of the Dalai Lama's earliest memories, from when he was still a toddler, is of his indulgent mother carrying him into the fields on her shoulders; while she worked or tended animals, they would play a game. He held on to her ears and "steered" her by tugging one or the other. "If she didn't go that way, I would shout and kick!" he says with a laugh, recalling how kind she was to him in all ways.

"I feel fortunate," he adds. "The first seeds of my compassion came from my mother."

In making his case that human nature is compassionate, the Dalai Lama turns to science, reason, and our own experience. The fundamentals of our biology and our shared experience as human beings show "we are social animals," the Dalai Lama reminds us, equipped with a "sense of concern for others' well-being."

When we are newly born, he adds, our mothers have enormous affection for us, and we fully trust them, relying on their care for our very survival over the first years of life.

That template of trust and bonding gets carried with us throughout life, and so we feel happier whenever we are surrounded by an atmosphere of affection.

A lack of affection, in contrast, whether in infancy or later in life, is harmful to our well-being.

"Little children don't care about someone's position, their education, rich or poor," he says. "It's the smile on your face" that they respond to.

The Dalai Lama shares a finding he heard about long ago: If newborns are consistently held with affection, their brains develop better than those of babies who are neglected and hardly ever touched, let alone held. Infants separated from their parents show fearfulness and helplessness, and monkeys separated from their mothers as infants grow up to be more tense and aggressive.

Being fondly held by a mother seems built into nature's design for the infant's healthy growth. "If we receive our mother's affection, then our body and mental state will be healthier," the Dalai Lama says. But among children who lack this, "Deep inside there's a sense of insecurity, harmful for health and proper mental development."

His conviction that infants are born with what amounts to a moral sensibility stems in part from scientific findings like those he heard about from Kiley Hamlin, a developmental psychologist at the University of British Columbia. She showed him a video from her research of infants as they watch a cartoon of three shapes: a circle, a square, and a triangle, each with cute big eyes.

The circle struggles to get up a hill, and the triangle comes along and gives it a crucial boost to the top. Then the circle struggles once again, and this time the square jumps on it, knocking it all the way down the hill.

Afterward, the infants, given the choice of toys in the shape of the nice triangle or the mean square, invariably choose the nice one. The same happens when a doggy puppet struggles to open a box and a bunny puppet helps—or another puppet slams the lid down.

The studies are done, with appropriate variations, with infants at three months, six months, or nine months, while they sit in their mothers' laps. The preference for the nicer choice occurs even with a three-month-old (who is too young to reach for either), as measured by how long she looks at a preferred puppet.

"When does goodness begin? Infants and toddlers already show its signature," Hamlin told the Dalai Lama. "Though we may think of them as interested only in their own desires, given the chance, toddlers under two show generosity. We find them willing to share—to give their treats away. And this makes them happy."

"They already know the map of emotions" in a rough way, the Dalai Lama says, suggesting that an inborn bias to good gives children a boost toward compassion, especially when their parents are themselves affectionate.

Jenny, just two and a half, reacted to a baby crying by giving him a cookie. When that didn't help, she began to whimper herself, then tried to stroke his hair. Even after he calmed down, she brought him toys and patted his head. That small moment of compassion was noted by Jenny's mother, who kept a journal as part of research on the roots of empathy.

A series of such studies done at the National Institute of Mental Health found that children before age two seem universally attuned to another child's distress and most often will try to help the other child in some way. When a one-year-old sees another baby cry, he brings his own mother over to comfort her. And if a baby at that age sees another hurt her finger, he is likely to put his own finger in his mouth to see if it hurts too.

But after two and a half or so, toddlers begin to diverge in their empathic concern. One factor seems to be how parents direct a toddler's attention. Children tend to become more empathic when their parents call attention to how their misbehaving upset another child. It turns out that "Look how sad you made her feel" has a better effect than "You were naughty when you hit her."

Some theorists point to this early-life empathic concern in arguing that human evolution was built around cooperation and altruism. We are born altruistic, the theory holds, but we can be socialized out of it by later experiences, such as competitive systems like school.

The Dalai Lama sees in parents' instinctive care for their young—who would die otherwise—another sign of a strong biological predisposition for caring and compassion. In contrast to this mammalian instinct, he notes, some reptiles and insects eat their offspring, given the chance.

The Dalai Lama has good company in basing this argument for innate compassion on science. As Harvard psychologist Jerome Kagan told the Dalai Lama, "Although humans inherit a biological bias that permits them to feel anger, jealousy, selfishness, and envy and to be rude, aggressive, or violent, we inherit an even stronger biological bias for kindness, compassion, cooperation, love, and nurture—especially toward those in need."

That innate ethical compass, he added, "is a biological feature of our species."

Wise Selfish

Some years ago, my wife and I had an unexpected bit of downtime with the Dalai Lama while he waited for an event to start in Montreal. He told us he had just come from Austria, where he had spent some time shopping.

That was startling—the Dalai Lama rarely shops. My wife asked him, what did he get?

"A toy for my cat."

It was a long wire with a small mouse-like object on the end, which he could use to play with his cat—and he glowed at the thought as he told her.

"Someone brought me a tiny, wobbly stray kitten," he explained. "If they had just left it on the street, it would have died. So I took care of it. Now it loves most the person who feeds it—me."

Positive emotions like love, joy, and playfulness are beneficial to health in many ways, from boosting immune strength to lowering risks of the same range of diseases. "The very constitution of our body guides us toward positive emotions."

In contrast, as the Dalai Lama puts it, "Constant fear, anger, hate, actually eat at our system." A wealth of scientific findings show that a steady diet of such negative emotions undermines the effectiveness of the immune system and contributes to diseases ranging from diabetes to heart problems; chronic hostility tends to shorten life.

People who live in poverty, for instance, have higher rates of heart disease than normal—and the emotional distress about the difficulties of their lives seems to erode both cardiovascular health and the capacity to recover from stress. On the other hand, feeling happy and upbeat in general speeds the body's recovery from the biological arousal caused by negative emotions. And so helping people to drop anxiety and distress and to feel happier, research finds, improves their biological health, including lowering the risk of heart disease.

As social animals, we have a biologically based need for the warmth of contact, the Dalai Lama notes, adding that loneliness can become a source of stress. Even more than mere physical togetherness, it's the affection, compassion, and sense of concern that we find so deeply reassuring—a sense of belonging to a group that cares about one another's well-being.

Then there's the commonsense argument. We've all seen, he told me, how a family that doesn't have much money but has lots of affection for one another will be happy. Even someone who just visits them will feel more relaxed there, sensing the affection.

By contrast, a family lacking such affection not only will be unhappy but will also send off signals of tension, so someone visiting will feel uncomfortable. No matter how elaborately decorated the surroundings, a lack of emotional connection leaves us cold.

"Oh, the visitor feels, I'd better be careful here," as the Dalai Lama puts it. "But with the affectionate family, as soon as you enter, you feel completely relaxed."

Being what the Dalai Lama calls "foolish selfish" means pursuing our narrow self-interest in ways that will work in the short term but might later bring animosity toward us.

The signs that such self-focus has become excessive, shading over into the destructive zone, include being more easily frustrated, clinging to wants, and being oblivious to others' needs. There's a narrowing of vision, limiting our ability to see things in the broadest context; rather, we see everything only in terms of self-interest, self-image—or the image we project for others, our social self.

"Wise selfish" means seeing that our own well-being lies in everybody's welfare—in being compassionate. Compassion is good for you, the Dalai Lama points out, not just for those who are its object. And that's his third point: The first person to benefit from compassion is the one who feels it.

The warmth we receive depends to a great extent on the warmth we give, but beyond that simple emotional equation, compassion also breeds an inner happiness independent of receiving kindness. That's why, he says, "Loving is of even greater importance than being loved."

There seems to be what some call a "helper's high," where brain circuits for pleasure—as when looking forward to dessert—activate while we mentally focus on helping someone else. Along with this inner reward, the circuitry that buzzes when we focus on ourselves and our problems quiets.

In Japan, responding to a tragic wave of suicide among young people there, the Dalai Lama suggested that Japanese youth would do well to volunteer to help the needy in Third World countries. Serving the needy brings a greater sense of purpose to our lives— a fact recognized by psychologists as a key to personal well-being.

By refocusing us away from the usual mental diet of worries, frustrations, hopes, and fears, compassion puts our attention on something bigger than our petty concerns. This larger goal energizes us. We are free from our inner troubles, which in itself makes us happier.

That shift from self-preoccupation resonates with an incident Eve Ekman told me about. A woman confided she was upset because her twenty-year-old daughter had gone away for two weeks with friends and hadn't contacted her once—not a phone call, not a text. She was on the verge of sending her daughter an angry, guilt-inducing e-mail.

And yet she could sense that something was amiss, that, as she put it, "I'm reacting in a stranger way than this deserves."

Eve asked if this was a common pattern for the woman—a routine inquiry in the CEB programs Eve teaches.

That led the woman to remember that, when she was young, her parents would drop her off at camp—and she'd never hear from them all summer. She felt unattended to, not cared about.

The woman could see that the strength of her feelings was out of proportion to the reality. "It wasn't a huge trauma," Eve told me. "But it's still in there, in her learned set of triggers."

So she practiced having compassion for herself—for her sadness when she was that young girl. As she did so, she felt a softening in her feelings toward her parents. "It sounded like forgiveness," Eve said.

And from that awareness of her reactivity to feeling ignored, she decided not to write the guilt-inducing e-mail. Instead, she realized she wanted her daughter to feel free to have a full life.

"Compassion reduces our fear, boosts our confidence, and opens us to inner strength," the Dalai Lama adds. "By reducing distrust, it opens us to others and brings us a sense of connection with them and a sense of purpose and meaning in life."

In the Dalai Lama's sense of the concept, compassion does not just imply sympathy or charity for someone else. It includes ourselves. "You need a word in English," he told a group of psychologists long ago, "'Self-compassion.'" To cultivate genuine compassion, we need to take responsibility for our own care and have concern for everyone's suffering—including our own.

A Sense of Oneness

Standing backstage at the San Francisco Civic Auditorium, the Dalai Lama had some downtime as he waited for the mayor, who was delayed on his way to offer an official welcome to the city. There were a handful of luminaries milling about nearby—but the Dalai Lama made a beeline to chat with one of the stagehands.

And when the Cold War was winding down, the Dalai Lama visited Mikhail Gorbachev. As he entered the vast and impressive Grand Kremlin Palace, I hear, the Dalai Lama paused to go over and shake hands with a guard at the door. That was the first time in his twenty-five years of standing there, the guard reported, that any dignitary had so much as noticed him.

I've seen this time and again: The Dalai Lama treats everyone equally, as he puts it, "whether high officials or beggars—no differences, no distinctions."

He models for us person-to-person caring based on an understanding of the essential sameness of people at a level beneath the surface differences of ethnicity or nationality, religion, gender, and the like. These are secondary differences; underneath, we are simply human beings, the Dalai Lama says.

Our sense of self-importance can be a further barrier between us. He senses this acutely in his own role as Dalai Lama.

"If I go around and tell people, 'I'm His Holiness the Dalai Lama,'" he says, sitting up in imitation of a pompous, puffed-up person, "then I'm trapped in a prison. It creates a barrier—I'm all alone. So I always say, 'I'm just another human being.' Then there is no barrier."

Once when we met, the Dalai Lama had recently visited his friend Dr. Aaron Beck, who had written a book called *Prisoners of Hate*. Mentioning that book, he noted, "If I emphasize, 'I'm the fourteenth Dalai Lama,' I would be a prisoner too!

"The sense of being special is a form of self-deception," he added.

"Don't think of me as something special or a stranger," he tells audiences. "Whenever I talk to a few people or to thousands, I consider them and myself the same—same emotions, same body. Then we feel a closeness."

Wherever he goes, the Dalai Lama emphasizes this message: Despite surface differences, we are similar under our skin; our hearts and minds are wired alike. He urges us to see the oneness of humanity, that, as he puts it, "we are all brothers and sisters," sharing common needs, so "their interest is my interest. Basically, every being is the same. Everyone has the right to be happy and to overcome suffering."

Understanding of our shared humanity, he says, leads us to compassion for everyone. Tolerance applies everywhere, across all divides. For instance, it extends to sexual orientation—so long as people do no harm and stay safe, there should be no discrimination on that basis, he says. "It's up to the individual."

What connects us at base, despite all our apparent differences?

In "our quest for happiness and the avoidance of suffering, we are all fundamentally the same, and therefore equal. . . . Despite all the characteristics that differentiate us—race, language, religion, gender, wealth, and many others—we are all equal in terms of our basic humanity."

Loving *Everyone*

People around the world admire the Dalai Lama for how he embodies qualities like humility, resilience, and compassion. But who, I asked, most inspires him?

The first person he names is Shantideva, an eighth-century Indian sage whose text *A Guide to the Bodhisattva's Way of Life* the Dalai Lama often speaks about. The *Guide* outlines a complete program of ethical discipline and mental training designed to achieve unstinting compassion.

Though aimed at monks of that early era, the general principles apply widely in modern times; the Dalai Lama's vision—such as the inspiration to start by reforming our own inner world—seems to reflect that text. But he recognizes there are many other routes to the same end.

"You have heard that they were told, 'Love your neighbor and hate your enemy,'" Jesus says in Matthew 5:43–48, adding, "But what I tell you is this: Love your enemies and pray for your persecutors, only so can you be children of your heavenly Father, who causes the sun to rise on good and bad alike."

In a London meeting with Christian contemplatives, the Dalai Lama was given this passage among several from the Four Gospels of the New Testament to comment on from his own spiritual perspective. The injunction, the Dalai Lama told the group of Christians, brought to his mind a question from Shantideva, who asked, "If you do not practice compassion toward your enemy, then toward whom can you practice it?"

Shantideva explains that if you can have this attitude toward enemies, they become "your best spiritual teachers," because they give you the opportunity to enhance qualities like tolerance, patience, and understanding.

That level of compassion, of course, bespeaks the higher reaches—not what most of us can do that easily. Hostility to those who harm us comes naturally. And so, the Dalai Lama adds, just being told to "love your enemy" will not move us to change.

Still, what the Dalai Lama calls "genuine" compassion includes *everyone,* without exception—not only those we like. He holds it out as an ideal, a goal we can move toward.

Even our enemies, says the Dalai Lama, "are still part of humanity. They are actually our brothers and sisters, so we must take care of them. And directly or indirectly, our future will depend on them."

It's a high bar to clear. Such genuine compassion goes beyond our innate tendency toward favoritism based on genetic closeness or surface similarity. As the Dalai Lama puts it, when we say, "I love my own cousin, those of my own religion or country or color," bias limits our affection.

But he insists that, with the right practice, from the ordinary level of affection we can develop an unbiased universal love, where "we don't care what their faith is, or their nationality, or social status—so long as they are human beings, they are our brothers and sisters."

The Dalai Lama recognizes that for many of us the ideal of such global compassion will sound like a mere wish. This part of his vision seems an aspiration, beyond our easy reach.

But more practically speaking, we aim in this direction whenever we are confronted with someone's suffering and respond to help, regardless of whether we know the person or not. Our compassionate action is not conditional—not dependent on how this person may have treated us or whether we have a relationship. When we see suffering, we do what we can.

The chorus of a rock anthem from the sixties urged, "Try to love one another right now." The operative word here is "try." Not so easy, especially with the added imperative "right now." Love cannot be ordered up on command—that seems a pipe dream (and in the sixties might literally have been so).

But as an aspiration, the Dalai Lama argues, such openhearted-ness represents a goal we can work toward gradually. As the Dalai Lama puts it, "In economics, we develop five-year and ten-year plans for change and growth. That's fine. But we need similar plans to cultivate warmheartedness and compassion."

What doesn't work: Merely repeating "compassion, compassion, compassion" a thousand times does nothing for us, the Dalai Lama says. Rather than espousing goodness but not acting on it, we need full conviction that we want to cultivate the capacity for compassion, based on recognizing its value and the self-confidence that we can do this. The real test lies not in what we embrace but in what we do.

Our natural biologically driven affection for those closest to us, the Dalai Lama advises, can be combined with the power of intellect to extend our love indefinitely. But gradually widening our circle of concern to embrace the whole of humanity does not come so natu-rally: The effort takes continued cultivation.

This, he advises, can be helped by reducing the grip of our own destructive emotions—our anger, or jealousy, or any of the others. Overcoming our harmful emotional reactions is itself a form of compassion, not just for ourselves but for everyone we connect with.

Anyone with the right motivation can move toward this, he adds. That map of emotions offers one aid, particularly in understanding what other attitudes of mind support compassion—tolerance, pa-tience, and forgiveness among them.

This approach relies on common sense and reasoning—no reli-gion required. Still, for those who hold to religious faith, reason can deepen convictions, he points out. "Faith becomes a method to increase our ability to practice compassion," the Dalai Lama says.

But there's a more universal path to compassion. While spiritual traditions have a long history of urging their followers to embrace caring, now cultivating compassion has found a new ally: science.

CHAPTER FOUR

Partnering with Science

Let's say you see two people win ten dollars, which they should in all fairness split fifty–fifty. Instead, the person who holds the money gives the other only one dollar, keeping the remaining nine.

But in this case there are special rules that let you force the cheapskate to give more money: If you give up two dollars of your own, he has to give four dollars to the victim.

That's the setup in "the Redistribution Game," which is used to gauge altruism, as measured by what a person does, not just what she says. Can cultivating a compassionate attitude make us more altruistic?

That question took on more meaning when Richard Davidson's Center for Investigating Healthy Minds, at the University of Wisconsin at Madison, had volunteers practice a method for cultivating a compassionate attitude. The compassion study assessed methods adapted from both Tibetan and Southeast Asian religious traditions. Rather than try to build such compassion-enhancing tools from scratch, scientists like Davidson are modifying them to fit a modern, even a skeptical, sensibility.

For instance, one exercise asked you to remember a time of your own difficulties and suffering—and then wish, with warmth and caring, "May I be free from suffering. . . . May I experience peace and joy."

Next you'd bring to mind someone you are affectionate with and make the same wishes for them.

Then you'd do so for an acquaintance and finally for everyone on the planet.

Another group of volunteers—the comparison group—learned a method from cognitive therapy for reappraising problems; this technique helped them think about an event from many different perspectives. After just two weeks of practicing the exercise for thirty minutes a day, each of the volunteers played the Redistribution Game.

At the start, everyone had the same amount of money. But then when they played the Redistribution Game, those who were randomly assigned to practice a compassionate attitude gave significantly more money than those doing the cognitive reappraisal training.

What's more, scans taken while the volunteers were shown pictures of people suffering—such as graphic images of burn victims—revealed that certain changes in two specific brain networks predicted how altruistic a person would be. The greater the activity, the more generous a person was during the Game with the victim of cheating.

One of these neural circuits helps us take the perspective of someone else, in this case the victim of unfairness. The other, surprisingly, was for positive emotion: It feels good to act with compassion.

The history of this study can be traced back years, to a moment after the Dalai Lama had spent several days in intense dialogue with a small group of scientists. The focus was a topic he had chosen, "destructive emotions."

At one point he turned to Richie (as everyone calls Richard Davidson) and said, in effect, In my tradition we have many time-tested methods for managing destructive emotions. Please take them outside the religious context, study them very rigorously, and, if you find there are benefits, spread them very widely.

That very mission has become a main focus in the neuroscience labs at the University of Wisconsin at Madison run by Richie, who numbers among the handful of scientists with whom the Dalai Lama enjoys a special closeness. When I asked the Dalai Lama to name scientists he knew well and admired, he said, "Richie, also, I love."

With the Dalai Lama's encouragement, Richie founded the Center for Investigating Healthy Minds (CIHM); part of its mission was to study the best routes to compassion. Take the kindness curriculum being tested at a preschool there. Preschoolers recite together a kindness pledge: "May all I think, say, or do not hurt anyone and help everyone."

Another: If the children do something kind for someone, they earn a "seed of kindness" planted on a big poster of a "kindness garden."

And they practice "belly buddies": Children put a favorite stuffed animal on their bellies, then lie down and quiet themselves by paying full attention to the buddy rising and falling as they breathe in and out. The kindness curriculum includes a variety of methods like these, all aimed at helping the preschoolers learn to be more calm and kind.

The preschoolers, four- and five-year-olds, are at the cusp of a developmental phase when kids are known to become more selfish, self-focused, and egocentric. In a test of the kindness program's effects, the preschoolers were given an apt challenge after a semester.

Each of them received some cool stickers (this at an age when kids are passionate about stickers) and was asked to allot the stickers to several envelopes: one with their own picture on it, one with a picture of their best friend, the third with a child they did not know, and the fourth a sick child.

Over the semester, a comparison group of preschoolers who did not participate in the program became more selfish in their sticker allotments—but not the kids in the kindness curriculum. The usual trend in five-year-olds toward selfishness can be offset. And this shift toward a warmer heart is not just for children.

A Boyhood Passion

On his first visit of many to Richie's brain-research units at the University of Wisconsin, the Dalai Lama was keen to see every device—the MRI, the PET scan, and so on. But what really caught his eye was the workshop full of precision tools, where those who maintain the brain probes toiled away.

Tools like those, he said a bit wistfully, were the kinds he wished he'd had when he was young.

The prominence of science on the Dalai Lama's personal agenda has its roots in his boyhood in Lhasa, where he loved tinkering with watches and anything else mechanical; he also repaired a broken headlight and tinkered with two cars that had found their way to that remote city (carried over the mountain passes, part by part, by porters). He fixed the generators that powered electric lights in his home, the ancient and enormous Potala Palace.

I once asked the Dalai Lama, "Why are you, groomed as a religious leader, so keenly interested in science?"

Spirituality and science, he told me, are not in conflict—rather, they are alternative strategies in the quest for reality. The Dalai

Lama envisions a partnership where the two work together, particularly in the service of compassion. As a basis for an ethic of compassion, he says, science can speak to a broader swath of humanity than can any religious faith.

In explaining his interest in science to a reporter from *The Wall Street Journal,* the Dalai Lama put it in terms of moral ethics and the universal need of people to find inner peace and have better responses to their problems. "If I offer methods from Buddhism," he said, "people will dismiss it as 'just religion.'" But if science says these methods work, "then, more openness."

In the years since making his way to refuge in India, the Dalai Lama has actively sought out contact with scientists, several of whom have become tutors. Among the first was the late neuroscientist Robert ("Bob") Livingston of the University of California, San Diego, whom the Dalai Lama recalls with great affection and who visited him several times in Dharamsala, acting both as science adviser and tutor.

On his many visits to the West, the Dalai Lama regularly met with eminent British quantum physicist David Bohm and his German counterpart Carl Friedrich von Weizsäcker, as well as with Wolf Singer, who for many years directed brain research at Germany's Max Planck Institute. The philosopher of science Karl Popper explained to the Dalai Lama the principle of "falsifiability," which states that scientific hypotheses should be formulated so that they can be either proved wrong or supported by further testing—a quality of the empirical approach the Dalai Lama admires.

And he continues to meet with Paul Ekman. The Dalai Lama, trained in debate, loves sparring with such "mature" scientists—particularly those he knows well—whom he often finds "more open-minded, more unbiased, than religious people.

"Science is not based on differences in faith or nationality," the

Dalai Lama says. "I find among scientists a genuine international-ism." He sees in this attitude of impartiality another strength of science.

On the other hand, while remarkably open to scientific methods and views, the Dalai Lama is not ready to abandon his own religious outlook for a blind faith in science. The Dalai Lama sees science as but one way of grasping reality, limited by its methodologies and assumptions, like any other way of knowing. Science knows well some aspects of reality but not the totality.

"Scientists themselves have emotions that create problems," he continues. "If we get helpful findings from science about how to create greater well-being and lessen destructive emotions, it's more convincing—and it will also help the scientists!"

One of the Dalai Lama's more provocative declarations: What we ordinarily think of as "psychological science" is at a mere "kin-dergarten" level when it comes to mapping the mind. Modern psy-chology, the Dalai Lama says, "needs to develop more knowledge, especially methods for dealing with destructive emotions."

While that judgment may make no sense to my fellow psycholo-gists, it does to me, in one way: comparing ancient Indian psychol-ogy with modern psychology when it comes to lessening the power of those turbulent emotions and cultivating positive ones like equa-nimity and compassion.

As it happens, as a pre-doctoral traveling fellow in South Asia, I studied a fifth-century text, a sampling of the "ancient Indian psy-chology" to which the Dalai Lama refers. I was amazed at the preci-sion with which this text delineated specific methods to shift our emotional and mental states (not to mention achieving transcenden-tal states, which to this day are largely off psychology's map).

Returning to South Asia as a post-doc, I studied the *Abhidharma,* a more detailed text that explains the dynamics of the ups and downs of our inner life. That ancient psychology lists fifty or so "mental factors"—elements of states of mind—and details a subset of a dozen or so that either further or hinder our well-being.

A key dynamic: When healthy (or "wholesome") states dominate the mind, the unwholesome ones vanish. In the vernacular of those days, for instance, agitation opposes composure; nonattachment vanquishes greed; torpor disappears in the presence of buoyancy and pliancy.

The Dalai Lama has urged melding these ancient sources with contemporary scientific findings in constructing that larger map of the mind. As he envisions it, this would one day subsume the emotional coordinates of Paul Ekman's cartography.

While the Dalai Lama sees how psychology could benefit from including these ancient insights, he has also been active in bringing modern science to the traditional Tibetan monastic education. In conjunction with Emory University—where he is a visiting Presidential Distinguished Professor—the Dalai Lama has helped introduce the biggest change in that venerable schooling in several hundred years: Textbooks on basic science have been specially developed and translated into Tibetan for inclusion in that curriculum.

Science, ancient and modern, in the right mix, yields a more potent sense of reality.

Science in Dialogue and in Translation

At one point in our time together preparing for this book, the Dalai Lama presented a small Buddha statue, wrapped in a gold-colored scarf. He explained that the devout, of course, regard Buddha as a *buddha,* an awakened being. But, he added, the Buddha can be seen differently—for instance, as resisting the caste system.

And Buddha told his own followers they should not accept his teachings out of blind faith or devotion but rather through their own investigation and experiment, which is more powerful than mere imagination or belief. "That's a very scientific way of thinking," the Dalai Lama continued, "so Buddha can be considered an ancient Indian scientist.

"If," he concluded, "you consider Buddha as a *buddha,* okay. But if you consider him a philosopher, a teacher, a social theorist, or a scientist—that's okay too."

In the early years of the Dalai Lama's interactions with scientists, he was uncomfortable about the phrase sometimes used to describe them: "a dialogue between Buddhism and modern science." Given his own tradition's thousands of years of exploration and systematic analysis of the mind, he viewed it as an "inner science" and felt it appropriate to acknowledge that this way of knowing had its own contribution to make: a dialogue between inner science and modern science.

That tension was resolved to a great extent when Francisco Varela initiated intensive weeklong dialogues between the Dalai Lama and groups of scientists; as the years went on, each side of the conversation grew to fully respect the other. These dialogues became the early core activity of the Mind and Life Institute, founded by Varela and businessman Adam Engle with the Dalai Lama.

The Mind and Life series of meetings with scientists continues to this day; as I write this, the Dalai Lama is in Kyoto, Japan, for the twenty-eighth such event, this one on new findings in brain studies of contemplatives. The seed that grew into this robust series of exchanges was planted in an almost-chance encounter between the Dalai Lama and Varela.

An eminent cognitive neuroscientist, the Chilean-born Varela taught at the École Polytechnique and the University of Paris and led a research group at the Centre National de la Recherche Scientifique. Varela first met the Dalai Lama in 1983 at a meeting in Alp-bach, Austria, when they happened to be seated together at lunch.

They talked about philosophic issues, biology, and cognitive science. At the end of the lunch, the Dalai Lama asked if Varela could come to Dharamsala and "teach him science."

Varela was both flattered and taken aback—but immediately said yes. On returning to Paris and thinking over that commitment, he realized he couldn't do this alone.

That insight led Varela to recruit other scientists to meet with the Dalai Lama at the first Mind and Life meeting on cognitive science and the Buddhist perspective on mind. Since then topics have ranged widely, from quantum physics and cosmology to that meeting on destructive emotions, at which Varela was one of the presenters.

The Dalai Lama had special affection for Varela, who died in 2001. He was by nature philosophical in his outlook—epistemology, or knowing how we know, was always a passion. Just a few years before his death, Varela had hoped to write a book on all the science meetings thus far, reflecting not on the content but on "what does it mean for two cultures and two views of mind to begin to talk to each other."

His wife, Amy Cohen, who now heads Mind and Life Europe, tells me that from the start of Varela's meetings with the Dalai Lama, "There was a real heart–mind connection between the two of them that swelled and strengthened over the years—a real friendship suffused with affection and mutual recognition."

The meetings, she adds, were always "an intense pleasure" for her husband; he enjoyed being in a space where "science, philosophy, and human affection came together in the particular dance, the dialogue, that was theirs."

These encounters with the Dalai Lama let Varela explore and

develop his intuitions about how Buddhist philosophy, epistemology, and ethics resonated with, and might alter, his scientific thought.

One of these "intuitions" resulted in Varela's spearheading a movement in cognitive neuroscience called neurophenomenology, which argues that brain research should take seriously people's accounts of their subjective experience—"first person" data. This can then be used to make better sense of "third person" data—the metrics yielded by brain measures (which usually are the *only* data gathered in neuroscience).

This approach, Varela saw, could act as a counter to the field's tendency to reduce the richness of experience to merely some measurable neurochemical activity in the brain. As a research strategy, this combination of angles of observation has proved invaluable in studies of contemplative practices.

The Dalai Lama appreciates this approach as a source of insight into the upper reaches of human goodness and into what kinds of training shape the brain in which way. And he enthusiastically endorses a next step: bringing any empirically grounded benefits outside the research lab to the widest human circle.

The movement from basic scientific research to a practical application makes all the difference for our well-being. Clinical trials of, say, a new treatment or drug are "translational research"—taking promising results out of the biology laboratory and testing them in forms that might help people.

The idea of translating basic research results into useful forms applies to any finding that might be helpful to people. For example, at a Mind and Life meeting on neuroplasticity, Michael Meaney, a neurobiologist at McGill University in Montreal, told the Dalai Lama about his research on the profound impact—even at the level of turning genes on and off—of a rat's licking and grooming her babies. The grooming not only released soothing brain chemicals but also tuned the babies' genes to create calmness under stress when they grew older.

For the Dalai Lama, that underscored the significance of earlier findings that physical contact and human connection help infants grow in a healthy direction.

But Meaney went even further, linking his findings to the stress-ridden homes of children living in poverty, who, more than most, suffer from abuse or neglect.

The growing brains of such children, Meaney said, likely exhibit a negative impact from their environment, akin to those of the stressed animals. The strong implication: Such kids need interventions designed to counter those impacts.

The Dalai Lama has particular praise for a Latin American program that improves the care given in orphanages—for instance, housing children in small groups with one caregiver (rather than in huge, impersonal dormitories) to create something akin to a family, with plenty of physical and eye contact, along with talk, for infants. Simple measures, he notes, can have lifetime impact.

An Investigative Mind

When Kiley Hamlin, the psychologist at the University of British Columbia, was showing the Dalai Lama that video of a three-month-old preferring the nicer triangle rather than the mean square, she concluded, "The very young already like goodness and enjoy being helpful and compassionate."

That, you'd assume, would please the Dalai Lama. But he didn't just take this in approvingly. Instead, he pointed out, "Thinking in terms of statistics, you've shown only one child. What is the average response?"

Hamlin reassured him that this test had been done with hundreds of children and in cultures around the world, with similar results.

He nodded in approval—but still queried, "And was their economic level taken into account?"

They had found the same in children from poorer families and from wealthy ones, she confirmed.

His probing the soundness of these results reveals a scientific bent to the Dalai Lama's thinking, which I've seen many times. Perhaps his training in logic and debate are at play.

In such encounters, scientists are frequently surprised at how spot-on the Dalai Lama's questioning can be after they have presented research findings to him. He sometimes pinpoints the next studies needing to be done in their field.

As for the usefulness of science meetings to the Dalai Lama, he once said he's collecting "ammunition," findings to support his message in his public talks—and with the press.

Just days after his interaction with Kiley Hamlin, the Dalai Lama told a reporter from *The Wall Street Journal* about the study, commenting, "Even three-month-olds show a preference for helping, not hindering," and suggesting this positive bias is a sign that biological seeds of compassion are built into our wiring.

But when a reporter once asked him if he might have become a philosopher of science had he not become the Dalai Lama, he nodded to the realities of his family's humble calling and replied, "In my case, to be fair, if I had not been recognized as the Dalai Lama, I'd be a farmer!"

He retains a deep respect for what he can learn from science. As he told a scientist at one conference, "I'm almost eighty, but I sit beside you as a student," adding with a laugh, "That way, I feel young too!"

The meeting the Dalai Lama refused to cancel on the day he learned he had won his Nobel Prize was the second Mind and Life dialogue, a two-day private meeting with a handful of prominent neuroscientists. That 1989 meeting was about the mind and the brain; among the handful of eminent neuroscientists in that conversation was Lewis L. Judd, at the time the director of the National Institute of Mental Health.

As Dr. Judd told me then (and as I reported in *The New York Times*), he was intrigued that the Dalai Lama's view of mental health included qualities like wisdom and compassion—literally off psychiatry's charts of the human condition.

"Our model of mental health is mostly defined in terms of the absence of mental illness" and such toxic states, Dr. Judd observed, adding that the map of the mind from Tibet "may have more positive ones that might be worth our study."

Tibetan training methods for "lucid dreaming," where the dreamer knows "this is a dream" and can consciously change its course, caught the attention of the neuroscientist J. Allan Hobson, then director of the Laboratory of Neurophysiology at Harvard Medical School. He told me, "Our research on dreams might benefit from their hundreds of years of experimentation."

And, said Antonio Damasio, a neuroscientist now at the University of Southern California, "Some Tibetan meditation techniques may enhance people's ability to monitor their bodily sensations. If we can train people in this," he added, "it might have clinical uses."

At that time, Jon Kabat-Zinn's pioneering work with medical patients to do just that—monitor their bodily sensations with mindfulness—was beginning, though today mindfulness seems to be spreading everywhere, from the medical clinic to the office and classroom.

Mindfulness, a part of Asian meditation practices for thousands of years, has now been empirically tested in hundreds of studies outside its traditional uses. The psychological benefits of monitoring the mind in this nonjudgmental, nonreactive way range from lessening the severity of eating disorders, deep anxiety, and depression to enhancing concentration in those with attention-deficit disorder.

Medical and nursing students learn mindfulness as a buffer against the emotional stress of their work. When preschoolers learn the rudiments of mindfulness, it accelerates their impulse control and readiness for learning. The uses seem legion.

Such practical applications of scientific insights please the Dalai Lama. Several times over the years, I've heard the Dalai Lama say to groups of scientists (among others) at one or another conference: "Is this just empty talk? Or are you going to do something—take meaningful action?"

Taking Compassion's Measure

Need to calm down? Try this. Take a deep breath, filling your lungs; hold it in for two or three seconds and then let the air out slowly. Take five to ten deep breaths this way. If you need help focusing fully on your breathing, you can make a mental note: "in" on the inhalation, "out" on the exhalation. Or you can imagine tension draining from your body as you exhale.

This deep-breathing exercise can calm and relax us as we start our day or anytime we feel the need. So suggests Thupten Jinpa in describing one of the many methods he adapted from traditional Tibetan sources to use in a compassion-training program. Like many of the methods now being studied in research on cultivating compassion, these have distant origins in spiritual traditions but have been stripped of their belief systems and simplified for more general use.

Jinpa, apart from being the Dalai Lama's main English-language interpreter, also directs the Library of Tibetan Classics, which translates texts from that culture's wide heritage. Drawing on this rich background, Jinpa developed Compassion Cultivation Training, or CCT, a variation of classical Tibetan methods he has rendered suitable for anyone. At the Dalai Lama's urging, this program became the centerpiece for testing at Stanford's Center for Compassion and Altruism Research and Education.

An evaluation of CCT by Stanford researchers found that it lessened people's worries and increased happiness. Even in those suffering from acute social phobia, the training helped lessen their anxiety and fears. When the program was tested with patients enduring chronic pain, their sensitivity to pain decreased after nine weeks, while their sense of well-being improved—and their spouses reported them to be less angry.

While the ways to cultivate compassion being tested are modern adaptations of ancient practices, the methodology of the research itself comes straight off the shelf of science. A network of scientific centers has joined in the study of compassion and how to foster it.

In research at the University of North Carolina, practicing an attitude of loving-kindness not only lessened depression and boosted positive moods but also increased people's sense of satisfaction with their lives, strengthening their connections with family and friends.

At Emory University, a similar adaptation was used with college students who were suffering depression. Initial results suggested that promoting an attitude of compassion not only fended off depression to some extent but also lessened the body's responses in the face of stress.

Early findings on cultivating an attitude of compassion suggest even biological benefits, such as lessened inflammation and lowered levels of stress hormones. Richie Davidson's research has shown that these modern adaptations of ancient methods create beneficial changes in the brain, in both its structure and its function.

The Dalai Lama urges the highest scientific standards for these evaluations. After telling an audience about some of these findings, for instance, the Dalai Lama made a proposal: "Give the tests again, after a year. And also ask their families—the people important in their lives—what changes they see."

At Germany's Max Planck Institute, neuroscientist Tania Singer teamed with Matthieu Ricard, a biologist-turned-monk, to assess several methods for cultivating compassion. They found a difference between building empathy (where you sense how the other person feels) and compassion (where you want to relieve their suffering); each enhanced the activity of different neural systems.

When we simply empathize, tuning in to someone else's suffering—for example, seeing vivid photos of burn victims and other people in grave distress—the brain fires the circuitry for feeling pain and anguish. Such empathic resonance can flood us with emotional upset—"empathy distress," as science calls it. Professions like nursing are too often plagued by such chronic anxiety, which can build to emotional exhaustion, a precursor to burnout.

It's not only nurses. When I last spoke with Eve Ekman, she mentioned she had been with a group of neurosurgeons just that morning, introducing the Cultivating Emotional Balance program at their hospital. "They want to learn how to respond to their patients' fears—showing empathy in a way that doesn't make the patient even more distressed," Eve told me. "They say it's easier in the operating room—you don't have to talk to your patients."

The surgeons' goal: keep their emotional balance—be open to their patients' emotions but not get overwhelmed. Too many workers in medical settings, Eve added, suffer from empathy distress, which leads to emotional exhaustion.

She told me that in the elevator at the hospital where she works, she'll hear someone ask a co-worker, "How are you?"

And the answer comes, "Nine more years." These people count the days and years until they can retire, they are so emotionally exhausted.

When Alan Wallace, a co-developer of CEB, first taught it to schoolteachers, he heard just that complaint from one of them. But by the end of the course, she had changed her stance; as Eve reports, she said, "I now believe I can make a difference; my work is meaningful. Instead of counting the days, I'm looking forward to each day I have left with those children, so I can help them."

CEB helps people cultivate loving-kindness, compassion, equanimity, and empathetic joy—rejoicing in the other person's happiness. Instilling the same openhearted capacities was also the aim of the program shaped by Matthieu Ricard and assessed by Tania Singer's research group.

The Singer group found that after people practiced feeling warmth and concern for others, they were able to view those photos of suffering without defensively looking away and so stay open to someone else's distress. Meanwhile, their brain circuitry for positive feelings became active—indicating their attitude of compassion and wishing well for the victim. Compassion, the findings suggest, serves as an inoculation against empathy distress, with more activity in the brain centers for caring, which builds resiliency instead of burnout.

"Some people have the impression that compassion is just good for the other person but you don't necessarily benefit—or even that feeling too much compassion somehow weakens you," the Dalai Lama says.

He told me of meeting an Indian woman who was working in medicine but who had become worn down by the demands and emotional turbulence of her patients—and so quit the field. But, the Dalai Lama was quick to add, research like Singer's shows that cultivating an attitude of genuine compassion can be part of that burnout inoculation.

When the Dalai Lama was once asked why he wanted people to be open and to empathize with the pain of the world, he replied that we all have a moral responsibility to face that pain and work to alleviate it. If we just get depressed and give up, he said, "The pain will have won."

The scientific findings on compassion give the Dalai Lama just the kind of "ammunition" he needs. "If I say be compassionate," the Dalai Lama points out, "then people will think, Of course he says that—he's the Dalai Lama, he's Buddhist. But if scientific evidence shows benefits, then it's more convincing. People pay more attention."

These days, as he says, scientific claims appeal to more people than do those of any given religion. While the Dalai Lama travels the globe, spreading his vision for a better future, he often supports what he says with scientific findings like these on compassion development.

The message of compassion is for us all—not only the religious. But just what the Dalai Lama means by "compassion"—and how that translates into action—took me by surprise.

PART THREE

Looking Outward

CHAPTER FIVE

A Muscular Compassion

When the Dalai Lama met President Nelson Mandela soon after apartheid ended, he was deeply impressed by Mandela's lack of resentment toward those who had put him in prison for so long. In that same spirit, South Africa's Truth and Reconciliation Commission, headed by the Dalai Lama's old friend Archbishop Desmond Tutu, heard thousands of confessions about atrocities of every kind from the days of apartheid and the struggle against it.

In only some of the crimes so revealed was the perpetrator granted amnesty. But there is no doubt the proceedings prevented a wave of vengeance-driven violence. Mandela's efforts to see that there was no personal revenge against the minority whites who had ruled (or against those who fought against them) was a major force in healing deep social rifts.

When it comes to conflicts or oppression like that under apartheid, "The wounds are everywhere," the Dalai Lama says. That's why a process like the commission is "very, very necessary, and very effective for healing."

The full disclosure of crimes on both sides—abuses by those imposing apartheid and atrocities by those rebelling against it—represents a model of transparency he admires.

He strongly advocates such openness in holding officials of every kind accountable for their misdeeds. This may sound ho-hum to many ears, but the driving force for his view caught me off guard: compassion.

The Dalai Lama's version of compassion is more muscular than Sunday-school stereotypes of a benign but soft and flabby kindness. He sees such full disclosure as one application of compassion in the public sphere, as is forceful action to right injustice of every kind.

His instincts are somewhat akin to those of the crusading author Upton Sinclair, as well as to the deliberate moves against corruption and collusion by Pope Francis. He calls for moral responsibility in all spheres of public life. There's "dirty politics, dirty business, dirty religion, dirty science," the Dalai Lama says, wherever serious ethical lapses occur.

His distaste for injustice, coupled with taking initiative to expose and reform corrupt systems—be they the misdeeds of banks or corporations, politicians or religious officials—is the singular application of compassion I least expected in the Dalai Lama's vision.

We talked about three principles that exemplify such compassion in action: *"fairness"* (with everyone treated the same), which depends on *"transparency"* (being honest and open) and *"accountability"* (being answerable for misdeeds).

Lacking any force to oppose it, corruption or injustice will continue.

But we can only remedy what we know about. Still, transparency about unfairness will not do it alone: We also need accountability.

The two are interactive. There is no accountability without transparency; transparency without accountability is toothless.

Compassion Takes Action

The Dalai Lama calls himself a "simple monk" and—despite his world tours and the entourage and security that surround him—lives a Spartan life, following a strict daily schedule. He resides in bare quarters and sleeps in a small room with sparse furnishings, as befits a monk. In warm weather at home, he prefers flip-flops of the kind worn by the poor farmers of India; his T-shirts fray from use.

On this point he feels a special kinship with Pope Francis, who likewise sleeps in a simple guesthouse room at the Vatican rather than in the more spacious papal apartment, drives an economy car, and prefers his most modest title, "Bishop of Rome," to "Pope." And the ways in which Pope Francis pushes the Church to become more active in helping the poor and the marginalized resonate with the Dalai Lama.

He was so pleased by Pope Francis's calling on Church officials to model austerity by living more simply—in a Church that "is poor, and is for the poor"—that he wrote him a letter of admiration. Religious leaders, the Dalai Lama says, should follow their own teachings through humility and simplicity in their living habits.

Then the pope did something that prompted another letter of praise: He demoted the German "Bishop of Bling," Franz-Peter Tebartz-van Elst, who had spent upward of $43 million on his private residence, replete with bronze window frames, a $30,000 bathtub, and a million-dollar landscaping job. In that second letter, the Dalai Lama expressed his appreciation to Pope Francis for "his tough stand, which carried a real teaching of Jesus Christ."

Commenting on the pope's reprimand of that German bishop for his indulgent lifestyle, the Dalai Lama said, "Even the religious can be corrupt." As he told an audience in Bangalore, India, "The prospect of religious people with no ethics is disastrous."

Compassion in action, he says, means not just relieving suffering but also getting engaged in rectifying wrongs—opposing injustice or protecting people's rights, for instance. And such compassion, though nonviolent, can still be quite assertive.

"In today's world there is a lot of fighting, cheating, bullying," the Dalai Lama says. "So altruism and compassion" are all the more important. But, he adds, "It is not enough simply to be compassionate" in our outlook. "We must act."

Constructive Anger

A social worker told the Dalai Lama that she and a group of her colleagues were furious at the huge number of cases they were given, which overwhelmed their ability to actually help their clients. Concerned for the children they were supposed to be helping, the social workers held a rally in protest—and got their caseload lowered.

As the social worker said, "We couldn't have done this out of resignation." It was the initial anger that mobilized them. A modicum of anger helps us stand up against unfairness.

The Dalai Lama sees ways a well-guided anger can be useful. Moral outrage can drive positive action.

His view on anger is not the blanket condemnation I expected from him. Just as with calmness, he makes distinctions in the varieties of anger.

When we feel outrage at an injustice, he urges us to marshal the positive aspects of anger: a strong focus, extra energy, and determination—all of which can make our response to that injustice more effective. But this becomes impossible when our anger takes over; then our focus dissolves into obsession, our energy becomes agitation, and we lose all self-control.

How we act matters too.

In general, he favors lessening our destructive emotions, including anger. "Tolerance means that you should not develop anger or hatred. But if another person does something harmful to us," and we do nothing, "the person may take even more advantage of us, and even more negative action may come.

"So we must analyze the situation—if it requires some countermeasure, we can take it without anger. In fact, we will see that the action is even more effective if it is not motivated by anger—we are much more likely to hit the target directly!"

But if such equanimity eludes us, the Dalai Lama advises "well-guided" anger, where you would take whatever actions are needed to protect against a real threat—someone harming you or others—but with restraint rather than hatred.

"Keep a calm mind, study the situation, then take a countermeasure. If you let a wrongdoing happen, it might continue and increase, so, out of compassion, take appropriate countermeasures."

Compassion includes everyone. "Even if a person's actions are destructive," he says, maintain a sense of concern for their well-being. But "if you have the ability, you must stop the wrongdoing," he adds.

One trick to the constructive channeling of anger lies in keeping basic compassion toward the person, even while forcefully acting to oppose their wrongdoing. This gets us to the challenge: Distinguish between what the person does and the person.

Oppose the act, but love the person—and make every effort to help him change his ways. Even as we oppose the action, the Dalai Lama urges, "Have compassion toward the actor.

"The real meaning of forgiveness," he clarifies, "is don't develop anger toward the person, but don't accept what they've done."

In their many hours of comparing methods for working with emotions, the Dalai Lama and Paul Ekman found a major point of agreement in this distinction between the actor and the act. Psychologists recommend just this cognitive maneuver to help people manage upsetting emotions like anger.

The Dalai Lama offers another reason for this mental strategy. When we need to counter someone's negative act, we will be more effective if we're not driven by our own destructive emotions.

That makes me think of a personal bête noire—a guy who got me involved in a business deal now gone wrong. When I bring him to mind, I very often become agitated and angry, focusing on his flaws. But if I've done my daily meditation practice, I notice I can reflect more calmly and clearly on the legal maneuvers that will end the deal—I can separate the actor from the act.

The Strength of Altruism

Ever since he first heard of Mahatma Gandhi, when he was a small boy growing up in Tibet, the Dalai Lama has been inspired by that Indian leader. Though they never met, the Dalai Lama calls Gandhi a "personal mentor."

Many aspects of Gandhi's life resonate with his own, starting with Gandhi's personal efforts to restrain the negative forces of human nature and develop the full potential of the positive. Another can be seen in the simplicity that marks the Dalai Lama's personal lifestyle, as it did Gandhi's. And a third is their making a common cause of the problems of the poor and oppressed.

Like Gandhi, the Dalai Lama strives to cultivate nonviolence and compassion in his own daily practice: "Not because it is something holy or sacred, but because it is of practical benefit."

He also values Gandhi's insistence on the importance of transparent honesty. "His practice of nonviolence depended wholly on the power of truth."

One way this power shows itself is when we face difficulties or obstacles. Then, the Dalai Lama observes, "Your own stand must be truthful, honest, and genuine, an altruistic attitude. But with that, with the strength of altruism, there's no reason to feel discouraged. But if we are hypocritical or saying one thing and doing another, our inner being weakens and we may not have the strength to face challenges."

Full honesty lets us speak truth to power. Such transparency in public life means getting beneath the surface to see what's underneath. "On the surface, people generally behave and try to look good, to practice restraint. But underneath there may be other things happening," he says. "Transparency acts as a deterrent to wrong motives."

He tells people in the media that they need a "long nose" to sniff out what goes on behind the scenes as well as in front; then they must report not just what is sensational but give an unbiased account of what really is going on in the background.

"In free countries, at least, the media has a huge role to play and can make a big difference. It's a different matter in countries with heavy censorship. For the time being, that is a difficult situation."

He declares the growing gap between the rich and poor "totally immoral!" He's witnessed the despair among the impoverished while on visits to Africa and Latin America and criticizes how corruption plays an active part.

And he puts it bluntly: "Corruption is like a cancer." Corruption helps both to create poverty and to keep it in place; all too often, for instance, funds donated to help the poor end up in the pockets of the rich.

The Dalai Lama advocates tackling corruption everywhere in public life. He sees as its root cause extreme self-centeredness, with no concern for others' well-being. In his view, the problem starts with modern education, which conditions us to think about personal success and money rather than moral principles. The assumption: "If you have money and power, everything will be okay." Business people and leaders are products of this system, he says, and so they think this way.

He cites the 2010 Commonwealth Games in India as one example of corruption. The games were intensely criticized within the nation's media, for problems ranging from contractors pocketing money and mass evictions of the poor to dangerous working conditions and child labor—plus there were questions of why a country with so many citizens living in poverty was spending billions for a sporting event.

"There are lots of scandals like that in India," says the Dalai Lama. "There's too much complacency. What's needed there is leadership that's tough, honest, and transparent. Then I think India can change—can transform."

I thought of his comment when I read recently about a global British bank that ran what's called a "dark pool." This private trading operation supposedly protected large investors like pension funds from financial "predators"—high-frequency computerized buying programs.

A high-frequency buyer would see the price a relatively slow large stock purchaser was offering, and in nanoseconds, acquire that stock at a lower price, and instantly turn around and sell it at a higher price to that purchaser. The result: The slower investors paid more than need be for their stock.

The New York State Attorney General accused the British outfit of falsely representing to the pension funds what was going on: While the bank claimed to protect the funds from predatory trades, it actually invited those same ultra-fast traders into the pool—or so the charges go.

All very arcane, like so many of the other gray zones in the financial sector that have come to light since the meltdown of 2008. As a law professor who specializes in banking said of the dark pool, "I think the lesson here is pretty simple. Bad things happen in the dark." That bank, he added, "was lying to customers. They weren't protecting them—they were setting them up."

In the Dalai Lama's view, the 2008 financial crisis laid bare not just a lack of moral responsibility and the key role of greed driving excessive speculation but also corrupt practices. Of course, he is not alone in suspecting a deep ethical flaw in the culture of the financial industry.

Some use the term "gangster capitalism" to describe how unethical or even outright illegal businesses thrive in an utter lack of transparency. Whether involving the close relatives of high-level politicians, political leaders getting rich through payoffs, or the pillaging of natural resources, such enterprises can only operate in the secretive dark.

"Be transparent," the Dalai Lama advised a group of business people. "Transparency brings trust."

The Empathy Gap

When the Dalai Lama quietly met with a group of students from mainland China who were attending colleges in the New York City area, he told them, "We need to support Xi Jinping," their country's new president, "in his effort to tackle corruption. It's quite bold, really wonderful—but he needs public support."

Remembering 1950s meetings with Mao Tse-tung in what was then Peking, the Dalai Lama says, "The Buddha was totally against the caste system, so even Mao described him as a revolutionary campaigning for social justice."

That remark brought to mind the time years ago I met John Ogbu, a Nigerian anthropologist at the University of California, Berkeley, who had come to do fieldwork in the small city in central California where I grew up. I was shocked to hear the focus of his research: the de facto caste system there.

He immediately saw that ethnic minorities were restricted to one part of town, while the white middle class lived in another—and that the schools as a consequence were segregated along what, in his eyes, amounted to "caste" lines. The moment he pointed it out, I saw he was right. But until then that glaring fact had been under the social radar for me—while I was going to those very schools, I hadn't given it a second thought.

Social inequality fades easily into the background of everyday life, woven into obliviousness by unspoken cultural norms and beliefs. One form transparency takes can be making visible these otherwise taken-for-granted forms of bias—as those active in women's and minority rights have long recognized.

The invisibility of social injustice creates indifference, particularly among those with power (those who suffer the injustice, of course, are quite aware of it). Research finds that such indifference begins at the person-to-person level, an invisible barrier to caring.

In direct encounters, the higher-status person tends to pay far less attention to someone of lower status than is true in reverse, according to results found by Dacher Keltner, a psychologist at the University of California, Berkeley, in a series of experimental studies. .

In a five-minute getting-to-know-you session between two strangers, for instance, the more wealthy person in the pair didn't make eye contact, nod, or laugh—all measures of engagement—as much as the less wealthy person. In the Netherlands, when strangers confided distressing moments in their lives, again the more powerful person in the pair was relatively indifferent. But, Keltner finds, the less powerful and the poor are keenly attuned to others, both up the status ladder and at their own level.

This differential in paying attention to people, according to Keltner's research, shows up within an organization when high- and low-ranking people are compared on their ability to detect a person's feelings from their facial expression. And when high- and low-ranking people in the same organization interact, the person of higher status not only shows less attention as indicated by gazing less at the other person but also interrupts more and monopolizes the conversation.

Those with few resources and fragile circumstances—like a single mother working two jobs to pay her bills who needs a neighbor to look after her three-year-old—depend on having good relationships with those they may one day turn to for help. "They need to lean on people," as Keltner told me.

In contrast, the wealthy person with a three-year-old can hire help as needed, whether an au pair or the services of a day-care center. And that, Keltner suggests, is but one reason the rich can afford to tune out other people—which includes ignoring their needs and their suffering.

When I mentioned these findings to the Dalai Lama, he added another complication: Followers of some faiths believe that a higher order determines people's destiny, and so because they somehow "deserve" their plight, there is no need to empathize or offer help.

Whether as tacit collusion with a caste system, or a belief in "the elect," or the idea that when it comes to the underprivileged, "God created them that way," such attitudes foreclose acting with compassion. The belief becomes an excuse for callousness. "That's a way religion can add to the problem," he observed.

People who dismiss others' dire needs as being due to some divine fate or karma, he adds, are "totally wrong."

On the other hand, we need to act, not just sympathize. "You can repeat 'equality, equality' a thousand times," he said. "But in reality, other forces take over." And where there is little such empathy, those who hold power in business and politics make decisions lacking a full understanding of how they will impact the powerless.

The inequality between rich and poor or groups disadvantaged due to bias becomes invisible, an unquestioned norm. Unequal access to power is taken for granted—particularly by the elites who enjoy its benefits. And those who suffer have no access to the power to make decisions that would improve their conditions.

And yet the mark of a compassionate society can be found in how it treats those people most distant from the center of power, whether because of group identity, gender, class, wealth, or those generations yet unborn.

Gandhi was keenly pained by the elite's indifference to the powerless. Among the notes found after his death in 1948 was this: "Recall the face of the poorest and the weakest man whom you may have seen and ask yourself if the step you contemplate is going to be of any use to him."

Gandhi's advice to picture a specific person's face has particular power in light of Keltner's findings: The intimacy of that act, and the image of the person in need, could elicit empathy, a direct counterforce to inattention. If we can empathize, we can better sense what's needed—and so act with more skill.

Structural Unfairness

The Dalai Lama cites figures like Gandhi, Mandela, Václav Havel, and Martin Luther King Jr. as highly effective activists with compassion as their motivation. Mixing their activism with nonviolence, he says, did not make them weak but instead took even greater courage and determination than turning to force.

"Nonviolence doesn't mean we have to passively accept injustice," he told an audience in New Delhi. "We have to fight for our rights. We have to oppose injustice, because not to do so would be a form of violence. Gandhi-ji fervently promoted nonviolence, but that didn't mean he was complacently accepting of the status quo; he resisted, but he did so without doing harm."

Knowing we represent the truth, adds the Dalai Lama, renders us calm and strong, with time and justice on our side. It's when people run out of sound arguments that they resort to fighting and violence. Calmness and nonviolence are signs of strength.

Fairness does not necessarily mean conforming to laws, the Dalai Lama points out. Corrupt or totalitarian governments can defend their injustices by saying they followed the rule of law. But laws fail to uphold justice—fairness to all—when in practice they are enforced in ways that support only the narrow interests of a ruling class. For a law to be just, it needs to protect the rights of everyone.

Some kinds of injustice are so intractable that transparency alone does not do the job. Despite decades of awareness, for instance, in many parts of the world unequal pay for women and minorities, "glass ceilings," and other forms of subtle and not-so-subtle discrimination—like caste—remain in firm place.

Then there's systemic oppression, the unfairness built into our social structures. Such wrongs meld with daily routine or seem so diffuse within an organization or government that no one feels responsible for speaking up.

A familiar scenario has an automaker getting internal reports that people are dying in its cars because of a defect, but reassuring the public not to worry. The company finally admits the problem only years later, after many more deaths.

"I suspect that every one of the people involved" at that automaker considers himself "to be an honest, ethical person," a commentator wrote about one such case. "Yet, collectively, they acted in a way that is absolutely stunning in its callousness."

The same can be said of similar incidents around the world that are the inevitable consequence of seemingly good people getting caught up in spoiled systems, where collusion, corruption, and the like twist behavior in ways that harm.

For instance, there's the daily degradation of nature resulting from a sad mix of political action funded quietly by partisans; investment decisions that finance despoiling nature; and unintended but toxic by-products of industry and commerce. Bureaucracies too can act as tacit weapons of injustice or exploitation.

"Sunlight," as U.S. Supreme Court Justice Felix Frankfurter said, "is the best disinfectant." Too little "sunshine" spotlights the action of elites, like corporate executives and politicians, with the power to make crucial decisions.

Nor is much attention paid to those whose work shapes our cultural beliefs and values and defines acceptable norms, such as religious figures or media gatekeepers, producers, and writers. On the other hand, any or all of those very people and forces can also operate for the good.

Impeccability

When I was talking with the Dalai Lama about where to send a portion of the proceeds from this book, the name of a group that handles funds he donates to worthy causes came up: The Dalai Lama Trust. The trust distributes its funds to address a wide range of needs, from typhoon relief in the Philippines through the Red Cross, to development of a science curriculum for Tibetan monks at Emory University.

In India as in Britain, this use of the word "trust" connotes a charitable organization. The Dalai Lama did not realize that in the United States "a trust" can signify a fund set up to avoid taxes on money that benefits oneself—not a philanthropic organization. Hearing this, he suggested changing the name to the Dalai Lama *Charitable* Trust, to make its purpose more apparent.

That he was concerned people might perceive the trust to be in his self-interest rather than as philanthropy bespeaks the Dalai Lama's sense of impeccability. He seeks transparency, fairness, and accountability in all he does—and wants the same for all of us.

At a Mind and Life meeting on compassion in economic systems, he was keenly interested when Ernst Fehr, an economist at the University of Zurich, told him about research in which people play games where they can either share or be greedy. At first, most people start out sharing—but if they see someone else be greedy, then they too start acting selfishly.

That changes, though, when the greedy are held accountable—when others can make clear there are consequences for being unfair. Once that becomes possible, cooperation soars.

This comes up anywhere people share a resource that all members of a group are free to use, like clean water. If people are selfish about their use, then there will be too little to go around.

The work of ecologist Garret Hardin on "the tragedy of the commons" takes a dim view of humanity's ability to share. He argues that greed and self-interest are powerful motivations that lead people to take more than their fair share—in this case, the residents of a grassy commons overgrazed their livestock, so destroying the commons itself.

But a closer look at the evidence shows that, throughout history, people also have worked together to manage shared resources—forests, fisheries, irrigation systems, as well as grazing land—to limit the damage individual greed might do. This too represents an application of compassion, which boils down to caring about others, not just ourselves.

"One of the most important things we all have to realize is that human happiness is interdependent," the Dalai Lama wrote in a foreword to a biography of Mahatma Gandhi. "Our own successful or happy future is very much related to that of others. Therefore, helping others or having consideration for their rights and needs is actually not just a matter of responsibility, but involves our own happiness."

The Dalai Lama's vision opens a complementary long-term strategy. As we—or future generations—learn to lessen selfishness and better manage destructive emotions while enhancing compassion, a social change might come. We just might end up with systems that actually have transparency, fairness, and accountability built in.

Consider what that might mean in the realm of economics.

CHAPTER SIX

Economics as if People Mattered

Whenever the Dalai Lama has a chance to speak to business people, he talks about the need for ethical values in their work. His main objection to capitalism is its lack of a compassionate moral outlook—its focus on acquisition of wealth to the exclusion of concern for people's well-being.

Capitalism needs compassion.

"I'm a Marxist," the Dalai Lama has often declared, at least when it comes to socioeconomic theory. With its emphasis on a more equitable distribution of wealth, he clarifies, Marxist economic thinking appeals to him because "there is a moral dimension."

Capitalism, as he sees it, assumes people are self-interested, focused on "making money—only profit, profit, profit," as he put it to me. Our motives determine the moral value of what we do, and our financial system largely rewards greed while ignoring costs to people and the planet.

He points to how commonly we find glaring poverty side by side with conspicuous consumption. This alone tells him there are deep troubles with our present economic system.

Wealth, he says, is for the good of society, not just for a single individual. He feels uneasy about the mercenary spirit of capitalism, which can be cruel and indifferent to the poor. As he told a group of business people, "The emphasis on 'me, me, me'—that's the source of the problem."

He raises the question of whether our very way of thinking about economics gives us satisfactory effects at the global level. Business has become perhaps the most powerful force in shaping our world, transcending governments and religion alike, he observes.

And yet the results—like the growing gap between rich and poor and the ongoing assault on earth's vitality—strongly suggest that business needs new ways of thinking. "It's not short versus long term," the Dalai Lama points out. "We need both. But there's too much obsessive focus on the short term regardless of long-term consequences."

Even so, he cautions against the pitfalls of stagnation and dictatorship of those socialist experiments that were "supposedly concerned for the working class" but in practice failed. While the name "socialism" may sound good, he adds, if in reality money secretly goes into private pockets, then the word is just a cover for corruption.

"It's not necessarily the system of economics that's the problem," whether capitalism or socialism, but "a lack of moral principle in the people involved in that system." Both "isms" can become corrupted by attitudes of selfishness and exploitation.

After the fall of the Berlin Wall, the Dalai Lama told his friend Václav Havel, who became president of the newly independent Czechoslovakia, that he wished the Eastern European countries, with their strong history of socialism, would come up with a new synthesis of socialism and capitalism. Instead, of course, those nations embraced the free-market models of capitalism.

A system like socialism, which fosters a more equal distribution of goods, ideally should operate by an active moral principle that capitalism lacks—which is why the Dalai Lama prefers it. But, he adds with a laugh, nowhere is Marxism practiced as it was originally proposed.

He sees how too-heavy state regulation dampens market dynamism and that the collectivist economic model is too top-down; he recognizes the need for entrepreneurial freedom too. Ideally, a system would balance freedom with altruism.

The compassionate economy the Dalai Lama envisions mixes entrepreneurial spirit with a sound social-support system and taxes on wealth—Sweden comes to his mind as a successful working model. Signs of a healthy mix in such countries, he says, can be seen in a smaller wealth gap and fewer ultra-rich.

While the Dalai Lama has been saying this for years, only recently has strong supporting data, such as French economist Thomas Piketty's *Capital,* emerged. That book analyzes data trends over centuries to show that those with money to invest will always earn more than those who labor for their wages. Capitalism enriches the wealthy far more than it does workers. A growing rich–poor inequality seems built into the free-market economy.

A few years ago, when the Dalai Lama was told about the climbing numbers of billionaires, he was puzzled. Why, he asked his translator Thupten Jinpa, would anyone want that much money? After all, he added, "You only have one stomach."

He argues that a healthy economy is signified not by how many people become billionaires but by the well-being of all. Capitalism can be a force for good only if it incorporates genuine concern for everyone.

That's what the Dalai Lama told a group at a conservative think tank in Washington, D.C. Since he makes no secret of his sympathy for a more compassionate version of economics, he said so to this audience. To the surprise of many, in his view the conversation went well.

A week or two later, the president of the think tank wrote an op-ed in *The New York Times* about the Dalai Lama's visit: "As with any tool, wielding capitalism for good requires deep moral awareness. Only activities motivated by a concern for others' well-being, he declared, could be truly 'constructive.'"

He added, "For the Dalai Lama, the key question is whether 'we utilize our favorable circumstances, such as our good health or wealth, in positive ways, in helping others.' . . . Advocates of free enterprise must remember that the system's moral core is neither profits nor efficiency. It is creating opportunity for individuals who need it the most."

While the phrase "creating opportunity" might resonate differently across the political spectrum, for the Dalai Lama the point is clear: One key to human flourishing is fairness and compassionate action on behalf of us all.

For an economy it means, as the op-ed put it, "practical policies based on moral empathy," like a safety net for the poor. "Washington," the op-ed concluded, "needs to be more like the Dalai Lama." I'd add London, Beijing, Moscow, and New Delhi to that list, for starters.

Rethinking Economics

Our dominant economic theories assume we operate like *homo economicus:* a rational, self-interested person who makes thoughtful judgments to fulfill desires. Economics predicts, for instance, that investors will seek to maximize profits, even if that means taking a risk. Neuroscience would tell us this particular motivation has a basis in the dopamine system for reward.

But investment advisers have long known that a very different brain system drives many people's decisions about their money: the neuronal network for threat, which worries about our safety. This drive for security leads people to be averse to risk, including with their money.

But what would an economics driven by our neural system for caring and contentment—not mere self-interest or fear—look like?

Some economists are already exploring that possibility. They think in ways that go beyond the assumptions of a selfish consumer as the field's basic unit, taking a fresh look at what people really want: lasting happiness, not just more stuff.

When I met with the Dalai Lama in Italy for this book, he had just received an invitation to a conference on the nature of happiness from Lord Richard Layard, whom my wife and I stopped off to see the next week in his office at the London School of Economics.

The aim of life, Layard told us, should be to create as much happiness—and as little misery—as we can in the world around us. The earliest articulations of economic theory by Adam Smith and Jeremy Bentham saw the measure of success for an economy in the well-being of its people. That ideal drew Layard himself to the field.

But, says Layard, in the twentieth century that basic premise got lost, as the universal metric for judging a country's economic health became its GDP, or "gross domestic product," the total value of goods and services produced (GNP, or "gross national product," is a close cousin). The assumption was that the more money at people's disposal, the greater their opportunities in life and so in their well-being.

Today's mainstream economics assumes we make rational decisions based on a clear sense of our own self-interest. The sum total of those rational decisions, the assumption goes, means markets will set the proper prices. That has been proved wrong by the popping of every pricing bubble through history since the Dutch tulip mania in the 1630s and, most recently and spectacularly, by the financial collapse of 2008.

Another great weakness of the GDP measure, Layard argues, has become glaringly apparent in recent years: A country can maintain a respectable overall GDP if a small elite becomes outrageously wealthy even while the masses sink. The ballooning wealth of a small percentage masks the lowering of well-being for the many.

If both parents spend long hours away from home, working just to survive—and to pay for day care for their kids—the profit at the day-care center adds to GDP. But the stresses on that family are ignored.

That's why nations that rank high on creating wealth do not top measures of well-being, especially when they have great financial inequities. Just measuring GDP misses completely costs of inequality like poor health care, education, housing, and food—all of which create hardships for children that make them more likely to end up poor as adults.

Another uncomfortable fact: The working poor, whose cheap labor creates more wealth at the top of the economic scale, have little chance themselves of advancing to a higher earning level.

Besides, the Dalai Lama cautions, economics based on a consumption-based lifestyle and the hope of limitless growth will gradually have to adjust to the reality of lower levels. The economic ideal of perpetual growth is not sustainable as a measure of success, a view articulated, for example, by the economist E. F. Schumacher in his book *Small Is Beautiful: Economics as if People Mattered*.

As my wife and I wended our way through the urban campus to lunch with Richard Layard, we passed the window of the university's bookstore, which prominently featured that influential volume by Thomas Piketty. *Capital* was clearly getting attention at the London School of Economics.

But Piketty's analysis, which draws on data from Europe and the United States, misses another point: how the poor have fared worldwide.

The rising tide of the global economy has lifted hundreds of millions—perhaps billions—of people at the lowest end of the scale: In the four decades after 1970, the numbers of those existing worldwide on a dollar a day or less fell by 80 percent. This raised the standard of living for workers in what were once "underdeveloped countries," like the BRIC group—Brazil, Russia, India, and China.

But that remarkable achievement has not lessened the rich–poor gap: The numbers of the ultra-wealthy worldwide mushroomed over the same period. As per Piketty, a problem with capitalism lies in the rules of the game: The pie being shared goes disproportionately to owners, at the expense of workers.

Nor does that higher tide lift all boats; the shift of manufacturing jobs from developed countries to undeveloped ones means, for example, that some workers in formerly prosperous countries now earn substantially less than did their parents at the same point in their career (even as cheaper workers in poor countries do better).

The Piketty rule holds that the rich–poor gap increases with time. Indeed, by 2016, the eighty wealthiest people in the world will have a net worth about equal to all of those billions on the lower half of the income ladder. The world seems to be heading toward islands of the ultra-wealthy few, walled off from the vulnerable many.

A global study of those at the low end of the pay scale concludes on a forced note of so-called good news: a projection that there will not be more than a billion people living in abject poverty in the future. Put another way, the poor will always be with us.

Traditionally, a capitalist's main focus is simply to make money, the Dalai Lama observes. But, he adds, capitalism needs to expand its theory to include benefiting the most people—and not just financially.

The Secret of Happiness

"What's the source of happiness?" a student at Princeton University asked the Dalai Lama.

Looking around at the students waiting for his answer, the Dalai Lama paused a beat or two, then called out: "Money!"

Another beat or two: "Sex!"

And then: "Nightclubs!"

His joke brought down the house.

Then he went on to say that when we see the world through a materialistic lens, we look to such sensory stimulation—even things like shopping, food, music, watching sports—as the source of satisfaction or joyfulness. But, he added, focusing *only* on sensory delights leaves us perpetually dissatisfied, because such pleasures are short-lived.

Immersion in consumerist indulgence as a way of life, so rampant in the First World and quickly spreading now throughout emerging economies like China and India, does not lead to real happiness but "cheapens life, feeding our lesser nature."

From time to time the Dalai Lama mentions once being the guest of a very wealthy family, at whose house he stopped for a lunch visit to break a long journey. In the bathroom, he says a bit sheepishly, he noticed the medicine cabinet door was open, so he peeked in—and found the cabinet full of tranquilizers and painkillers.

The Dalai Lama's critique of modern economics goes to its very assumptions about the basis of fulfillment. "Many people feel money is the source of a happy life. Money is necessary, useful—but more and more money does not bring happiness. Relying on money to be happy is too materialistic."

A flaw in that way of living is that even if we enjoy ourselves, "such joyfulness can go together with much worry at a deep mental level. It's a painkiller: The pain is still there, but you forget it for a moment while you are distracted."

We may feel some temporary relief, but then when something causes that deeper worry to stir, we forget the happiness. So "we need a deeper basis for contentment."

He clarifies: "The proper way to reduce pain is to work at the mental level itself, not through sensory gratification." The challenge lies partly in reorienting our attitudes toward the source of satisfaction and away from materialism.

"This is difficult to change. Our real hope is the people of this century"—today's young and those not yet born—getting what he calls a "proper education" about values and the true basis of a satisfied life. "I think that's the only hope."

He adds: "Nowadays, many people have the belief that if material progress continues, then everything will be okay. That way of thinking is a mistake. Material goods provide comfort for the physical body but not for the mind."

Money, as the song lyric has it, can't buy you love—or happiness.

Happiness, Layard's research shows, depends much more on the quality of our personal relationships than on our income. In many ways, the most important external factor in well-being is whether we feel this closeness.

By the same token, the Dalai Lama points out that feeling kindness, affection, and trust within our circle of family and friends makes us happier than do luxuries. He cites social-science research showing that the emotional benefits of gaining wealth are temporary—and that the overall level of people's contentment in a society is better the more evenly distributed its wealth is. That seems to be why countries like Denmark continually rank at the top of ratings of satisfaction and happiness.

If the goal of government were its people's well-being, Layard argues, then it would regulate the economy to be more stable rather than in ways that help a few people become extremely wealthy.

While economists' faith in the GDP has held that money represents a person's happiness, Layard points out an irony: The very economist who first developed the GDP warned against using it to gauge people's welfare.

A great deal of data, Layard says, shows that factors like your health and the quality of your relationships matter the most for happiness. Income accounts for only about one percent of the variation in people's happiness.

Layard stands at the forefront of a movement among economists to find a more meaningful metric for well-being than the GDP. He believes that countries should be judged by how satisfied their citizens are with their lives. Layard, a member of Britain's House of Lords, has helped move this agenda into government policy there.

As a result, first Britain and now all countries in the Organization for Economic Cooperation and Development (which seeks to further worldwide economic growth and employment and to raise standards of living) include measures of life satisfaction in their official statistics.

The Dalai Lama encourages such progressive thinking beyond economics alone to promote well-being. Despite the innovative creativity that drives economic activity, we have yet to provide the bare essentials for living to billions of people. Only an economy oriented around compassion, he argues, can overcome the vast disparities between the poorest and wealthiest.

Given that true happiness begins with a modicum of material comfort but then depends on cultivating qualities of mind like contentment and caring, the purpose of economic development, in the Dalai Lama's view, can be found in furthering both goals.

He has applauded groups that encourage countries to define the success of their policies in terms of "Gross National Happiness." But, he adds, he's still waiting to hear about creative ways this ideal of a compassionate economy might become action—not just talk.

Action for Happiness

Layard's data shows plummeting levels of trust among people and rises in anxiety and depression even as GDP grows. The true mark of a society's progress, he argues, should be its people's well-being—as reflected by their levels of happiness, rather than simply by financial gain. While controversial among economists, that argument swayed many, including some surprising allies.

One was Gus O'Donnell, who at the time was cabinet secretary, head of the U.K.'s civil service, a post so powerful, some say, that he was widely known by his initials: GOD. O'Donnell was instrumental in changing how government policies—ranging from health and education to pension and employment—were evaluated, so that the impact on people's well-being was taken into account too.

With that success, Layard and his allies sought to stir a supporting social change that would offer an alternative to the predominant self-obsession with financial striving. They wanted to spread a better vision of what a happy, fulfilling life looks like. Religion had offered such moorings in earlier times, but, given the lack of religious affiliation throughout Western Europe, there was an institutional void.

And so began Action for Happiness, a secular movement that captures many of the ways in which religion aims to give people an

ethical and emotional anchor—teaching how to engage life with
meaning and how to treat others well—but that also appeals to people with no particular religious interest. As a sign of his endorse-
ment, the Dalai Lama agreed to be the organization's "patron."

On joining Action for Happiness, people pledge: "I will try to
create more happiness and less unhappiness in the world around
me." That means taking action to improve their own well-being but
also to help create happier neighborhoods, workplaces, schools, and
communities, says Mark Williamson, the group's director.

While Action for Happiness's membership numbers in the hundreds of thousands, and about 60 percent of those live in far-flung
countries, "The magic is in small, face-to-face groups," Williamson
says. The model seems a bit like Alcoholics Anonymous, in that
anyone who qualifies can initiate a local group where people meet
regularly around a set format.

Each meeting starts with a few minutes of mindfulness and expressions of gratitude, with a discussion at the heart of the session.
The meeting ends with people choosing an action to take, along the
lines of helping someone in need or connecting with a lonely person.
One group launched a Happiness Café, where like-minded people
can connect and share ideas to create a happier and more supportive
local community.

In Exploring What Matters, the main Action for Happiness program, the group meets for eight weeks, with each session focusing
on a single big question for discussion. They start with "What really
matters in life?" and then "What really makes us happy?" These are
followed by sessions on dealing with adversity, having good relationships, caring for others, and creating happier workplaces and
communities. They end with "How can we create a happier world?"

This progression from personal meaning and happiness to compassion often leads people to find ways to help other people. For

instance, Jasmine Hodge-Lake came to Action for Happiness because of her chronic pain. Degenerative spine disease, carpal tunnel syndrome, and fibromyalgia created a toxic mix of suffering that had brought her life to a standstill.

Unable to work and in constant pain for more than a decade, she spent her days in despair. A pain-management course that brought no relief left her feeling more helpless, plunging her deeper into depression. "At the end I felt, I have no hope," says Hodge-Lake. "This is my life: no life."

Adding to her funk, she felt isolated. "I didn't want to be around other people and thought that no one really cared about me," she recalls.

By chance, she stumbled on the Action for Happiness website, which includes a simple list of Ten Keys to Happier Living—connecting more with people, for example. For Hodge-Lake, that list brought the realization that there were practical steps she could take to become happier. And so she joined the eight-week course.

Her first "lightbulb" moment in the course came as she was listening to a taped talk by Jon Kabat-Zinn about mindfulness and saw that she could change her relationship to her pain: Accept it rather than fight against it. That internal shift lessened her emotional distress, even as the sensations of pain remained.

Another lightbulb came during the week devoted to what makes work meaningful and fulfilling. Hodge-Lake, realizing she had lost passion for just about everything, resolved to work with other people suffering from chronic pain, to see how she might help them too.

"I was still fairly depressed, but I started to do more things," Hodge-Lake says. "It was amazing how the tools that Action for Happiness gave me helped. I found there were things I could do that would make a big difference. I started to feel hopeful about the future."

With that inner change, she thought about how to improve support for people who live with chronic pain. "I realized we need a new approach—one that is more hopeful and uses some of the ideas that I had learned from Action for Happiness."

Hodge-Lake now informally counsels others with chronic pain about ways they might be helped—and she seeks to give them hope. She's in the process of becoming a "patient voice" in a program to improve patient-care guidelines for Britain's medical system. And she's spreading the word about Action for Happiness, passing out their card on Ten Keys to Happier Living—and encouraging people to get involved.

"I wouldn't be where I am now without Action for Happiness and that course," she contends. "I still have bad days, and life certainly isn't perfect. But it has really helped me so much. Now I'm trying to be the change I want to see."

Doing Good While Doing Well

The cavernous brick-walled factories of Easthampton, Massachusetts, prospered in the nineteenth century but by the twenty-first had become abandoned derelicts, with shattered windows and graffiti-scrawled walls. Recently, one of these factory buildings, now known as Eastworks, has been restored to use, housing ventures like Prosperity Candle, which fills a spacious loft, well lit by huge windows. There Moo Kho Paw, an immigrant from Burma, has learned to support her family with a new craft: candlemaking.

Paw, mother of three, went from abject dependence in refugee camps on the Thai–Burma border to earning her first paycheck as a candlemaker, allowing her to support her kids and pay her rent and a babysitter. She joins ten other refugee women in candlemaking for Prosperity, which also employs twelve earthquake victims in Haiti and about six hundred women (many of them war widows) in Iraq. All have found a livelihood that lifted them from poverty.

And that was the plan. Prosperity Candle is no ordinary company: Founded as a "social enterprise," its legal status lies somewhere between a charity and a business. "We are a for-profit company with the heart of a nonprofit," says the founder, Ted Barber. "Our purpose is to make the world a better place."

That's no trite platitude but rather the explicit aim as defined in the company's state charter to do business. It's one way some companies are heeding the call for business decisions that incorporate an ethic of fairness and compassion and for heightening the ethical standards of business.

Take another such for-benefit corporation, the Greyston Bakery in Yonkers, New York. The bakery hires, trains, and houses people who were homeless, ex-convicts, drug addicts, on welfare, battered wives, or illiterate—all well-trodden paths to despair.

Tutored in skills like baking, the bakery's workers have a solid livelihood. The bakery supplies a vast amount of brownies daily to Ben & Jerry's ice cream factory in Vermont, where they are mixed into flavors like Chocolate Fudge Brownie. The company's motto: "We don't hire people to bake brownies; we bake brownies to hire people."

The Dalai Lama was delighted to hear about the bakery and the class of businesses it represents. Called "B Corporations" in the United States, these businesses have an explicit mission to benefit society or the environment, as well as to make a profit—doing good while doing well. This double mission encourages a company to meet goals for the greater good, not just to make money.

Beyond B Corporations, an even more purposeful way of doing good while doing well can be seen in the "triple bottom line": profits, people, and planet. Having targets beyond profit alone redefines how a company does business.

For example, Patagonia, the American maker of sports clothing, became a B Corporation in 2012. That move gives the company legal cover to let environmental and social benefits of its operations take as much priority as—or more than—financial return alone. So, for instance, the company was able to support time-consuming research, taking many years before any financial payback, to refine rubber for its wetsuits derived from a desert shrub instead of from petroleum.

Then there's Warby Parker, a firm that makes eyeglasses frames—and gives away a pair of glasses to a person in the developing world for every frame it sells. And Jonathan Rose Companies, a green-construction firm, builds housing for the poor that also meets the high environmental standards of LEED certification.

These companies re-create capitalism to be meaningful, not just profitable. One of the first such social enterprises was the Grameen Bank in Bangladesh; its founder, Muhammad Yunus, famously pioneered micro-loans for people in poverty, which helped them start their own small businesses, eventually paying back the money to be loaned to others.

The bank represents a nascent movement that goes by many names, from "conscious capitalism" or "purpose-driven business" to "impact investing." All share the same goal: Business becomes a force for good.

Many large corporations now put at least some value on showing corporate social responsibility, or "CSR," as it is widely known. At a minimum, CSR means simply following ethical business practices, but many businesses go beyond their own needs, to further the social good.

Cisco Systems, for instance, has an engineering culture built around its business of making and installing digital networking systems and providing that expertise to other companies. But what most people who know the company's name don't realize is how seriously they take their CSR.

For example, about a third of Cisco's sixty thousand employees live and work in India. When a million people were left homeless in South India by a once-in-a-hundred-years flood, the company's employees helped rebuild 3,223 flooded homes, as well as a health-care center. While they were at it, the Cisco experts left four remote schools wired for distance learning.

Responding to a crisis in unmet medical needs for the world's poorest children, the company's CSR arm applied its expertise to devise a care-at-a-distance technology. Cisco's system, for instance, lets pediatric specialists anywhere in the world consult with doctors in remote places, even on rare or hard-to-treat cases. Some are deployed in hospitals within the United States, but others are in Brazil, China, and Uganda—and in that flood site in India.

I told the Dalai Lama about how some businesses are retrofitting to become a force for good by building caring values into the very operations of an existing corporation. The global conglomerate Unilever, for instance, has announced as part of a larger sustainability goal its plan to source raw materials from a half million small farms in the Third World, all new to the company's supply chain—by giving them technical aid so they can become dependable suppliers, giving them steady incomes.

Development experts say that helping small farmers increase their business like this stands as the best way to improve the health, education, and economy of the world's poorest rural areas.

Hearing this, the Dalai Lama once again exclaimed, "Really wonderful!"

"The problem is profitability at the expense of humanity," as Marc Benioff, CEO of the cloud computing company Salesforce, told me just weeks before my meeting with the Dalai Lama. "Corporations have immense resources—take these and use them for good. With compassionate capitalism, you can be both successful and also do good."

Benioff's company follows a "1:1:1" principle, giving one percent of profits, one percent of product, and one percent of employees' time to worthy causes—a model he has been urging other tech firms to emulate.

Along the same lines, Warren Buffett and Bill Gates have challenged other billionaires to donate more than half their wealth to charities, as they have done. More than two hundred have taken a "giving pledge" to do so.

There are many such examples of compassionate capitalists—though arguably not nearly enough. The Dalai Lama himself, to my mind, offers a model of generosity that we all could emulate to some extent. In whatever way we can, he told a business group, "help others."

If it is the emotional temperature of our days that makes them good or bad, even the workplace offers a chance for greater warmth. I was a bit startled to hear the Dalai Lama tell a small group of business people what amounted to some practical managerial advice. While it might have come straight out of a human-resources manual, it was based on his homespun compassion.

A businessman told the Dalai Lama he was concerned about how stressed and at a loss his younger, entry-level employees seemed. The Dalai Lama's response: "For their peace of mind, let the younger staff have an internal conversation—maybe once a week or every month—about their state of mind, their emotions, not the business."

They could share ideas on how to be resilient, confront challenges, be more effective, he added. Along those lines, he praised the emotional climate at some Japanese businesses that foster a sense of loyalty and security, as though they are a "family" of sorts. Boosting people's well-being at work marks another way business can be of benefit.

In talking with a group of CEOs, the Dalai Lama spoke of "positive capitalism," where "you move forward but also make it possible for others to move forward too."

The Dalai Lama even envisions businesses working together for the benefit of all of them, an alternative to ruthless winner-take-all thinking. "Business needs a sense of responsibility to work together more cooperatively—less emphasis on secrecy, fear, negative competition. Trust is the key factor. We need positive competition: If I progress, they should too, so they are not left behind.

"The global economy," he says, "is like a roof over all of us. But it depends on individual pillars for support."

That fits the career advice he gave a crowd of college students: "First take care of yourself financially. Then, step by step, stand on your own feet in order to help others."

CHAPTER SEVEN

Care for Those in Need

"My friends, come help. . . . A woman froze to death tonight at 3:00 A.M., on the pavement of Sebastopol Boulevard, clutching the eviction notice which the day before had made her homeless. . . . Each night, more than two thousand endure the cold, without food, without bread, more than one almost naked.

"Hear me; in the last three hours, two aid centers have been created. . . . They are already overflowing, we must open them everywhere. Tonight, in every town in France, in every quarter of Paris, we must hang out placards under a light in the dark, at the door of places where there are blankets, bunks, soup, where one may read, under the title 'Fraternal Aid Center,' these simple words: 'If you suffer, whoever you are, enter, eat, sleep, recover hope, here you are loved.'"

This heartfelt appeal came during the harsh French winter of 1954, airing on Radio Luxembourg, a radio station heard throughout much of France.

The voice on the radio—and author of the same statement re-printed in the country's largest newspaper—was Abbé Pierre, a priest and activist for the homeless in France, once prominent as a Resistance fighter during World War II.

The response was overwhelming nationwide, with hundreds of millions of francs being donated as well as mountains of blankets and supplies. Abbé Pierre immediately founded the Emmaus houses for the homeless.

They were supported in part by a vineyard the project had been given, which the Dalai Lama was to visit years later. The abbé particularly impressed the Dalai Lama: "He was wonderful, a great friend of mine."

Likewise, when it comes to putting love and compassion into practice, it's no surprise that Mother Teresa immediately comes to the Dalai Lama's mind. He met her briefly, and after she passed away he visited her successor, Sister Nirmala, at the Missionaries of Charity in Calcutta. There he was moved by the dedication of the sisters in aiding the sick and poor, with no thought for themselves; they were vibrant examples of the Christian ideal.

He admires such faith-based groups that, for instance, go to live in remote rural areas in places like India and Africa, sacrificing comfort to improve the health and well-being of people in dire need, by setting up schools and clinics. Such missions are "wonderful," he told me, "a community serving God's creation."

But, he added, it's all the better when the groups' goals are simply to relieve suffering rather than to serve an agenda of conversion. Fewer such hidden agendas, if any, go with the service to the world's poor of countless NGOs ("non-governmental organizations"), which pursue a wide range of goals for social betterment. They serve at the front lines in a worldwide force for good.

There's a Tibetan phrase for such compassion in action: *men la lhakpar tsewa*. It translates as "being specially concerned for the underprivileged," defending the defenseless, helping those who are in poverty, disabled, diseased, or otherwise need care.

"Mentally," the Dalai Lama told me, "sometimes rich people just look down at people in need and maybe give them something. But there's no genuine respect in that. These are the same human beings, with the same abilities. We all have the same potential but not the same opportunities," he added, noting that progress here depends on how society changes.

That brought to my mind a set of worldwide data on IQ analyzed by psychologist James Flynn. He found that in nations with a privileged and underprivileged group, the better-off children had a large IQ advantage.

But when the poor children got better nutrition and education free from discrimination against their group—for instance, if their family immigrated to another country—that IQ disparity vanished in a single generation.

Both the advantaged and disadvantaged groups in society have a responsibility to work toward change, the Dalai Lama says. Those better off should, first, become attuned to what's needed to help the downtrodden and then offer resources to help with education, job training, and the like. The aim is "to help them stand on their own feet."

Those in need, for their part, can take responsibility by helping themselves. "No matter your difficulties," he advises, "don't feel you are hopeless or helpless. You have the same right as anyone to a happier life."

With these efforts, he says, "Circumstances can change for the better."

If we adopt the attitude of the oneness of all people, we naturally see that "we all have an equal right to become a happy person." We can't just dismiss the plight of the needy with pity, saying, "Oh, you are unfortunate," and doing nothing to help.

"When you translate compassion into action," the Dalai Lama told a group of college students involved in service projects, "you need sincere motivation—and also some insight into the dynamics that created the problem. Look at the root causes," for instance of the rich-poor income gap. And, he added, you need both clear vision and compassion.

For those who believe in God, he says, "In the eyes of God, all seven billion human beings are equal: the same nature, same right to happiness, same desires. So serving humanity, particularly poor people, is the best way to serve God."

For those with no religious belief, he takes another approach: "We are social animals, and even animals sometimes practice generosity—share their food and care for each other—even simply licking. If you are happy and have plenty of food but your neighbor is having difficulties, it's completely natural to be generous.

"So in whatever way, we must help and serve needy people; we should develop generosity."

Helping People Help Themselves

Walk the dusty streets of India long enough and eventually you are likely to come across a leper huddled by the side of the road, a tin bowl for coins on the ground nearby. The leper's body may be missing fingers, toes, even limbs—a sad consequence of the disease's progression as it numbs nerves.

The Dalai Lama has often donated to facilities for people with leprosy. One that has particularly inspired him is the Anandwan community, founded by his friend Baba Amte, who in his younger days had devoted himself to Gandhi. Baba Amte believed that what lepers needed was not charity but dignified work.

Baba Amte himself suffered from a debilitating progressive spinal degeneration, which left him bedridden most of the time, yet he actively led despite his suffering. Baba Amte made a vivid impression on the Dalai Lama, who visited an Anandwan community in western India—a village of homes, workshops, schools, and a hospital, with verdant gardens on what had been barren earth, built entirely by people with leprosy or other handicaps.

As the Dalai Lama recalls, he sat on Baba Amte's bed, holding his hand. "I told him that whereas my compassion is just so much talk, his shone through in everything he did. Here was someone who was a living example of compassion in action, an inspiration to us all."

Anandwan today cares for more than two thousand leprosy victims and more than a hundred of their children, another several hundred blind or deaf-mute children, plus orphans and those born to unwed mothers.

Prevailing social norms would have treated these denizens of Anandwan as outcastes or pariahs, relegating them to begging on the mean streets. But not Baba Amte, who lived among them in the community he built.

"When I visited there," the Dalai Lama says, "everyone was full of self-respect and dignity, everyone equal. They all had jobs, a livelihood. When they became old and retired, they were still looked after. They were handicapped but full of spirit. I was really very much impressed."

Baba Amte put it bluntly: "Charity destroys, work builds."

The residents of Anandwan support themselves by making products ranging from carpets, school notebooks, and greeting cards from recycled paper, to metal bed frames, crutches, and special protective footwear for those with leprosy.

Though Baba Amte passed away in 2008, his two sons, both physicians, carry on his work. At last report, Anandwan—and two sister communities—employed over five thousand residents.

"Their mental attitude makes a big difference," the Dalai Lama recalls from his visit to Anandwan. "Their work gives them self-confidence and self-respect, so they are full of enthusiasm."

When it comes to helping those in need, the Dalai Lama—like Baba Amte—emphasizes people helping themselves. Here, attitude is crucial. "Sometimes poor people feel they cannot do much to help themselves."

But, he adds, it's the root causes of their difficulties that need to change. They have the same potential as anyone else. But they need to believe in their own ability and to make an effort. Then, given the same opportunities, they can be equal.

He told me how some hard-liner Chinese Communist officials had spread propaganda saying that the Tibetan brain was "inferior," and he said that some Tibetans had adopted that self-defeating view of themselves. But when given the same schooling and chances in life, Tibetans did as well as anyone else—and that convinced many Tibetans that they were not inferior after all.

He had used this example with a post-apartheid resident of a shantytown in Soweto, whose home he was visiting. The man told him that African brains were inferior and so Africans could not be as intelligent as whites.

The Dalai Lama was shocked and saddened by this. "I argued that this is totally wrong. If you ask scientists if there are any brain differences due to color, they would definitely say no. The real point is equality. Now that you have the opportunity, you must work hard. You can be equal in every way."

The Dalai Lama argued energetically to convince the man that Africa had great potential and that long colonial rule had created a lack of self-confidence in Africans, which could be overcome—as with the Tibetans—with social equality, opportunity, and education.

After a lot of argument, the man sighed and in a low voice said, "Now I'm convinced: We're the same. I believe we are equal."

"I felt a tremendous relief," the Dalai Lama recalls. "At least one person's way of thinking had changed."

Self-Mastery

Of course those who have wealth—like those in developed countries seeking to help impoverished areas like rural India or Africa—should help with "education, training, and equipment," the Dalai Lama says. But, he adds, that's just half the answer: The downtrodden also must help themselves. Any group that finds itself economically disadvantaged or discriminated against needs to fight against defeatist attitudes, he contends, and find the grit to attain a better life.

"The only way to reduce the gap between the rich and the poor," whether in Africa, America, or anywhere else, he says, is not through complaining and anger, frustration and violence, but rather through "developing self-confidence, hard work, and education."

Take Mellody Hobson, the youngest of six children (the oldest is more than twenty years her senior) born to a single black mother in Chicago. Hobson met her father only twice. And money was always an issue in their household.

Recalling what it was like to grow up without a stable and consistent income, Hobson says, "There was this overwhelming sense of financial insecurity. There were times when we were evicted from our apartment and we would move all of our furniture and belongings into an older sibling's studio apartment. And for a time, we would live there with four or five people.

"This kind of financial insecurity meant we were not surprised when our car was repossessed. It meant that sometimes when we would buy food at the grocery store, our insufficient-funds checks would be posted at the checkout counter, as a warning to the cashier not to accept checks from us. It meant many occasions when my mother would borrow five dollars' worth of gas from the station owner to get me to school."

Though they never lived in a homeless shelter or slept in their car, the lack of real security was haunting.

Still, her mother was both ambitious and industrious, buying dilapidated buildings cheaply and then fixing them. Hobson credits her mother with instilling a "can-do" spirit, telling her she could achieve whatever she desired if she worked hard.

"She always told me, 'You can be anything,'" Hobson remembers.

The uncertainty and chaotic living drove Hobson, who by age five was telling her mother that she was never going to be poor.

"I would just look at my circumstances and say, this is never going to happen to me. I hated it." She was, as she tells it, "obsessed," fanatically studying for hours, locking herself in the bathroom and sitting on the floor while running water to drown out the household noise so she could focus on her schoolwork. She was always among the top students in her class.

Hobson attended the Ogden Elementary School, one of the top public schools in Chicago, located in an upscale neighborhood. But since her mother couldn't really afford the rents in that neighborhood, she recalls, "I experienced a lot of moving—we got evicted a lot, a lot. It wore on me—especially since I worked so hard to hide it from my friends and others."

The Ogden School, one of the first in the United States to offer the high academic standards of the International Baccalaureate program, was one stable element in a chaotic life. "School was everything to me at that point—everything. It provided all the order and structure that I craved, and it was dependable. I always went to the same school, even if I didn't always go to the same home," Hobson told me.

Industrious like her mother, Hobson from early on had a concentration and drive that let her study for hours and even today rules her routine: up at 4:00 A.M. for an intense physical workout—running, swimming, or spinning—and ready to start the day's work at 6:00 A.M.

"I've always been very disciplined," says Hobson, "but that discipline comes out of a bit of paranoia, I think. I always had the sense that I needed to be so in order to get ahead."

That resolve made Hobson highly independent in getting what other children at the Ogden School took for granted. If she wanted to go to a birthday party, she would have to figure out how to buy a present and get there and back on her own, because her mother was often working.

Because most kids at Ogden were very well-to-do, Hobson "knew what the other side looked like and I wanted it."

From Ogden, a public school, Hobson went on to a Catholic college-prep school, on a partial scholarship. She remembers being called out of class one day and told not to come back until her mom could pay the tuition. "I was apoplectic," Hobson recalls. "I had to miss school for a few days until my mother could raise the few hundred dollars."

Hobson went to Princeton University with a combination of loans and scholarships. There her senior thesis at the Woodrow Wilson School of Public and International Affairs was on South African children living under apartheid. Their struggles deeply moved her and put her own life and challenges in perspective. Their parents worked far away, in the cities or in coal mines, and these children were really on their own. Many became highly politicized, creating part of the political will that eventually brought down the system of apartheid.

From Princeton, Hobson went to work at Ariel Investments, where she has worked ever since—likely making her a rarity among the 1,100 other graduates in her Princeton class. "That would make sense to you if you understood my craving for stability," she notes. "I lived in my first apartment for four years and my second for fourteen, though both were really, really tiny. Financially, I could have moved long before I did, but I wouldn't, because I hate moving."

Starting at Ariel in client service and marketing, she rose rapidly through the ranks. When she was just thirty-one she became president, the job she still holds. In addition, she serves on several corporate boards, including Starbucks and Estée Lauder, and is chair of DreamWorks Animation SKG.

"Oh, wonderful!" the Dalai Lama said on hearing Mellody Hobson's story.

He liked it even more when I added that she had worked with or helped to establish programs for public-school kids in Chicago, designed to help children lacking in financial resources get the education and confidence that would put their lives on a positive arc.

After School Matters offers twenty-two thousand inner-city teens a rich range of choices, from lessons with members of the Lyric Opera of Chicago or the Joffrey Ballet to classes in rebuilding computers, making robots, animation, fine arts, hip-hop—about one thousand such programs. In the summer, After School Matters provides jobs to eight thousand teenagers and is the largest employer of teens in Chicago.

More than 95 percent of the high schoolers are minority, and most live below the poverty line. "We provide teens with opportunities that will enrich their lives and give them the foundation for a successful life," says Hobson, who chairs the organization.

The Ariel Community Academy, a public school sponsored by Hobson's company, sits in what was once one of Chicago's toughest neighborhoods, one that is only now gentrifying; 98 percent of students are African American, and 85 percent are poor enough that they get free or subsidized lunches. Yet from pre-kindergarten through eighth grade, academy students are held to the highest academic standards in a curriculum that emphasizes financial literacy.

In a novel experiment, Hobson's firm gives each class $20,000 to invest over the course of their grade-school years. Upon graduation, the students give $20,000 back to the incoming first-grade class so that the program can be self-perpetuating.

Half of whatever profits exist are split among the whole class. For all children who choose to put their share of earnings in an investment plan for college, Ariel Investments adds another thousand dollars.

Says Hobson, "We want to socialize them" to invest in retirement plans and let them know the value of any matching funds from their company, "which is free money." In this way, they are thinking about retirement savings as children—well before the start of their careers.

Any remaining funds go to a charity the students choose. In a sentiment the Dalai Lama would surely applaud, Hobson told me, "We don't want poor kids to always think of themselves as recipients of philanthropy. We want to teach them philanthropy as well."

Something in this mix pays off. Year after year, the students' scores on statewide math tests place them among the top in the entire state, and the school has consistently won an award for closing the gap in academic achievement between children in poverty and those better off.

Those results strongly suggest the academy students are, among other benefits, getting a boost in a mental faculty crucial for success in life: cognitive control, the power to stay focused and ignore distractions, to delay gratification now in pursuit of a future goal, and to put a damper on destructive emotions.

This capacity has been measured in children as young as four years old by one of the most famous experiments in the annals of psychology, the "marshmallow test." Conducted at Stanford University, the test gives four-year-olds the choice of eating a marshmallow immediately or waiting several minutes and then getting two. Surprisingly, when the kids who were able to wait were tracked down at the end of high school, they had a huge advantage over those who gobbled it down on the spot in their scores on the college entrance exam.

Another thirty-year study of cognitive control found that this singular ability predicted children's future financial success and wealth better than did their IQ and the wealth of the family they grew up in. Citing economic research that shows learning such skills in childhood boosts lifelong earnings, the scientists who did the study strongly urged that cognitive control—a learnable ability—be taught to every child, particularly those who are disadvantaged.

"This is very important," the Dalai Lama said when I told him about these studies, "to help children get better at this—teach them how."

This key skill comes down to a single teachable attitude, though psychologists have described it in many different terms. Carol Dweck, a Stanford psychologist, calls it "mindset"— the simple belief that you can succeed. If you face a problem a bit too difficult for you, the question is whether you have the attitude "I can't do this" or you simply feel you have not solved it yet. With the latter attitude, you keep trying—and so are far more likely to succeed. The belief that they could get better at math, for example, predicted well which students would stay with and do well in a tough course.

At the University of Pennsylvania, psychologist Angela Duckworth studies this can-do attitude as "grit"—persevering toward long-term goals despite setbacks and obstacles. Combined with cognitive control, she finds, these personal skills predict success. For instance, grit predicted both grade-point average at an Ivy League school and level attained by contestants in the national spelling bee, over and above the person's IQ.

Both these concepts are updates of an older construct in psychology: the distinction between feeling yourself to be a "pawn" or an "origin." With the outlook of a pawn, a person feels helpless in the face of larger forces in their life. But feeling yourself to be an origin means you believe you can make efforts to change circumstances for the better.

Gandhi advocated something quite similar, using the Hindi concept of *swaraj:* self-mastery or self-rule. Regarding how we help someone in need, he urged people to ask: "Will it restore him to a control over his own life and destiny? In other words, will it lead to *swaraj* for the hungry and spiritually starving millions?"

Women as Leaders

On a bus heading for school in Pakistan's remote Swat Valley one day, a man boarded and called for Malala Yousafzai—and shot her in the head.

Malala was targeted because she had become the spokesperson for educating girls, a movement opposed by violent Taliban extremists. But Malala was not deterred, using the shooting and attendant publicity to further her crusade. Her book, *I Am Malala,* became a global bestseller, and she became the youngest person to win a Nobel Prize for Peace.

The Nobel was shared between Malala and Kailash Satyarthi, an Indian activist who combats forced child labor—all too often, children are sold into bondage by their dirt-poor families to weave rugs, labor in textile factories, or risk their lives burrowing through tiny tunnels in coal mines. Both Malala and Kailash are passionate about the rights of all children to an education, a right denied not only to both the poorest but also, disproportionately, to girls.

In a letter to Malala after the Nobel announcement, the Dalai

Lama wrote how moved he was by the "tremendous strength" she showed while recovering from the shooting. "That you have continued, unbowed, to promote the basic right to education earns only admiration."

Malala embodies female leadership, which the Dalai Lama urges for the future. It's a topic he mentions frequently, and when I asked him about it, he told me a story that at first seemed a digression.

A Swiss doctor who had treated the Dalai Lama for an eye problem became friendly enough to invite him to his small mountain chalet, a hunting lodge.

There the doctor showed the Dalai Lama his guns and a collection of hunting trophies—the stuffed heads of animals he had shot, hanging from the walls.

The Dalai Lama told me with a laugh that what he thought to say was along the lines of "Butcher!" But, in keeping with decorum, he said nothing.

After that tale, the Dalai Lama came back to my query, pointing out that hunting is, typically, a male sport—a holdover from earlier times, when men needed to hunt for food to help their families survive. That coincided with a period in the sweep of human history, he conjectured, when there was apparently no concept of leadership.

Some historians (particularly those with a Marxist lens, he noted) argue that originally humans had no class distinctions, lived in small groups, and shared whatever they had. When the human population increased with the discovery of farming, he went on, then came the concepts of "my land, my possessions."

And with that emerged thievery and an increase in robberies and such—and so people felt the need for strong rulers who could prevent crimes and impose justice. Leadership in those days required physical strength, which favored men; it was an era when "hero" meant mercilessly killing, he said.

"Times change, reality changes," the Dalai Lama said. While so-cial norms and cultural heritage have held women back, now is "the time to change these things. Gender, color, no difference. In modern times, equality."

But the numbers of women in leadership ranks are nowhere near what fairness would dictate. So, he says, now that "education has brought more equality, we need women to take up more positions of responsibility and leadership."

He argues that our times require leaders who are more sensitive to human needs and who have concern for others, with an emphasis on warmheartedness, and women tend to be more biologically at-tuned than men to the suffering of others.

Here science provides a key finding. Scans reveal that the neural response of the brain's pain centers to seeing someone in pain is to mirror that of the person suffering.

And this sensitivity to another's suffering—the essence of compassion—occurs more strongly in women than in men. Science also finds that women have greater accuracy in reading emotions than men do.

The Dalai Lama sees in such data an indication that women are naturally more prepared for compassion, "because they are more sensitive to others' pain—more empathetic. So biologically, women have more potential for compassion.

"These days, nurses or others who care for people are, for the most part, female," the Dalai Lama said, adding, a bit impishly, "The majority of butchers are males."

By the same token, macho political leaders seem more likely to create crises as a show of strength. Judging from history, he conjec-tured, there should be less danger of violence if in the future more leaders are women. And more women leaders, he said, would take a more active role in promoting human values like compassion.

This more concerned and caring style of leadership can, of

course, be found in many men too—the Dalai Lama himself embodies these traits. But in general he, like many of us, sees such compassion as coming more naturally to women.

But in order for more women to emerge as leaders, the Dalai Lama urges, the unequal treatment of women in societies throughout the world, from the outright oppression suffered by Malala to more-subtle forms, must be abolished.

Barefoot College

Consider Kamala Devi, who comes from a poor family in a rural village in the Indian state of Rajasthan but now heads a program to teach impoverished women how to build, install, and maintain solar-powered lights.

Devi first learned there was such a thing as solar power when the night school she attended replaced its kerosene lamps with solar ones. How, she wondered, could a lantern give light without a flame?

It was years before Kamala Devi learned the answer. Married off early, as was the local custom, she was able to go to night school only after completing her daily chores—and after overcoming resistance from her husband and his family to getting an education at all.

Once Kamala got to night school, she was lucky enough to be chosen for a training workshop in solar engineering being given at a nearby town. That workshop changed her life.

The men in her family scoffed at the idea that a woman could understand how to assemble and repair solar equipment—but after months of training, she was adept. And now she heads the local school for training other women like her in the manufacture and repair of solar units.

That school and Kamala Devi's training were part of the mission of the Barefoot College, founded in 1972 by Sanjit "Bunker" Roy, another friend of the Dalai Lama's. By elevating the social and economic status of women in the poorest regions, the college not only changes how women (and men) there view their traditional role but also boosts public health: Children get better food and education.

Roy has now spent more than forty years living in a small village in rural Rajasthan, a far cry from his privileged upbringing. In 1965, shortly after finishing college, Roy volunteered to help in villages in the destitute state of Bihar, which was suffering a famine.

Inspired by Gandhi's teachings to help the very poor, Roy worked for five years digging wells in Tilonia, a village in Rajasthan where he later founded the Barefoot College—and pioneered training solar engineers like Kamala Devi. That training is unique: The students are typically unschooled grandmothers from hardscrabble villages. But when they return to their hometown as solar experts, suddenly these women have new status and respect—another goal.

"For me, the best investments are in training grandmothers," Roy told the Dalai Lama. "These women, most between forty and fifty years old, are illiterate. But they are the most mature, the most tolerant, and they have so much courage."

The instruction is given through sign language, gesture, and demonstration rather than on the printed page. This has meant that even women from rural Africa can be trained as solar engineers—such as the group from a village in Mali, two days by road and seven days by boat from Timbuktu, itself an icon of isolation.

Even though designed for those who cannot read, the training does not skimp on technical expertise. The students learn to make sophisticated equipment, like charge controllers and inverters, and how to install solar panels and link them together in a local power grid.

By now the Barefoot College has turned out hundreds of solar engineers, who have brought this sustainable electrification to some six hundred Indian hamlets as well as to twenty-one African countries—even to Afghanistan. This means poor villagers in those places can supplement their income from a day's work by making handicrafts at night in their newly lit home, and older women who had been relegated to second-class status are now wage earners with a valued skill.

It also means that children can study and go to school at night after looking after their family's cattle or goats during the day. More than seven thousand children attend some one hundred fifty night schools founded by the Barefoot College and lit by solar units.

Among the Barefoot College's other services to the rural poor are glove puppets used by health workers "to talk about social messages like why you should not beat your wife, why you need clean drinking water, why you should send your child to school," Roy told the Dalai Lama at a conference on altruism and compassion in economics, at a Mind and Life meeting in Zurich. The puppeteers spread their messages in places "where there is no radio, no written word, no television," as is true still in many parts of rural India.

As Roy finished, the Dalai Lama put his hands together and gave a *gasho*-like bow, in honor of Roy's work and his message. Then he told Roy, "The real transformation of India must start from the countryside and village, and you really have done that. This is an example for the rest of the world of how to help poorer countries, particularly in the Southern world."

The Dalai Lama had first been alerted to the importance of rural development in alleviating global poverty on his visit to China in 1955, during the years that the Communist government was courting his favor—four years before he fled to India. On that trip he met the then-mayor of Shanghai, "a very nice person," who told him he felt that the key to China's economic development was in building up rural areas rather than Shanghai itself.

"That's a socialist way of thinking," he told me, "spending more money to help the majority—needy and poor people in rural areas. That's an immensely helpful way to build a country."

The Dalai Lama said he was impressed seeing the efficiently mechanized small farms of Taiwan and Japan. There the farmers seemed prosperous. The local villages and towns had hospitals and even regional universities—all of which signify a healthy economy. "I'm always saying that the real transformation of countries like India and China must take place in rural areas, not just in a few big cities."

China too could learn about village development for the rural poor, he added, gesturing toward Bunker Roy, from this "Indian guru—not from Karl Marx!"

And then he invited Bunker Roy to teach solar engineering in Tibetan settlements throughout India. Roy accepted on the spot.

CHAPTER EIGHT

Heal the Earth

"At the height of the last Ice Age, when glaciers covered much of North America, there was a sheet of ice about a mile high where we sit today, and sea levels were almost four hundred feet lower." The Dalai Lama heard those words spoken at an MIT meeting by John Sterman, head of the systems dynamics group at that university.

The earth's temperature during that Ice Age averaged nine degrees Fahrenheit colder than at present. And by 2100, Sterman continued, the average temperature will be nine degrees Fahrenheit warmer, if we stay to our present course.

Sterman's research group had created a computer model of the link between carbon emissions and the earth's temperature. Showing the direct relationship—the more emissions, the hotter the temperature—he asked the audience at MIT, "When do we need to start lowering emissions to keep the planet's temperature at a range we can stand?"

The consensus came back: around 2016—in about two years.

"Wrong," Sterman said. "We need to cut emissions *now*," not just by using less fossil fuel but by restoring forests and lowering CO_2 levels in a range of other ways.

The Dalai Lama was listening intently. He praised the precision of Sterman's science and then took this to another level. "It's a question of the survival of all the beings on the planet," he emphasized, and it's our moral responsibility to keep everyone safe—around the world as well as in future generations.

Our planet is our home, the Dalai Lama says, so caring for the environment means caring for your own home. But just as it would be foolish to burn the furniture in your room to keep warm, he cautions, the way we are living on the planet is consuming it.

"A genuine concern for humanity means loving the environment."

But so many of us look only at our immediate interests. Even if people know of the long-term consequences, he adds, "They think, It doesn't matter—that will all be in the future. I'm just concerned with now. But it's a problem no one will be able to escape."

To bring that home (at least the Dalai Lama's home), take the Bara Shigri glacier, just about one hundred mostly impassable mountain miles to the northeast of Dharamsala. That glacier has been shrinking by more than ninety feet yearly, a sign of what's happening throughout the Himalayas.

The Dalai Lama saw a recent image of Bara Shigri glacier, shown to him by Diana Liverman, a former chair of environmental sciences at the University of Oxford, who now teaches at the University of Arizona. Liverman used Bara Shigri as an example of how the human impact on our planet has accelerated in the last sixty years.

That impact does more than make glaciers melt, she added. It poses threats to life that range from waning water supplies and unbreathable air to the death of species and acidifying of oceans—and more.

While some trace the beginning of the human assault on the planet to the Industrial Revolution, Liverman focused on what she calls the Great Acceleration, which began in the 1950s. Starting in that decade, there were sharp increases in such drivers of planetary troubles as population, numbers of cars on the road, and the use of water, chemical fertilizers, and paper.

Fertilizers, for instance, run off into rivers, lakes, and oceans, altering nitrogen levels and depleting the oxygen needed by sea life. Paper, of course, depletes forests. And cars both burn carbon that warms the planet and spew particulates that kill millions of people each year from respiratory disease.

This litany of environmental disasters will come as no news to many of us. But Liverman went deeper in her analysis, showing how this "acceleration" attacks specific systems that are crucial for supporting life as we know it. Carbon dioxide, as we hear often, is a greenhouse gas that warms the planet—but so are methane, which is a by-product of farms and landfills, and a handful of other industrial chemicals.

Then there are the effects on the water cycle, the nitrogen cycle, the burden of toxic chemicals that earth, water, and air can bear, and on and on. Besides heating the planet, these cause a sharp loss of forests, of species, of water that can support life.

The Dalai Lama is particularly troubled by the environmental damage in Tibet since the Chinese Communist occupation in the 1960s. Chinese lumbering operations have clear-cut once verdant forests that protected river systems from silt and flooding. But for years now those same rivers have repeatedly caused major floods in northern India, Bangladesh, and throughout China.

"The Chinese central government tried to restrict lumbering," he says, "but, through corruption, some Chinese, simply to make money, have found ways to continue cutting trees."

He also sees trouble in how the Chinese are exploiting Tibet's rich mineral resources. "Of course it's worthwhile to use those resources," he says, "but this should be done with careful planning, without so much environmental damage."

The research of a Chinese ecologist, the Dalai Lama once heard, shows that the effects on global warming from the Tibetan Plateau are as great as those from the South and North Poles. "So Tibet is the Third Pole."

One surprise: The biggest cost from the melting of Himalayan glaciers may not be flooding in the rivers they feed but drops in the monsoon rains that so many people rely on. Most major Asian rivers from China to Pakistan find their source in the Himalayas.

"One billion people's lives depend on those rivers," the Dalai Lama observes. So conservation in Tibet—like reforesting clear-cut forests that protect watersheds—helps all those people.

The recent environmental woes in Tibet range wide and are likely to get worse as Chinese development of that area's natural resources increases apace. Unregulated dumping of chemicals from mining and industry pollutes a high percentage of waterways. Most of China's lithium and all its chromium—used in electronics like mobile phones—are mined in Tibet.

"When I came to India as a refugee from Tibet, I had no awareness about the environmental issue. In Tibet we could drink any water we saw. It was only in India that I first heard people say, 'Oh, this water is polluted—you should not drink it.' As I gradually met with environmental activists and scientists, I came to realize this is a very, very important issue—it's a question of our own survival."

By 1986, the Dalai Lama wrote: "Many of the earth's habitats, animals, plants, insects, and even micro-organisms that we know to be rare may not be known at all by future generations. We have the capability and the responsibility to act; we must do so before it is too late."

Now, he says, "I think awareness about the environment is far stronger than it was fifty years ago."

He sees the obsession with profit at all cost as a driver of the damage. "In India and China, where the environmental issue is so important, there's a lack of responsibility," he observes. "It's just money, money, money," and so people exploit natural resources at any environmental cost, "to get rich."

What's happening in Tibet is symptomatic of our worldwide crisis. The ongoing ecological damage to the planet creates a different set of powerless victims—not just species at risk for extinction and future generations who will live under increasingly arduous conditions but also the people of the poorest countries, whose health and environment are being disproportionately harmed by the consumption habits of the rest.

"If you look at the poorest people in the world, most of them depend on nature for their survival," Dekila Chungyalpa, at the time with the World Wildlife Fund, told the Dalai Lama at a meeting on the environment.

"In fact," she continued, "we could consider nature their grocery store or pharmacy. It's where they go to for food, medicine, and wood for fuel. And there are many studies that show if we harm nature, we essentially make poor people poorer, that harming nature contributes to poverty."

Many scientists call the current geological age the Anthropocene ("anthropos" means "human" in Greek), in recognition of how human activities deteriorate the planet's life-support systems. The carbon cycle and global warming are the best known of these but are just two of many. For example, rampant species loss has pushed biodiversity, one of these systems, past a safe boundary. These impacts come as a byproduct of everyday activity. Our systems for energy, transport, construction, industry, and commerce create an array of insults to nature. Unfortunately, these are either too macro or micro for our senses to take in; we have no perceptual apparatus to sense directly global warming or lung-damaging particulates from auto exhaust.

Moreover, the time horizon at which such assaults occur spans decades and centuries—too slow a pace to notice.

"The sight of violence, whether in reality or on television, makes us recoil, but climate change and the damage we are doing to the environment don't provoke us in the same way, because they take place more stealthily."

What we need, the Dalai Lama adds, is compassion at every level—including for the planet.

Radical Transparency

Because we are largely blind to these impacts, the Dalai Lama contends, we need "deeper transparency."

Showing him my smartphone, I proposed that transparency could be deep enough to track the life cycle of any such electronic device and its ecological, health, and social impacts along the way. That life cycle might start with the mining of rare earths in China and Africa—some from areas controlled not by governments but by militias that deploy slave labor.

It might end with its "recycling," when poor villagers somewhere in, say, India expose themselves to toxic chemicals as they tear it apart to recover the valuable bits (for example, pouring a toxic mix of cyanide over circuit boards to recover gold).

Yet "we have the illusion," I told the Dalai Lama, "that we know everything about it."

To highlight all those impacts, life cycle assessment, a new method for ecological transparency, measures each of the myriad consequences of, say, a drinking glass, at every step of the way—from gathering sand, to mixing in chemicals, to cooking it all at high temperatures, and so on. Each of almost two thousand steps, measured in ultra-thin slices, can be analyzed for levels of polluting emissions into air, water, and soil—and countless more environmental impacts.

Now software makes that information available to anyone, comparing specific products—including mobile phones—against competing ones and ranking them from most to least harmful to the planet. A life cycle assessment would detail a far wider range of impacts, from the particles emitted to the contaminated water released.

I gave as further examples the ways we make steel, cement, glass, and bricks, which are roughly similar to how we've done it for centuries, even millennia: mixing together the raw materials and heating them at a very high temperature for hours or days. This Bronze Age technology's huge carbon footprint is only the most obvious of many adverse impacts.

Then there are the grim human realities. The Dalai Lama named miners who risk their lives in unsafe, unprotected conditions as an example of such extreme—but invisible—exploitation of workers. We agreed that a full disclosure would be powerful if it pulled back the veils on such impacts of what we buy and do.

Such radical transparency when we buy our smartphones—or anything else—could alert us to how that purchase connects us to far corners of the earth. We would get measures of true costs to the environment as well as ways our purchase might unwittingly support criminal activities, deplorable working conditions, or practices dangerous for laborers and local communities alike.

Just such transparency about the otherwise-invisible suffering that sometimes accompanies the production of what we buy can be found in the Social Hotspots Database. This index lets companies (or customers) track their products' supply chains, to see whether they involve workers who are in dangerous conditions or stressed by too-long hours, too-low wages, forced labor, and the like.

"Nowadays, big companies are quite concerned about their image," the Dalai Lama said to me. "Keeping customers' trust is very important for their success."

This favors their embracing transparency about such ecological and labor realities and choosing ethical practices. To the extent that companies are becoming ever-more sensitive to their public image, such transparency might motivate more to do the right thing.

Of course, many companies are already taking steps to be more sustainable and responsible on their own. But even they would be aided by any added market force for good—consumers voting with their dollars for the better alternative—that full eco-transparency might encourage.

Further, if this translates to better choices in the industrial supply chain, the improvements would be magnified. And ecological virtue would translate to a competitive advantage.

As the Dalai Lama advised a group of CEOs who had come to meet with him, "Think of the reputation of your company."

Trade-offs, Innovations—and Education

During the Indo-Pakistan war in 1965, the Dalai Lama was brought to South India for safety. There he met a disciple of Gandhi who was adamant that Indians should not travel in cars but instead use the then-common bullock carts to get around.

That, the Dalai Lama felt, was too extreme; people needed to travel more quickly. I see his worldwide itinerary, for one, as argu-ably having great benefits for those thousands who attend his events.

But there is a trade-off between speed of travel and its cost in carbon emissions; the greater the speed, the more carbon emitted, with air travel having the worst impacts. To better understand how to think about these trade-offs, we might turn to a method that analyzes the "true cost" of the products we use and of our activities in terms of the toll they take on the earth's resources.

A plane trip, for instance, can be analyzed for its true cost in impacts like carbon emissions. Each leg of an itinerary will create a certain amount of emissions—and those can be offset by, say, planting a given number of trees in an arid or deforested area.

With the help of a user-friendly website, I calculated the total airborne carbon added by plane flights for this book: 15.79 tons of CO_2. In a remarkably quick fashion, I was able to make this calculation and purchase carbon offsets, which cost about $184 for all six airplane flights, some for both my wife and me, including a transatlantic round trip. Those offsets will take the form of carbon-replenishing acts like distributing more-efficient cooking stoves to families in Ghana.

Why does the efficiency of a cooking stove matter? The poor half of the world's population—about three billion people—largely depends for cooking and heating on open fires. That adds a huge quantity of carbon to the atmosphere. Over a lifetime of use, those better stoves my offset bought will reduce atmospheric CO_2 by about two tons.

The benefits go further. There are about four million premature deaths each year from exposure to polluted air; women and children suffer the most from the portion due to these cooking fires. Another bonus: less deforestation by families cutting tree branches to cook and heat. Plus the stoves are made by local ceramicists, which boosts the economy.

All this lends itself to a simple math of benefits and harms. For instance, the Dalai Lama tries to be more aware of the ecological consequences of some of his habits and change them for the better. He makes a point of not taking baths. But there's a trade-off: He takes a shower each morning and evening, and so, he jokes, "Maybe no difference!"

By American plumbing standards, filling a bathtub takes between thirty and forty gallons of water, while a shower uses five to twenty gallons per minute. So the trade-off depends on how long the shower lasts, how much water flows per minute, and the size of the tub. Since the Dalai Lama shaves his head, he does not need to wash his hair—and so two very quick showers per day may still use less water than would one bath.

Pico Iyer, a longtime friend of the Dalai Lama's, tells of a moment when the two of them were leaving the lama's private quarters. They had started to walk off, when suddenly the Dalai Lama turned, hurried back to the room they'd just left—and switched off the light.

And when he was offered several pieces of paper towel to dry his hands, I hear, he said, "One is enough."

In the scope of things, these may seem small gestures. But changing these and other habits, if taken to global scale by everyone, can make meaningful differences. Beyond such simple efforts, there is far more each of us might do for the planet, but so few of us do much at all. The problem comes down to lack of motivation.

As the Dalai Lama points out, our continuous diet of bad news, such as the scientific evidence for severe environmental dangers, comes without adding what concrete actions we might take to counter the perils. The result: We feel powerless, that things are out of control.

The Dalai Lama heard from Elke Weber, a cognitive scientist at Columbia University's Earth Institute, that our "footprint" of negative impacts makes people feel guilty, ashamed, or otherwise uneasy. This, Weber added, leads people to tune out in order to feel better.

To avoid that tune-out, Weber endorsed using the "handprint" as a way to track our personal impacts and the sum total of our better ecological practices—like turning off light switches, biking instead of driving—and continuing to enlarge that number. The brainchild of Gregory Norris of the Harvard School of Public Health, the handprint engages our positive motivations and so keeps us going.

Rethinking Every Thing

The chart looked like a complex spiderweb overlaid on a map of the globe. That web portrayed the supply chain of an item most of us carry these days: a mobile phone. The Dalai Lama watched with fascination as Gregory Norris walked him through some of its intricacies at the twenty-third Mind and Life meeting.

That web had spokes touching 131 countries around the globe. The supply chain for a single phone, it turns out, involves an astounding 6,175 independent processes, like mining coltan, a rare mineral, at a remote site in the eastern Congo.

At such points, some alarming facts emerge: Armed gangs, it is said, which finance conflicts in that region of the Congo, "tax" workers in the mines and extort the people who smelt coltan into tantalum, the mineral used in phones. Other "social hotspots" include places in that supply chain where workers are exposed to toxic chemicals or dangerous conditions, are paid too little, or where children labor away when ideally they should be in school.

Norris teaches students how to come up with such data in his class on life cycle assessment (or LCA). The method lets a specialist unpack, with remarkable precision, the hidden impacts of any product on a wide spectrum of such environmental, health, and social factors.

The LCA gives us the footprint of a manufactured object, so telling us how much it has taken away from the health of the planet. As Elke Weber says, footprints can be depressing. That's what Norris found when he had his students at Harvard calculate their personal footprint—the impacts of everything they owned and did. Many of them felt the world would be better off without them.

That led Norris to an insight: "I realized that no one's footprint would ever get to zero, because everything we buy carries a history of impacts."

Simply using less helps, he saw, but that's not enough. How do I give more than I take? he wondered. His answer: the handprint, a metric that tells us the positive impact of all the ways we help the planet, from recycling to encouraging better practices by companies—or by their many suppliers—for the better. Through the Harvard T. H. Chan School of Public Health, Norris has brought together five companies—Johnson & Johnson and Owens Corning among them—that are experimenting together with using the handprint to lower their impacts. As a learning community, they are sharing how to apply the concept to their operations and the difficulties as well as the opportunities of the method. The goal: to pave the way for more companies to do the same.

When the CEO of Owens Corning told his board of directors they were trying to become a net-positive company—with a handprint bigger than their footprint—he was applauded. "Employees from all parts of the company are saying they want to be part of this," Norris told me.

The handprint initiative led Owens Corning to donate three hundred water-heater blankets to a school project on energy-saving in Maine, where such insulation can greatly reduce energy loss plus save on heating bills. The plan: stimulate a "virtuous cycle," where families who got the blankets would give back some of their savings to the school project, which would pass that money on to another school in turn to buy water-heater blankets and repeat the process—creating an ongoing chain of energy savings from neighborhood to neighborhood, town to town.

The blankets do more than just reduce energy consumption. Gregory Norris did the handprint eco-math, which calculates the point at which the footprint of the blankets' manufacture and transport becomes net positive. For the blankets' climate change and biodiversity impacts, payback comes at just two months, for particulate pollution impacts on human health, at seven months.

A single blanket saves a typical household five dollars per month in the Northeast; blankets last about ten years, for a total savings of six hundred dollars. Since the program allows the school to donate blankets to another school, and that school to another, in an ongoing chain, the eco-benefits multiply. After five rounds of the program, for instance, it will have prevented twenty-three years of life lost to respiratory disease from air pollution.

Then there is the entrepreneurial opportunity in reinventing our material world so that it meshes with nature. Plastics and Styrofoam, for instance, never fully decompose and flow back into nature. The centers of the world's great seas have circling gyres with high concentrations of the partial breakdown of plastics and Styrofoam, which kill sea life and worsen the composition of the ocean, among other negatives.

The Dalai Lama was intrigued by an inventive alternative created by two college students, who came up with a Styrofoam substitute that is 100 percent degradable back into nature. Why? Because it is made from farming wastes, like rice hulls or corn husks, combined with mycelium, the root system of mushrooms.

Ecovation, the company founded by those two college students, may have developed one of the world's first net-positive products: insulation made from the same sort of natural ingredients. Norris says another candidate might be solar ovens made from discarded junk in the Third World. Both the insulation and the ovens have a handprint that grows and grows as they are used.

When the Dalai Lama heard about such radical innovations, he was enthusiastic, agreeing that this was just the kind of rethinking we need for everything man-made—and we need it now.

He noted that with natural resources under intense threat and more people adding to the earth's population, the urgency to rethink has become greater than ever. Hearing how to move toward solutions makes it easier for people to engage seemingly overwhelming problems without becoming too discouraged to act.

While our ecological trajectory looks dim, the Dalai Lama points out, at the same time people are paying more attention, with more awareness of climate disasters. So I asked him, "Is there a role for mindfulness in compassion for the planet—for instance, being more mindful of what we buy?"

"First of all," he replied, we need to "open our eyes and know what to be mindful of. Then we can respond appropriately when we encounter situations in life that correspond to what we have learned."

How Did That Get Here?

It was a cloudy, chilly December day at the Smith College Campus School, in Northampton, Massachusetts, when Robbie Murphy brought a small crate of clementines to share with her second-graders. Each year, around when the nights drop to freezing, these easy-to-peel seedless tangerines appear in stores there.

A favored delicacy locally, the clementines sparked a buzz of excitement, even cheers, in these seven- and eight-year-olds, as they gathered into a circle on the floor. Ms. Murphy asked, "These don't grow around here—how did they get here?"

The students brainstormed the steps those clementines might

have taken on their journey: Someone grew them on a farm, picked them, placed them in the box, put stickers on it, and sent them to the store where their teacher got them.

She took out a globe and showed the students where to find the clementines' origin—Morocco—asking, "How many people did it take to bring this clementine into our lives?"

The class came up with this list: a farmer, pickers, box builder, truck driver, boat or plane pilot, store clerks—and then truck makers, boat makers, plane makers, store builders, then people who get the fuel for those trucks, boats, and planes, and the makers of the steel for those vehicles . . .

How many people altogether? Guesses ranged from twenty to hundreds.

"There's a really big idea here," their teacher said. "It takes a lot of people to get a clementine to Northampton in December."

Another big idea: Ms. Murphy reminded the class of how "there's sunshine in the clementine," just like "there's a cloud in a piece of paper"—that is, it takes water to manufacture the pulp for paper— and that "everything in the world is connected." These seven- and eight-year-olds were getting glimpses of how the earth's natural systems entwine with the tentacles of the global supply chain.

Ms. Murphy passed around the clementines so each kid had one, then led them through several mindful steps: "Peel it, smell it, look carefully at all its parts and how beautiful that fruit is. Give all your attention to the clementine."

Then she guided them, "Think about just one of the people who made this possible. Close your eyes, picture that person, and send a quiet thank-you . . . then pick another one and thank them . . . send them a wish."

After a silent minute or two, she asked, "Who are the people you thought about?" The boat pilot. The person who grew the tree. The store people. All the people who made the metal in the plane . . .

And the wishes? "That they have a good life. Be happy. Not be bored."

This exercise stretched those second-graders' minds in at least three ways. Paying close attention to the clementine exercised the mental muscle of focus. Wishing well to the people who made having this fruit possible and thanking them widened the circle of caring. Awareness of the chain of people who brought that fruit from Morocco to their school suggested systems thinking.

Surveys today find that concerns about the environment are low on most people's priorities. But as ecological crises escalate in coming years, today's children will be living with ever-more-dire consequences and thus be far more aware and motivated to take action.

So, the Dalai Lama says, "More education is very important." We need, he adds, to educate children so they can take responsibility to look after the environment, to take care of the earth. This means "an education based on the explanations of experts, about the growing problems"—the invisible ones as well as the obvious.

By the time, say, the pollution is so bad that we have problems in breathing and our eyes are stinging, he cautioned, "It might be too late. We need an education where taking care of the planet is a natural part of our life."

The Dalai Lama told a meeting on the environment: "I think one of the differences between younger and older people is flexibility and open-mindedness. Young people pay attention to new ideas, whereas older people like me have more-fixed ideas."

He added, "I am from the last century, and our generation created a lot of problems. The youth of this century are the planet's real humanity now. Even though global warming increases in intensity, they can work together in the spirit of brotherhood and sisterhood, share ideas, and find solutions. They are our real hope."

CHAPTER NINE

A Century of Dialogue

It was an emblematic moment from the days of the Irish Troubles, when young soldiers were sent to calm those in Northern Ireland who were rebelling against British rule. The divide was drawn to some degree along religious lines: the Protestants of Northern Ireland against the Catholics.

Just months before in a nearby town, twenty-six unarmed and nonviolent protesters—along with bystanders—were shot by British soldiers; fourteen of those died. That "Bloody Sunday" marked one of the lowest points in Northern Ireland's Troubles.

A crowd of young men was hurling bricks and rocks at some soldiers, who hid in a shelter. One of those soldiers, Charles Innes, was serving with the Royal Artillery in Londonderry, where there was particularly vehement tension and anger. Innes was, he now admits, frightened.

He faced three alternatives. He could run out of the shelter and yell at the kids to go away—and risk being killed by someone down the road with a rifle and scope. He might shoot his own weapon, but then someone else could be harmed.

Or he could fire his rubber-bullet gun, a hollow tube that flung hard projectiles several yards. At a few feet, those bullets could be very harmful, after about twenty yards, less and less so. The rubber bullets rarely hurt anyone—the children of Northern Ireland collected them as battleground souvenirs.

Or so Innes told himself. That day, however, he fired a rubber bullet that, from around ten yards, hit a bystander, ten-year-old Richard Moore, who was walking home from school. The bullet struck the bridge of his nose and eventually blinded the lad (who, as we learned in Chapter Three, years later became a friend of the Dalai Lama's).

This was a double tragedy for Richard's family. His uncle had been one of the victims killed in the Bloody Sunday massacre. And now young Richard was the victim. But, as we've seen, after his initial turbulent feelings settled, Moore did not pity himself, and in short order he replaced any hard feelings with forgiveness toward the soldier who fired that bullet, whoever he might be.

For his part, when Innes learned what had happened to the young Moore, he was flooded with sadness and regret—feelings he carried for decades. Then, twenty-one years after firing that ill-fated rubber bullet, Innes got a letter from Moore, who had tracked him down—and now wanted to meet him.

At that poignant encounter, Innes admitted his deep distress, and Moore let him know he held no resentment, telling Innes, "We can't undo what has happened, but we can go forward."

After discussing their feelings about the tragic incident that linked them, they went on to talk about their lives and families—and ended up forming a friendship.

Over the years, the two have told their story of tragedy and forgiveness to many audiences, including at a Tibetan school in

Dharamsala, where they shared the stage with the Dalai Lama, who introduced Moore as "my hero."

Charles Innes has traveled to Northern Ireland many times to visit his friend Richard Moore. The first time they gave a talk together there, he recalls, the atmosphere in the room was one of hostility toward Innes—but by the end many were in tears.

This friendship exemplifies a change that the Dalai Lama envisions anywhere there are violent conflicts and hatreds across group lines.

When it comes to altering the mind and emotions, it only makes sense to talk about individuals like Moore and Innes, the Dalai Lama sees. "So the initiative must come from the individual. In a change from a warrior-like society to a peaceful one at the worldwide level, the more peaceful world starts with the individual. Why? It takes an emotional change: compassion."

Once we feel such compassion alive in our minds, the Dalai Lama says, "You see no basis to killing, to bullying, cheating. All these unhappy ways of acting are based on the concept of us-and-them. We think we should just look after ourselves; I should look after me, and not care about anyone else. The worst: We exploit others."

If we start by getting our own destructive nature under control, the Dalai Lama insists, we can better follow a path of respecting one another. "If we consider each other to be brothers and sisters" in the human family, he adds, "then meaningful dialogue can come."

To be sure, we don't readily control the decisions governments make—but we do control how we ourselves act; in our own lives we can opt for dialogue instead of conflict. We can lengthen the pause between impulse and act, taking time to think about what we *really* need in the long run.

Of course, a dialogue does not mean we will all agree, the Dalai Lama acknowledges. "We have different views; there always will be disagreement. You need patience but not a foolish patience," in other words, putting up with just anything. "You don't give up your own needs and interests—that's not patience."

But dialogue, not violence, is the answer, he insists. "Invariably, violence creates more problems than it solves. The only way to solve problems is not by the use of force but by talking. So that's why I say the coming years should be a century of dialogue."

Take what happened with the Mekong River, which winds 3,100 miles from its source in the Tibetan Plateau through China's Yunan Province, Burma, Laos, Cambodia, Thailand, and Vietnam to its outlets in the South China Sea. The second-most biodiverse river in the world, the Mekong is a lifeline for transport, water, and protein for more than three hundred million people.

All that was under threat by proposals to build dams along the Mekong for hydroelectric power. But a dam on the river's main stem would disrupt the spawning migration of one hundred fifty species of fish, change seasonal water patterns that farms depend on, and block sediment from rebuilding the river's delta, which was already eroding from rising seas, displacing millions.

The Dalai Lama heard about this predicament from Dekila Chungyalpa, who hails from Sikkim but for many years worked for the World Wildlife Fund. Dekila was part of a WWF team helping to find a workable settlement among all the varied interests at play—and in conflict—along the Mekong.

WWF identified which institutions were, as Dekila put it, "the best levers to bring about policy change, benefit the community, or benefit the species we were trying to protect." And they reached out to form partnerships with these key players.

They worked with riverside communities to ensure their fisheries were sustainable, with area banks that would invest in the dams, even with Coca-Cola, which wanted to preserve the region's fresh water. WWF became a technical adviser to the Mekong River Commission, an intergovernmental body that oversees the Mekong River. And they persuaded the supreme patriarch of Theravada Buddhism in Cambodia to be a spokesman for preserving the river—in those parts, when he speaks, people listen.

Then WWF mapped the river in terms of fisheries, showing what the impacts would be if a dam were put low on the main stem (tragic) or on one of its many tributaries (much less harmful). By spotlighting the consequences of a dam being built on a given site with a certain design, WWF simplified the decision-making—and clarified what the financial returns would be for the banks that underwrote them.

The result: The premiers of three countries—Vietnam, Cambodia, and Thailand—all called for leaving the river's main stem free of dams. Laos, the poorest of the region's countries, has gone ahead to build a controversial main-stem dam far upstream.

Even so, Dekila said, other key decision-makers have put the needs of biodiversity, local communities, and their own long-term interests ahead of a short-term economic gain. What's more, the stakeholders along the Mekong are now mobilized and engaged to preserve the river's future.

Dialogue and negotiation, she concluded, have been key.

Beyond Us and Them

Fresh from a stop in Hawaii, the Dalai Lama told students at San Diego State University that he had heard there a native island chant meaning, "Your bone is my bone; your blood is my blood." That attitude, he said, echoes the one he urges for us all: "Your life is my life, and your health is my health."

This fits that profound recognition of the basic sameness and interconnection of all humans he calls "the oneness of humanity."

Without this inclusive sensibility, he tells us, the growing collective challenges we face—like climate change and competition for natural resources, rising population, and especially frictions among peoples and cultures—will become increasingly vexing.

The last century has been marked by violence spurred by people who cling to difference, not similarity. "The very concept of war," the Dalai Lama said to the students, stems from too much emphasis on us-and-them. "If we really develop a sense of the oneness of humanity, then there is no basis for war, no basis for violence."

The Dalai Lama objected once when he heard someone talk about differences between people in the "West" and in the "East," saying he felt there was too much emphasis on such divisions. "I don't think this is right. We're all the same human beings, with the same emotions. There is too much demarcation of we-and-they. The feeling that this person is somehow different limits our compassion."

What divides us, he emphasized, is far more superficial than the factors we share: Despite differences in ethnicity, language, religions, gender, wealth, and the like, we are all the same when it comes to our basic humanity. The Dalai Lama pointed to genomic research that shows, for instance, that "racial" differences account for a tiny fraction of our genetics; we all share the vast majority of genes. So why pay so much attention to minor differences?

We are out of focus when we fixate on the secondary level, putting far too much importance on what are really just surface differences. Because of that, "We have lots of problems. The legacy is violence—and children, old people, suffer the most."

By emphasizing instead our similarities, the Dalai Lama argued, we can empathize with one another across the boundaries that divide us. Our common humanity means we can find the ways we are connected rather than focusing on our differences.

If we can hold this attitude, we can more easily build empathy and trust. Person-to-person connection makes this more likely.

The dismissive blame-the-victim attitudes of the rich toward the poor, for instance, could be overcome by more contact, the Dalai Lama conjectured. He envisioned a place where children of the wealthy met and played on an equal basis with children from the slums. And so it would go with other damaging stereotypes.

For instance, when Vamik Volkan was a young boy, his native Cyprus was bitterly contested by the Turks and Greeks living there; a civil war led to partitioning the island between the two groups. He remembers growing up in his Turkish family pre-partition and hearing rumors that each knot on the local Greek priest's cincture stood for a Turkish child he had strangled. And then there was the disdain with which he heard about how the Greeks ate the meat of pigs, considered too filthy to consume by his own Turkish group.

Years later, as a psychiatrist at the University of Virginia, Dr. Volkan cited those formative memories as typical of the ways inter-group hatreds are stoked over generations, the seeds of hostile prejudices. His theory holds that the more we cling to the identity of our own group, the more we need to demonize other groups.

That demonization, oddly, becomes strongest the more similar us-and-them are. Greeks and Turks on Cyprus, for instance, are so similar genetically that they share a rare blood disease, and visitors find it difficult at first glance to know if a given person is Greek or Turkish.

This happens worldwide, of course. Violence between an Uzbek minority and Kyrgyz majority in Kyrgyzstan, between Hindus and Muslims in the Punjab, between Catholics and Protestants in Northern Ireland—all present cases in point.

Freud called this overemphasis on what distinguishes virtually similar groups "the narcissism of minor differences." He observed how trivial distinctions between people who are otherwise alike be-come exaggerated to justify hostility toward them. As the bias hard-ens into outright prejudice, anything that disconfirms the negative stereotype gets dismissed or ignored.

And yet in all such intergroup hatreds, there are people who have friends on "the other side." To see what might repair such us–them divides, social psychologist Thomas Pettigrew tracked down more than five hundred studies on the question from more than thirty-eight countries—with responses from a quarter of a million people. The evidence was clear: An emotional involvement, like a friendship or romance, with someone from the other group over-came whatever prejudice people might have learned.

American blacks and whites in the South who played with one another as children—even though their schools were segregated—ended up having little prejudice, as did rural Afrikaner housewives who became friends with their African domestic workers.

This warming impact is not just from the casual contact but also from the intensity of the emotional bond. The warmth we feel for one member of a group gradually widens to include the whole group—even across tense divides. While the stereotype might stay on in a mental closet, the strong negativity that went with it fades. And if emotions shift, so does behavior.

The globe is becoming much smaller and more interdependent. "In ancient times we were indifferent to this, lost in self-interest," the Dalai Lama reflected. "But in today's world, North, South, East, and West are heavily interdependent."

In today's reality of an interconnected world, he said, we have to live together—even if we do not like our neighbors, we have to get along. The world economy connects us so that we have to depend on others, even on hostile nations.

"Under these circumstances, it is always better to live harmoni-ously, in a friendly way, than to maintain a negative attitude," as he put it. "Our own survival depends entirely on others. Therefore, showing concern about others brings benefit to us."

The Dalai Lama gave as an example what might happen if this attitude of connectedness could take hold across the regions and groups in Africa now caught up in conflicts. If they could then make peace and unite, he believes, they would "become a real power." Those nations together have the potential to become a world force, "an African Union, like the European Union." Perhaps the continent could become a demilitarized zone among those nations, he added, but with a single army for defense.

The reverse tendency—us-and-them thinking—creates obstacles to such unity. If our compassion is to be global, excluding no one, then dividing people by nationality, religion, ethnicity, or any such grouping poses a blockade by emphasizing our differences. As the Dalai Lama says, there are no such limits to genuine compassion.

The Power of Truth

The Dalai Lama was awarded the Nobel Peace Prize to honor his rejection of violence in resolving the tensions between the Tibetan people and the Chinese Communists, who have occupied and annexed his country since the 1950s.

Instead of calling for violent revolt, the Dalai Lama had long sought dialogue with the Chinese government and proposed a nonviolent middle way, where Tibet would be within Beijing's authority yet semi-autonomous as a zone of peace, with genuine protections of Tibetan religion and culture. The Nobel citation underlined his "constructive and forward-looking proposals for the solution of international conflicts" as a model everywhere.

From his perch in India, he spent decades as the leader of the

Tibetan government-in-exile—and fruitlessly sought negotiations with the Chinese to protect his people and their cultural heritage.

Speaking of his years of seemingly futile attempts to negotiate with the Chinese Communists over the status of Tibet, the Dalai Lama said, "They rely on the power of the gun, which uses fear. Our struggle uses the power of truth." He sees preserving Tibet's traditions as a struggle for survival of a culture of compassion for the benefit of humanity as a whole.

But he distinguished between the Chinese officials as responsible for the brutality and their status as human beings for whom he had compassion and wished well-being. "They also want a happy life.

"They want harmony, peace. But harmony comes from here," he said, motioning toward his heart. "That leads to friendship, trust. But if they use force, that doesn't lead to trust."

So, he continued, "Any counter-action on our part, like criticizing their actions, was out of a sense of compassion for their own well-being. In the long run, the power of truth, of honesty, of compassion, is much stronger than the power of the gun."

"Does this imply," I asked, "that because you believe the power of compassion will win out in the end, that you still have hope, even if they are unwilling to dialogue?"

"We make a distinction between the government and the people of China," he replied. Since the 2008 crisis in Tibet, with open protests taking place in many parts, "People in China are paying attention, and then they realize that the Tibetans are very truthful, but not their own government.

"Of about a thousand Internet blogs and articles about Tibet by Chinese in the Chinese language," he said, with about two hundred of those from within mainland China itself, "all support our 'middle way' approach and are very critical of their own government's policy. I've met numbers of Chinese in other countries who show solidarity with Tibetans, and the numbers increase year by year."

He continued, "The world belongs to its people, not to kings or queens, not to rulers. America belongs to about three hundred million citizens, not the Republican or Democratic Party. So China, after all, belongs to the Chinese people, not the Communist Party.

"They are very powerful, but they cannot remain forever—it's the people who remain. The Communists have to use lots of censorship, which is actually a sign of their weakness—it shows their fear, that they have something to hide. Our side is completely transparent. These are some of the reasons we never lost hope."

Mahatma Gandhi's principle of *ahimsa*—nonviolence—inspires the Dalai Lama. Just as Gandhi followed this path in the struggle for India's independence (and Martin Luther King Jr. did in the civil rights movement, and Nelson Mandela in South Africa), the Dalai Lama has put this philosophy into practice in his dealing with the Chinese to restore human rights and freedoms to Tibetans.

Mahatma Gandhi's struggle for freedom through nonviolence was laughed at and dismissed at first. Now nonviolence has become a common strategy throughout the world, especially for those protesting injustice.

"These," the Dalai Lama says, "are clear examples of the power of truth, sincerity, and honesty. These are the key motives, because we are not working only in our own self-interest but in the interest of life."

As a strategy, violence can lead to short-term gains, resolving some immediate problem, the Dalai Lama notes, but those gains tend to be transient, resulting in other problems over time. So while nonviolence may take more time, its long-term benefits are greater.

But nonviolence in the political realm means more than simply abstaining from violence; the true expression of nonviolence in the Dalai Lama's view is compassion. And compassion is not just a passive stance but also a stimulus to action.

He adds, "To experience genuine compassion is to develop a feeling of closeness to others, as Gandhi-ji did, combined with a sense of responsibility for their welfare. His great achievement was to show through his own example that nonviolence can be implemented effectively not only in the political arena but also in our day-to-day life."

Seeing so clearly the futility of war, the Dalai Lama remarked on the first anniversary of 9/11: "The attacks on the United States were shocking, but retaliation that involves the use of further violence may not be the best solution in the long run."

That insight, of course, has proven prescient. Since violence fails to bring lasting solutions—or to bring a better world—dialogue offers a potentially constructive alternative, both to threats of war and to the inevitable problems of peace.

And, given the failure of war, the Dalai Lama envisions a far-off future of complete demilitarization, where armies will be dispensed with and the arms industry closed down, its resources put to better uses. The Dalai Lama approvingly mentions a Swedish toy company that decided to no longer sell toy weapons—a very small step in the right direction.

And yet he recognizes the complexity of our political reality: "Arms destroy life, but at the global level the free world needs to be strong."

To my surprise, the Dalai Lama says that warfare itself can be relatively humanized if it is fought with a compassionate motivation, taking care to minimize casualties and civilian deaths. He contrasts that with impersonal, mechanized destruction, "full of hatred," where "murder is seen as a form of heroism."

Even so, he says, resorting to force never addresses the underlying causes of conflict, failing to resolve them and often making them worse—not to mention the needless pain, suffering, and destruction left in the wake of force.

Harmony Among Religions

It was a radical experiment back in 1958 for the island nation then known as Ceylon, when a high school teacher took his students—all from privileged families—to a poverty-stricken hamlet to help villagers there. That initial *shramadana* has given rise to a movement throughout Sri Lanka involving almost fifteen thousand villages, about half of all those in that nation. And that former teacher, Dr. A. T. Ariyaratne, founded and has led Sarvodaya Shramadana (loosely, "donating time for the uplift of all"), the organization guiding this work, for all these years.

Sarvodaya's philosophy resonates with the Dalai Lama's view that those in need are best helped by being empowered to help themselves. In Sarvodaya villages, everyone comes together to identify their most pressing needs—clean water, a school building, sewage—and then works together to provide them.

The villagers learn skills like how to give basic health care, put in water pumps, and build housing and roads. In a country where the government has long ignored such essentials, these actions also instill the sense that people have the power to determine their own destinies. Sarvodaya initiatives have helped villagers to build some five thousand preschools, health clinics, libraries, even roads, and to found village banks and dig wells and latrines.

The motto "We build the road and the road builds us" speaks for the sense of empowerment villagers get as they work together on such projects. And the strengthening of ties within these villages across ethnic groups—Sinhalese Buddhists and Tamil-speaking Hindus, Christians and Muslims—offered surprising resilience during one of Sri Lanka's darkest hours.

The movement for an independent state by Hindu Tamils in the north of Sri Lanka had begun to smolder in the 1980s, and it flared into a bloody civil war a decade later with the ruling Buddhist Sinhalese. From the very beginning of hostilities, Dr. Ariyaratne, known as the "Gandhi of Sri Lanka," had been leading marches and rallies to protest the war.

When the government forces ratcheted up their fighting in 2005, Dr. Ari (as he's widely known) called for a giant peace rally. Several hundred thousand Sri Lankans gathered amid ancient ruins at Anuradhapura, once the site of the island's capital. Those gathered represented both sides of the battle, as well as every other religious and ethnic group on Sri Lanka.

At one point, Dr. Ari led them in a loving-kindness meditation, where they directed wishes for well-being to all—including those who, as he said, "have taken up arms and killing, so their minds will no longer harbor hatred." The Dalai Lama sent a message to those at that rally, applauding how, despite the ferocious civil war, people from all the diverse religious and ethnic groups on that island were calling for peace.

After the terrorist attacks of September 11, 2001, the Dalai Lama often spoke up to defend Islam. In Washington, D.C., at the National Cathedral's first-anniversary memorial service for the attack's victims, he said the fact that the attackers had Muslim backgrounds did not justify prejudice and stereotyping of the religion.

If a religion had its bad actors, it would be unfair to blame that entire religious community for the actions of a small minority or one individual.

Of course, it's not just between religions—much strife around the world occurs among ethnic groups of the same religion. Even minor distinctions can become fuel for these fires. The Dalai Lama uses his prominence as a religious figure to protest such hatred and violence, particularly between faiths—and even within them.

"When I hear both sides crying 'God' while they kill each other, it doesn't make sense," the Dalai Lama says, pointing to "Catholics and Protestants hating each other while both believe in Jesus Christ. Even among the Buddhists, we have at times quarreled and even killed each other."

Those who foment an us-and-them attitude on the basis of religious beliefs, the Dalai Lama says, are distorting those beliefs. This pathology of the natural instinct to care for one's own group comes at the expense of others. It amounts to having a divisive self-centeredness in common, with religion in the service of hatred.

What seems to happen in such cases, he observes, is that instead of "using their religious faith and resources to transform their own personality and character, they impose their personality on the religion. It's very tricky when people manipulate religion."

"There's too much conflict in the name of religion," he continues. When religious voices are divisive—viewing those of other religions as the "enemy"—the Dalai Lama sees a lack of moral principles at work. He has frequently taken public stands against such intolerance.

For instance, though the area of Ladakh is culturally Tibetan, it lies in the Indian province of Jammu and Kashmir, which has been racked by conflicts between Muslim secessionists and the Indian army. The Dalai Lama told Ladakhi Muslims that his friend Farooq Abdullah, former minister of their state, had told him that the true meaning of "jihad" has nothing to do with attacking other people but rather with combating our own destructive emotions: It means the self-discipline to restrain yourself from harming anyone. The Dalai Lama added, "I respect Islam. They are good philosophers, and it is a very important religion."

In the present atmosphere of suspicion by and of Muslims, he feels, more contact with people of goodwill from other groups would be beneficial, as would more-modern education in the Arab world. He was pleased, for instance, that Jordan had taken many steps in that direction and felt that this could counter the influence of hard-liners.

He has visited Israel four times, Jordan twice. In both countries he met with religious leaders, spreading his message of interfaith harmony. He encourages visitors he meets from the Emirates and other parts of the Arab world to be more active in supporting such attitudes, which he hopes might reduce violence in the Middle East.

And it's not just Islam; every religion, he says, has its hard-liners. He has, for example, spoken up to protest the brutal violence fomented by extremists among Burma's Buddhists against a Muslim minority there.

But, the Dalai Lama concedes, there will be a clash of ideas and conflicts as long as we humans exist—it's only natural. For that reason, he says, we need a means to resolve differences through mutual understanding and dialogue.

By his long-standing practice of making pilgrimages to the holy sites of the world's religions, he affirms the underlying unity of faiths. As he told me, "The real purpose of faith is the practice of love—it's all the same."

Following the terrorist attacks of September 11, 2001, the Dalai Lama said in a statement: "I believe no religion endorses terrorism. The essence of all major religions is compassion, forgiveness, self-discipline, brotherhood, and charity. All religions have the potential to strengthen human values and to develop general harmony."

And, he added, the challenge of finding effective methods for taming the unruly corners of our minds has arguably become more urgent than ever. The range of ingenious weapons spawned by our cunning brains means that when human intelligence is controlled by negative emotions like hatred, the results are disastrous.

Look at the serious problems in the world, the Dalai Lama observes, mentioning what were then crises of the day in war-torn

Ukraine and the Middle East. "All these are man-made troubles due to emotions out of control." He points to self-centeredness, us-and-them thinking, and hatred. And he doubts whether those who carry out hostile policies—even if they feel some fleeting satisfaction at killing someone—are happy with themselves deep inside.

External disarmament starts with inner disarmament. Our peacefulness is not just for our own benefit but also helps the people around us.

Toward a Century of Dialogue

When the Dalai Lama was invited to speak to a conservative think tank in Washington, D.C., many in his wider circle objected. "When I heard that," he said of the objections, "thinking we are leftist, they are rightist, and we should not speak to them—that's wrong!"

Despite the warnings, he went, hoping to share another, more compassionate view. Both sides, left and right, he said, agree on a common objective: what's best for people. There should be a conversation between the sides, he urges, not silence or hostility. Share your viewpoint; make critiques of the other position.

"Dialogue. That's the only way." Still, dialogue means defending your values, not compromising them.

At a meeting with environmental scientists, the Dalai Lama heard one activist trace her own evolution. She recalled, "When I was younger, I was always yelling, 'Everybody should change!' What I realized through experience is that by not yelling, we're able to create partnerships where the partner responds, and that's ended up being much more beneficial."

Her point resonated with the Dalai Lama. He replied, "You need to reach out to those who are receptive, emphasizing benefits in common."

Dialogue, he notes, has become essential today to grapple with the global problems we face: a growing population with dwindling natural resources; the drastic rich–poor gap; environmental damage. These are not problems one or two countries can address, nor can they be solved using force; they require cooperation among humanity as a whole.

By thinking of humanity as one—"us"—we can better enter into conversations and negotiations that will leave everyone winners. "Dialogue," as he told a crowd in Slovenia, "is not a luxury we may choose to enjoy, but a simple necessity."

In the days before the second American invasion of Iraq, there was a ripe moment when, the Dalai Lama conjectures, he might have intervened by going to Baghdad (as he was urged to do at the time) with a group of Nobel Peace Laureates and reasoning with Saddam Hussein. They might have argued that war with America would be suicidal, and that, even if out of simple self-concern, Saddam should de-escalate.

But the Dalai Lama felt that he personally had no connection to Iraq—the idea was impractical. Still, this quickened his thinking about a group of Nobel Laureates and other highly respected figures who might undertake such high-level interventions.

His good friend Václav Havel, the president of Czechoslovakia, had begun such a process by founding Forum 2000, a group of people from diverse countries, cultures, religions, and academic disciplines, who convened once a year to identify key global issues and look for ways to de-escalate conflicts.

At the forum, the Dalai Lama—with Havel, the Jordanian prince El Hassan bin Talal, and F. W. de Klerk, who oversaw the end of apartheid—started the Shared Concern Initiative, to address important world challenges like human-rights violations. The initiative made appeals for human rights in Burma, Russia, and China.

The Dalai Lama's impulse to engage world problems remains strong; he thinks there is a place for a group of Nobel Peace Laureates, along with other well-respected thinkers, scientists, and retired politicians no longer tied to any government. Beyond being well known and respected, they need be beyond reproach, with no hint of hidden agendas, and completely honest and trustworthy, selfless and sincere.

In a situation where tensions are building, such a group might intervene and calm things, he hopes—at any rate, they could try. If there's a positive outcome, "very good, if not, nothing to lose."

Such groups represent a new kind of leadership on the world scene, not based on some national interest or tied to any governments, not open to veto (as so often happens in the UN), and fully transparent, with no agenda other than the best interests of humanity. This body would represent the world's billions of people, not the world's governments. Its power would reside in the respect and esteem people have for it and its recommendations on world problems.

Put-Ups and Win–Wins

The year was 1987, the place a high-society party in a fashion designer's swanky apartment on Manhattan's Fifty-seventh Street, and attended by a most unlikely person: A. J. Ayer, one of the most famous philosophers of his day. A retired Oxford don, Ayer was spending the year as a visiting professor at Bard College.

Ayer was chatting with some partygoers near the door of the living room when an upset young woman came rushing in, saying that she had just come from a bedroom where a friend was being assaulted.

Rushing to the scene, Ayer found Mike Tyson, according to Ayer's biography, forcing himself on Naomi Campbell, who at the time was still an unknown.

Ayer insisted that Tyson desist, at which point Tyson turned on him, saying, "Don't you know who the _____ I am? I'm Mike Tyson, heavyweight champion of the world."

To which the bantamweight Ayer replied, "And I am the former Wykeham Professor of Logic. We are both preeminent men in our field; I suggest we talk about this like rational men."

As they began to talk, Campbell slipped out of the room.

When I heard that widely reported encounter I realized it echoed one reported by a teacher at an inner-city middle school in New Haven.

Three boys were heading to gym class, where they would play soccer. One, a bit pudgy and unathletic, was the target of ridicule by two others walking behind, both "jocks" who excelled at the sport.

One of the jocks said, his voice dripping with sarcasm, "Oh, so *you're* going to play soccer?"

At that the pudgy fellow stopped, took a deep breath as though bolstering himself for a nasty encounter, turned, and said, "Yes, I'm going to play soccer. I'm not very good at it. What I'm good at is art: Show me anything and I can draw it real well. You—you're really great at soccer. Someday I'd like to be as good as you are."

Hearing that, the youngster who had been so sarcastic changed his tone and said warmly, "Oh, you're not so bad. Maybe I can show you a few moves that will make you better."

And he put his arm around the pudgy kid in friendship as the two walked together to their gym class.

Some basic emotional moves in the Tyson–Ayer match and in the one between the two boys are essentially the same. The intervention: You say something positive about the other person (Ayer to Tyson acknowledging his "preeminence") and say something positive about yourself (Ayer announcing his high-status philosophy chair).

This conversational strategy at the middle school was no accident. That maneuver is taught as an on-the-spot response to bullying. Called a "put-up," it tends to deflate the energy behind the put-downs and taunts bullies deploy.

If disarmament begins with each of us and then spreads outward, we all could use more skill at disarming on the interpersonal level.

Just such methods in this microcosm of peacemaking are taught in that New Haven middle school as part of "social development," an add-on to the standard academics. An even fuller spectrum of constructs and tools for disarming schoolyard hostility is offered in the Resolving Conflict Creatively Program; its roots go back to the 1980s, when a school-district superintendent asked for a program on peacemaking in the schools.

It was during the Cold War, and some children were frightened by the apocalyptic danger of nuclear war; at the same time, violence was rampant in too many students' lives—about eighteen students a day died from violence across the United States. The superintendent wanted an approach that started with students managing their own hostile impulses and that could radiate into society as they grew up.

One who answered that call was Linda Lantieri, a former teacher and principal in the New York City schools who was then a curriculum developer. It was a fertile moment for nonviolent approaches to conflict. Marshall Rosenberg had begun teaching his approach to Nonviolent Communication, and faculty at the Harvard Law School had just published their primer on positive negotiation, *Getting to Yes.*

Drawing on such sources, Lantieri teamed up with Tom Roderick, director of the Morningside Center for Teaching Social Responsibility, to put together ways this could be taught to children from kindergarten up through high school. "For the young kids," Lantieri told me, "a common conflict might be who goes first in a play-ground game.

"So we used puppets to show kids arguing about who goes first and to model different outcomes: a lose–lose, where they end up fighting and the teacher says neither of you can play; win–lose, where one kid bullies the other. And then the puppets lead the students in brainstorming win–win outcomes, like flipping a coin to see who goes first, timing each other to take turns, and so on."

With older children, the program teaches "active listening," where the children practice hearing what the other kid says in a dispute, but without reactive judgment, and letting the speaker know they have understood by paraphrasing them. Then there's the "I-message," where, instead of an accusation or blaming, you say how you feel when the other child does something that upsets you, which opens the way for a resolution. All these methods and more are used in these schools by peer mediators from the upper grades, who roam the playground to work out disputes as they occur.

Now called Resolving Conflict Creatively, the program also teaches ways to enhance acceptance and appreciate diversity, as well as to counter bias. For younger children, it's talking in pairs about their similarities and differences. By fourth grade, they use a panel where kids from different groups and backgrounds tell their stories—including what they never want other kids to say about or call their group, because it's too upsetting.

"It helps other kids understand how they may be hurting them," Lantieri said. In one such panel, she told me, Lisa, a Korean immigrant, related how when she had just arrived in the United States, a young African American man almost pushed her onto the subway tracks. As a result, she said, "I've never touched a black person."

To that, Abdul, a black classmate, walked over to her and said, "I'm going to extend my hand to you." Trembling, she took his hand—and then they hugged.

These programs have been spreading across schools in the States and even to homeless street kids in Brazil and Puerto Rico, where youth violence, Lantieri said, "has been off the charts."

One week in a high school in East Harlem, the topic was how to handle yourself in a tense encounter—a common predicament for the students there. They went through exercises on how to manage emotions to stay calm and be open, so you can make a good decision.

As it happens, the very next week one of the seniors, Raymond, was getting off a subway train on his way to school when three guys surrounded him, demanding he give up his sheepskin coat. One of the three had his hand in his jacket pocket, possibly hiding a gun or knife. In those days, sheepskin coats were highly prized; coat wearers had been shot in robberies.

So Raymond kept his cool, saying in a friendly tone, "This is incredible—I was just getting ready to do that." As he talked, he unzipped his coat, asking to which of them he should give it. At that, one guy grabbed his coat and the three ran off.

When Raymond got to school—after walking three blocks in freezing cold—he was fuming with rage. A teacher called a group of kids to gather around as Raymond explained what had happened and how enraged he was. He had stayed calm but lost his coat.

Then something completely unexpected happened. One of the kids listening asked, "How much was that coat?"

"A hundred nineteen dollars," Raymond replied. It had been a hard sum for his mother to save up.

"There are ninety-two seniors in this school," the other student said. "That's a little over a dollar each."

Three days later, the senior class had collected enough to get Raymond a new sheepskin coat.

"We each have a responsibility," the Dalai Lama tells us. "If you make the attempt now, then within this century, a more peaceful world can be achieved."

Yet given the realities of conflicts small and large around the world these days, I asked the Dalai Lama if his proposal for dialogues, not conflict, was mere wishful thinking.

He responded, "People of the twentieth century"—as he calls those who are now toward the end of their lives—"are not so open to change; their minds are fixed. For them, not much hope of change. The only hope is the younger generation. Education can overcome distorted ways of thinking. That's the only way.

"I will not see this in my lifetime," he admitted. "These problems will remain. But slowly educate the children. The next generation, future generations . . ."

"That's the hope?"

"Yes!" was his emphatic response.

CHAPTER TEN

Educate the Heart

The fourth- and fifth-graders from Vancouver's Walter Moberly Elementary School were visibly excited, but well behaved, as they waited for the Dalai Lama to arrive. They were seated in a circle, and as he and his party of security agents and Tibetan officials swooped in, the Dalai Lama walked the circle's rim, greeting students and laughing warmly.

At the invitation of their teacher, Jennifer Erikson, he joined them in this "gratitude circle," a familiar activity for these students. The kids passed a talking stone from hand to hand as their gratitude zoomed around the room: "I'm grateful," they said, "to be alive," "to meet the Dalai Lama," "for the ocean," "for peace in the world," "for my family," "for sports."

When the rock reached the Dalai Lama, he paused, then told the children, "We are basically all the same in a big human family. When we meet, we find we have the same emotions, same mind, same body. All love the same things, like friendship."

Then, looking at the rock in his hand, he added, "I'm grateful for joy," and handed the rock to the youngster next to him.

As the circle completed, the teacher asked, "How does gratitude help us?"

An answer came from a girl: "It teaches us we have lots to be grateful for instead of moping that we don't have enough."

And a boy: "By releasing a chemical called dopamine that makes me feel joyful."

The Dalai Lama, pleased with the science angle, said, "Absolutely right!"

And a girl added, "It makes other people happy too."

Another: "And it makes me feel calm."

"Calm. That's right," the Dalai Lama agreed. "That's a very important feeling. Wonderful!"

"As they give gratitude," Ms. Erikson explained, "they learn to understand how others feel." The growing sense of closeness also increased the students' trust, so they could relax and learn together rather than pull back out of fear.

And then they all stood for a photo, gathering around the Dalai Lama, who beamed at being with this class before heading to his next engagement.

That gratitude circle, a special demonstration for the Dalai Lama, took place in the library of the John Oliver High School. Like its feeder Moberly Elementary, the high school stands amid a working-class area in South Vancouver, one with a thick mix of immigrants from places like the Philippines, Southeast Asia, and China.

As have so many children of immigrants over the years, the students at Moberly and John Oliver strive to fulfill their parents' dreams of success by working hard in school. But high academic achievement, the Dalai Lama argues, in itself does not reflect a complete education.

He sees modern schooling as needing fundamental reform, beyond the standard body of knowledge. The Dalai Lama calls for an education of the heart, with ethics and the capacity for living by compassionate values being essential.

This education would include basics of how the mind works, such as the dynamics of our emotions; a healthy regulation of emotional impulse and the cultivation of attention, empathy, and caring; learning to handle conflicts nonviolently; and a sense of oneness with humanity.

Time and again, the Dalai Lama returns to the idea that in the long run the right kind of education will help in solving many major problems, from global warming and a decaying environment to economic gaps and conflicts. He looks to this radical overhaul of our educational system as one key to lasting answers.

Educating the heart would strengthen the brain's compassion and caring system, which in turn might lead, for instance, to entirely new economic behavior among those so educated. In short, his vision for the world would be passed on to coming generations as they are schooled.

Mind Training

Simran Deol, an eleventh-grader at Moberly, sat with her eyes fixed on a dot in front of her, as EEG headgear she wore projected a line onto a large screen, tracking her concentration level. As her mind stayed focused, the line drifted upward, or, as she got distracted, it bent downward. The Dalai Lama observed with keen interest.

A teaching assistant, a graduate student at the University of British Columbia, explained to the Dalai Lama that Simran would try to concentrate as other students attempted to distract her. At that, two of her friends went up to her, talking and tugging at her sleeve— and the line on the screen drifted down.

So the Dalai Lama coached Simran. "When training our mind, it's useful to make a distinction between the mental and sensory level. When you look at the dot, the main work is mental but also sensory—'eye-consciousness.' If you rely on eye-consciousness, it's very limited—what's in front of you is a prop.

"But at the mental level we can ignore eye-consciousness. If what you focus on is in your mind, then you can focus better even if there are disturbances around you," he advised, telling her to hold the image in her mind's eye.

Simran closed her eyes to focus better on that mental image, and the line inched up. It trended down again when her friends once more distracted her—but rose again as her concentration strengthened.

He advised her to practice this one-pointed focus against such challenges: when someone who angers her showed up, as well as when friends did.

He listened with fascination as the teacher, Joanne Martin, quizzed Simran's classmates on what was happening in the girl's brain. He was pleased when one answered, "There are more neurons connected when she's focused."

That lesson in focus has wider implications for education: Both concentration and the ability to squelch destructive impulses activate the same neural circuitry, which is also crucial for the readiness to learn. As a feelings map might show, strong negative emotions are powerful distractions; the more concentrated we become, the less pull such emotions have on our focus.

When a student asked, "How can we be focused and happy each day?" the Dalai Lama's answer, at first, seemed off point: Imagine a large airplane flying through the sky, he said, adding, "It's very hard to understand all the parts that help it stay in the air."

But then he took the metaphor home: "It's the same with the

mind and emotions. Some emotions disturb our mind, and others are so useful—for instance, helping with calmness."

After that he suggested how they might apply that emotions map he encouraged Paul Ekman to draw up. "To develop long-lasting peace of mind, we should have more knowledge about the map of emotions. No concern for what's good or bad—simply some awareness. Then, according to our daily experience, apply it.

"Once we have some kind of awareness about this, then as we face daily experiences we can notice when we're irritated, not happy. We can analyze," he urged, pointing out that irritation is part of an emotions family that includes fear, distrust, and anger, among others. An opposite group numbers among its members a calm mind, self-confidence, compassion, and affection.

Those positive states, he told the students, bring peace of mind. Fear and anger eat at us. "The disturbed mind is harmful—our blood pressure goes up, we feel stressed, our sleep is destroyed, we have more frightening dreams. But what's the counterforce? Not drugs, alcohol, not any external means."

We need to take the time to develop peace of mind, he advised. This emotional shift will not come overnight. "So we need some training."

Reinventing Education

The Dalai Lama had come to John Oliver High School for an in-person session on Educating Hearts and Minds. Several hundred students were packed into the school gym for the event, which was live-streamed as well to thirty-three thousand others across the province.

There he told the young crowd, "I'm quite old, about eighty. My life is now mostly completed. But yours are just beginning. It's up to you whether you lead a happy life, whether you make a positive contribution for the well-being of humanity.

"I've had the opportunity to meet lots of different kinds of people—leaders, beggars, respected scientists, and spiritual practitioners. I'm convinced a happy life is not dependent on being wealthy, or even having a good family.

"I always listen to BBC every day. The news tells me there's lots of pain in our world, lots of problems and violence. These problems are man-made." Yet the people causing them are often smart.

That, he added, shows that today's education does not bring inner peace or moral principles. We can't change this by force, and a religious sermon cannot reach all the billions of us on the planet, let alone nonbelievers. The only way is through an education that aims for a universal good: Everyone wants to be happy.

A thousand years ago in the West, the education systems of the world were the domain of the Church, he observed. As the hold of religion on education waned over the centuries, so did the reach of teachings about caring and responsibility. Applied ethics took a backseat, particularly as science and technology developed over the last century. And today the foundations of education are for the most part materialistic.

"People who grow up in this system don't learn the importance of inner values but rather tend to think that progress, money, and material values are more important," he said. "So how can we bring balance to this?"

Rather than base an education on blind belief in values like compassion, he pointed to the new science showing how peace of mind and a healthy body are related to a concern for others. With that grounding, he said, such values can be brought back into education.

The Dalai Lama, as we've seen, has a conviction that we are born with a predisposition toward kindness. "When children are very young, this is quite alive," he said, but this part of their nature can remain undeveloped. "In the existing system of education, there's not much emphasis on that."

Instead, children are exposed to influences that breed distrust, anger—the opposite side of their nature. "We need an education for the positive in them. Otherwise, it lies dormant. We need an education that brings out this positive side."

There's the slogan "healthy body, healthy mind," he said, but then pointed out that the modern education system neglects the part about a healthy mind.

He sees an urgent need for refocusing education. Today's system of modern education, from his point of view, is lacking in moral education, ethics, and what he calls "the oneness of humanity"—the sense of a single human family, all equal in our quest for happiness. "What's missing are moral principles."

While in ancient times a tribal notion of the separateness of peoples ruled, in today's interconnected world we need to use reason to extend our compassion beyond just our own group to a sense of concern for everyone. The Dalai Lama turns to education as a tool for extending our biological instinct for compassion toward our loved ones outward, toward everyone.

Many students study business and economics with the aim to become rich, he continued. So they work "tirelessly, without sufficient sleep, always busy, busy, busy. But there's no compassion in that— it's just for themselves.

"If you only want to make a profit, if the thing that matters is money, then there's this growing gap between rich and poor. Whether you call it compassion or just a sense of responsibility, if humanity suffers, if there's too much violence, then there is huge suffering. So it's in your own interest to help the world."

Reinventing how children are schooled has been a theme the Dalai Lama returns to in outlining virtually every aspect of his vision of a force for good.

"Everyone's future depends on dealing with these problems. So then there's the question, What to do? Then show the method," he told me.

"The method?" I asked.

"Education," he answered, adding, "But if our educational system pays little attention to the problems we face, they will increase. Nobody wants that."

It's not enough for just a few people on the margins to talk about the changes needed, he says. He calls for a movement, "a revolution in modern education," based on new ideas and new thinking.

Social and Emotional Learning

Victor Chan first met the Dalai Lama in 1972, after an unlikely adventure overland from Europe that included being kidnapped for a time in Afghanistan. He has written two books with the Dalai Lama. In 2004, Victor Chan first brought his old friend to Vancouver, to give public talks about the need to educate the heart.

That visit led Chan to found the Dalai Lama Center for Peace + Education. And that visit triggered a movement to include "social and emotional learning" (or SEL) in schools throughout the entire province. This brand of schooling soon became a focus for the center's activities. By 2013, 90 percent of schools in British Columbia had such programs.

SEL takes many forms; there are more than one hundred curricula in use by schools around the world that teach life skills like managing upsets, empathy, and cooperation—in short, emotional hygiene and compassion.

On a later visit to Vancouver, the Dalai Lama, though pleased to hear about the spread of SEL, expressed surprise that teachers did not get any training in how to teach this while studying in schools of education. So now the University of British Columbia not only includes SEL training in its education for teachers but also has one of the first master's programs in the topic.

At John Oliver High School, the Dalai Lama said, "People might start this work with skepticism, but just watch, you'll see the results. Start with one school, then ten, then one hundred. Here you're implementing a pilot project." He noted that he really appreciated the teachers and students involved.

"Day by day, this kind of education can teach affection, a sense of responsibility. It's very important for your own happiness, for your family. And as families become more compassionate, society becomes more compassionate. This is for the survival of humanity."

Victor Chan told me the Dalai Lama "wants us to have an impact on the sixteen hundred schools and half million kids in the province of British Columbia. We need hard evidence, so we're working with researchers at the University of British Columbia."

Scientists there, like Dr. Kimberly Schonert-Reichl, are doing research into SEL's effects. For instance, she designed the Heart-Mind Index, which assesses abilities in five-year-olds like solving conflicts peacefully, getting along, and being attentive. Such soft skills mark a kindergartner as more ready for school.

The best programs go beyond the classroom to promote an emotionally literate school culture, include parents, and offer activities beyond the school day. Schonert-Reichl's research shows, for example, that students have more optimism, self-control, and well-being when they feel emotionally supported by their teachers. And if teens from poorer neighborhoods (who are at long-term risk for heart disease) volunteer to tutor younger children, their cardiovascular health improves.

Millions of children have gone through such SEL programs around the world by now. A meta-analysis of more than two hundred seventy thousand students, comparing those who had SEL and those who did not, found the programs increased positives, like good school attendance and behaving in class, by ten percent while decreasing problems such as bullying and violence by the same amount—with even more benefits among the students who needed help most.

What's more, academic-achievement test scores went up by 11 percent. Clearing your mind makes you a better learner.

A Call to Care

At the Smith College Campus School, fifth-graders in Emily Endris's class sit in a circle. They have each been given the name of a classmate and the assignment to observe that person carefully and note what they admire about him or her. Now they are telling that very person what they appreciate.

Ms. Endris instructs them to look each other in the eye as the compliments come: "You listen and don't interrupt." "You always keep trying in gym." "When we went to get a drink at the water fountain, you let me use the higher one, and that made me happy." "You smile a lot and are happy most of the time."

The person who receives an appreciation thanks the one giving it and then gives the next, as the admirations sweep around the circle. Then they each reflect on how it feels to notice someone carefully, to say something true and complimentary to them—and to be the one on the receiving end.

The verdict: lots of smiles and good feeling. But in the discussion afterward, they zero in on the need for compliments to be sincere lest they ring hollow—a blanket "you're great" doesn't help. Another take-home: When you really pay attention, you see aspects of the person you hadn't noticed.

These exercises are part of an ongoing R & D mission at this "lab" school for Smith College, where teachers in training try out their skills and college students taking courses like child development come to observe different age groups. As a site for research, the school continually tries out innovations in pedagogy.

These two classes are part of a larger innovative experiment. A handful of teachers, Robbie Murphy and Emily Endris among them, are developing and trying out learning opportunities like the clementine and mutual-appreciation exercises, as part of Call to Care, an initiative to build an elementary-school curriculum that enhances mindfulness and compassion.

While mindfulness has of late been trendy in schools—as well as in businesses and medical settings—Call to Care extends such careful attention to relationships and adds thoughtfulness, concern, and compassion.

The need for children to enhance their focusing skills "has been amplified in our world of distractions," as Sam Intrator, the head of the campus school, told me. "Now more than ever, schools need to teach how to monitor your 'attentional' landscape and how it connects with others.

"Much of mindfulness in schools seeks to give individual students tools for inner work. Yet the classroom is a busy, crowded space," Intrator, a professor at Smith College and well-known education thinker himself, added.

"Mindfulness fits better in schools if it helps you think about your relationships. Settle yourself, but then how do we share, connect, and mesh?"

The campus school was invited to be a pilot site for Call to Care by the Mind and Life Institute, which happens to have its headquarters several miles up Route 9, in the next town. While the institute was originally founded to foster dialogues between the Dalai Lama and scientists, in recent years he has urged the institute's president, Arthur Zajonc, to tackle a wider mission, including rethinking education.

The Dalai Lama himself donated some of the funds that allowed the launch of Call to Care. When he did so, he asked that the curriculum be acceptable everywhere. Toward that end, a handful of other schools in the United States, as well as in Vietnam, Bhutan, Norway, and Israel, are lining up to take part.

The schools will develop exercises like those at the campus school for a curriculum guide suggesting how teachers can integrate the program into what they are already doing. Call to Care represents an evolution in social–emotional learning.

The Dalai Lama has been mentioning the program in his world travels and is eager to connect interested educators with Call to Care. He contacted Arthur Zajonc to get a progress report, which, as I write this, nears completion.

Another key point: Call to Care should meet impeccable scientific standards. As more pilot schools come on board, evaluations of how this program affects, for example, students' sense of connectedness to school and classmates will be evaluated on metrics like attendance and referrals to the principal for fights, bullying, and the like. The goal: an empirically tested program.

The Dalai Lama has his own ideas of what the program might be like one day.

That map of emotions, he has suggested, might be part of the mix. Then, as students master the topic, he foresees that their responses to unhealthy states would become as automatic as washing their hands when they get dirty—an emotional hygiene as deeply embedded as the physical one. And his hope is that one day this approach would become part of universal standards for education, similar to standards for math.

Such an education in the emotions could be part of the curriculum for every child, from kindergarten on, the Dalai Lama proposes. If taught hand in hand with compassionate ethics, this would give children the practical inner tools that would let them more readily act on those values rather than merely mouth them.

A parent might have great hopes that one day a child in kindergarten will become a great scholar or scientist and knows this will take years of step-by-step education, the Dalai Lama said—and it's the same with educating the heart. "The child's mind develops similarly, step by step over the years, gradually cultivating a compassionate attitude."

The topic at every level, as he envisions it, would be half theoretical understanding, half practical applications in life. Part of this curriculum might even draw from ancient Indian psychology, combined with recent psychological findings, to widen and deepen our understanding of emotions and lay the groundwork for change. This, he suggests, could itself become an academic subject.

Making this an academic topic would give SEL a strengthened knowledge base. The curriculum would be adapted to children's level of comprehension, empathy, and emotional regulation skills, becoming more nuanced as they went through higher grades, with its fullest articulation in the college years.

The Dalai Lama pictures introducing emotional hygiene inductively at first, letting children discover for themselves their own internal map's main coordinates. After all, he notes, from birth an infant knows the happiness of being at her mother's breast, and every toddler feels more secure in his parent's lap. Children intuitively know the basics of their emotional terrain.

So, he suggests, a teacher might show very young children two faces, one angry and the other smiling, and ask, "Which face do you prefer?"

And the children will say, "Oh, a smiling face."

But, the Dalai Lama notes, it must be a genuine smile, not a "tricky smile," a distinction he learned from Paul Ekman's research: A heartfelt smile has crow's-feet around the eyes, while a forced one does not. Such facts would also be a feature of learning the intricacies of the emotions map.

As in SEL generally, the lessons would readily apply to children's lives. The Dalai Lama gives this example: When children have some disagreement or conflict, their immediate reaction, instead of just fighting, should be to "solve their problem through a meaningful dialogue"—not through force. This response should be a natural part of their thinking.

And, he adds, the children should take these methods back to their families. "When they see their parents quarrel, they tell them, 'Oh, no! This isn't the right way—you should talk, not fight.'"

This emphasis on teaching emotional and social skills by no means slights academics. He recognizes a place for healthy intellectual competition among students too—but "healthy" here means a motive like self-compassion, not preventing others from having their success.

The goals of the education the Dalai Lama envisions are not just good minds but good people. As he told an audience at Princeton University, "Our existing modern education system is oriented toward materialist values. We need an education about inner values to lead a healthy life."

His advice at Princeton: "Keep your high standard of education, but it would be more complete if you also included something about warmheartedness."

PART FOUR

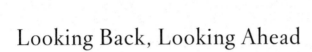

Looking Back, Looking Ahead

CHAPTER ELEVEN

The Long View

"When I was born in 1935," the Dalai Lama recalls, "the Sino–Japanese War had begun, followed by the Second World War, the Chinese Civil War, the Korean War, the Vietnam War, and so on. For most of my life, I've witnessed war and violence taking place somewhere on this planet."

However, he believes that, as a whole, a positive change took place in the twentieth century. "At the time of the First World War, people thought the only way to solve problems was through the use of force," he says. In the past, when nations declared war, people proudly joined the war effort.

"By the end of the century, though, more people had become thoroughly fed up with violence, and there were strong movements for peace. People who had previously considered each other as historical enemies now viewed each other simply as neighbors."

This note of optimism, powered by his long view of history,

thrums in the background throughout the Dalai Lama's voicing of his vision.

He redirects our focus from how bad things are to how our world could be better. He looks beyond just what's urgent now, for ourselves, and calls for action that will matter for all, including generations far ahead.

The daily news, as we've seen, highlights wars, murders, and other human cruelties and crises. From this mirror on events, our world seems more violent than ever. But more objective data tells us a different story, one in keeping with this optimistic view of what can come.

For the scientific case here, consider studies of the risks of dying violently at different points along the arc of human history. Ian Morris, a Stanford University historian, surveyed millennia of archaeological data and found that during the late Stone Age, about ten thousand years ago, 10 to 20 percent of deaths were murders—perhaps interclan violence.

The paradox, Morris says, is that during the dawn of civilizations, while wars helped build huge empires, those very kingdoms eventually became a force for peace within their own borders. The death rate plummeted—very likely, says Morris, because suppressing violence made governing easier.

Today, according to United Nations statistics, just 0.7 percent of people worldwide die a violent death—and that number includes all those caught in the smaller conflicts still smoldering around our globe. The decline in the rate of violent deaths over ten thousand years: from one in every five-to-ten deaths to one in every 140 or so. This may be the safest era yet, not the most dangerous.

To be sure, the tragic legacy of the twentieth century is that, despite its great leaps in technology, it was an era of unparalleled violence, with more than two hundred million deaths from hostilities. Yet during the Cold War, with both sides armed with nuclear weaponry that could annihilate much of humanity, we avoided a world-wide conflagration.

Morris sees our ability to evolve culturally as the capacity that lets us live in bigger, more interconnected societies than ever and keep the peace. The historian of war concludes, "The age-old dream of a world without war may yet come to pass."

Are Things Getting Better or Worse?

"In 1996, I met the Queen Mother, someone whose face I had been familiar with since my childhood," the Dalai Lama said. "Since she had observed almost the entire twentieth century, I asked her if she felt things were improving or not. She replied without hesitation that they were. She said, for example, that when she was young, no one talked about human rights or the right to self-determination, as they do now."

That hopeful outlook flavored his remarks in Matera, a hot, dusty, and poor town in the south of Italy that had been considered a potential site for the country's nuclear waste dump. Instead, the Dalai Lama's friend and fellow Nobel Laureate Betty Williams came up with another way to help the local economy: a plan to make the town the site of an orphanage for refugee children.

When Williams and he visited Matera to dedicate a building for that purpose, he said, "In this part of Italy and in this part of the world, this project will be like a seed of peace. We need to plant such seeds elsewhere. This is the beginning of a way to create a happier world."

A woman told the Dalai Lama she was discouraged because she saw no connection between anything she might do and what could happen fifty years down the road. In response, he took the long view.

He told of hearing from the late Carl Friedrich von Weizsäcker, a German philosopher and his tutor in quantum physics, that within his own lifetime the Germans and the French were at first bitter enemies, killing each other. And yet a few decades later, Charles de Gaulle, who had led the Free French Army against the Nazis, became close friends with the German chancellor Konrad Adenauer. They teamed to support the concept that led to creation of the European Union.

"In the early part of the twentieth century, this was unthinkable, but it happened by mid-century," the Dalai Lama observed. "Impossible things become possible. So what seems impossible to you at this moment can change if you make the effort."

For instance, in most parts of the world, the eighteenth century was a time of harsh treatment of children, animals, the insane, the poor, debtors, prisoners, and slaves. By the end of the nineteenth century, such cruelty became rarer—and by the end of the twentieth century it had become criminal in most places.

The last century or two have seen rises in the world's well-being, as tracked by data on health, education, inequality, and safety. For instance, two hundred years ago, just one in five people could read; by 2000, four out of five worldwide were literate. In the last one hundred thirty years, life expectancy leaped from less than thirty years to around seventy years globally.

He pointed out that much of what we take for granted today once would have sounded like mere pipe dreams: universal education, outlawing slavery, worldwide response of immediate aid to grave disasters anywhere on the globe, instant access to the world's knowledge base. In the last century or two—or decade or two—each has gone from outlandish dream to commonplace reality.

That may be one reason the bad news from Tibet—for example, the wave of Tibetans immolating themselves to protest Chinese Communist rule—does not seem to have dimmed the Dalai Lama's long-term optimism about his homeland's future. True, the Chinese Communist regimes have left Tibet's (and China's) culture and environment in tatters.

But, he said, it will also be their responsibility one day to fix these. What Tibetans can offer when that day comes will be their unique cultural perspective and values, including living together in harmony and peaceful coexistence.

The Dalai Lama's concern about Chinese repression of Tibetan culture focuses less on externals, like how people dress, than on these cultural and spiritual values "that have proved to be of true benefit to people both in Tibet and abroad."

He noted that even as the Chinese government represses Tibetans in their homeland, increasing numbers of the four hundred million or so Buddhists in China are following Tibetan teachers, even among the power elite and intellectuals. "That's a positive sign."

Yet he is no wide-eyed Pollyanna. He warns against complacency and wants us to face facts.

The Stories We Tell Ourselves

Can the Dalai Lama's optimistic vision have any hope of reversing that tide of negativity we hear about in our daily dose of the day's events?

Then again, how well does the news reflect day-to-day reality? Might that negative slant on events—on what's possible—be due to a shared myopia? Let's rethink that ominous tide for a moment.

Imagine a fraction that reflects the ratio of kind-to-cruel acts in the world. For the top number, put a rough estimate of the number of acts of cruelty committed by people around the world on any given day—everything from bullying to murder.

For the bottom quantity, guess a number for the acts of kindness of all varieties everywhere on that same day—from the countless gestures of nurturing that parents give their children, to everyday civility, to someone helping another person in need. On any day of the year, the denominator of kindness will be vastly greater than the numerator of cruelty.

And if you look only at those acts of meanness, there's an equally telling fraction that can be made. At the top, put that same number of cruel acts committed. Under it goes the number of such cruelties that *might* have been committed but were not: murderous or simply mean impulses not acted on, arguments and even near-fights that did not lead to violence, and the like. The *potential* for cruelty is far greater than the aggression actually acted out.

This may seem hard to picture given the onslaught of human callousness, corruption, and cruelty offered up in our daily media diet. The news skews our perceptions toward the fewer acts of negativity and away from the far more numerous acts of goodness in the world at large.

But the media focus on what's wrong with the world rather than on what's right comes as a by-product of the perennial function of news itself: to get us to pay attention to what needs fixing, to what may be dangerous, or to alert us to potential threats. What's wrong makes the news; what's fine does not. This lens on "what's news" inevitably distorts the picture, reversing the ratio of kind-to-cruel.

That parallels what happens in our own minds. The vast majority of information we take in never reaches our awareness. Of the small portion that does, a prominent strand features problems, mistakes, or threats—so we can find solutions, make corrections, or better prepare.

One main function of awareness, cognitive science tells us, is to notice and fix such wobbles in life. When things go well, we needn't pay particular attention to them. The brain habituates to business-as-usual, tuning out so we do not notice the routine and familiar.

This allows the brain to economize on glucose, its energy source, but it also renders relatively invisible the vast amount that's right in our personal lives. Likewise, at the collective level, the headlines mainly feature just the select strand of what's awry.

"I always tell people in the media they have a responsibility," the Dalai Lama said. "They focus on the sensational, negative things, while the positive they take for granted. Then you can see why people who always hear the negative will develop the attitude that basic human nature is negative—and so the future of humanity is doomed.

"And yet if we truly analyze," he pointed out, "the acts of compassion are much, much greater than acts of anger."

His remedy here surprised me. Instead of simply saying that media should change the ratio of good-to-bad news to favor the good, the Dalai Lama suggested something else.

"I say this to the media. I tell them that in this modern time they have a special responsibility to bring awareness to the people, not just report on bad news, but bring people hope.

"You must report the bad news," he insisted, clarifying, "but at the same time you should also show the possibility to change or overcome these things. Otherwise, all the very negative reports are overwhelming and demoralizing.

"You should speak out," he advised, adding that "media people should be more serious—not just advertising or some picture of a beautiful girl, not just murder and scandal and all these negative things, but serious matters."

As a journalist myself, I had the thought that though this twist appeals to me, there's not much likelihood that many in the news media will make this change (to be fair, a few news sources do some of this already, and others may take this charge to heart).

Tell the positive side, suggest solutions, he insisted again. For example, we have this environmental problem, but here's what we can do to prevent it rather than just continuing with things as they are.

If told only the negative side, people feel helpless. The Dalai Lama suggests showing them the "we have the ability to change" story. "That will motivate."

Thinking in New Ways

The Dalai Lama remembers a conversation in 1973 with professors in England who were telling him about the huge differences in wealth between the world's richest and poorest people, particularly in the industrialized "northern" world versus the agricultural "southern" world. Even then they were questioning whether there were enough resources to go around.

These days, with the rapidly rising living standards of those once-poor nations—like China, India, and Brazil—and the prediction of ten billion people by the end of this century, the question of scarce resources looms larger.

"We shouldn't say, 'Oh, until now things have been like this, so things as they are should be okay.' That's wrong! The population is increasing, major disasters increasing, global warming too, while resources are getting more limited. It's quite certain there will be more and more problems and possibility of conflicts over the economy or for major resources," driven by the self-interest of the Western powers, Russia, and China.

In addition, with the growing number of major natural disasters (or at least a greater global awareness of them), the Dalai Lama noted, "Nature seems to be telling us that now the world needs more cooperation.

"We have to think about this seriously," he cautioned. "Now it's totally wrong to take for granted that we can carry on with this way of life, our ways of thinking. The next several decades will be very difficult. So we have to think in a new way." For example, when the Dalai Lama was in Australia, he saw that adopting Israeli-style drip irrigation was creating fertile land from the arid outback at the rate of two hundred kilometers a decade.

He proposed that "wasteland can become green" at a more rapid rate by adding to the new irrigation the building of solar-powered water-desalination plants, which together could green even more-vast areas of desert. But his imagination did not stop there.

"So," he told Australians on his most recent visit, "you can take in more poor immigrants."

The plight of Africa, particularly, has concerned him—one of his closest friends, Archbishop Desmond Tutu, has kept him up to date on this troubled continent. That's one reason the Dalai Lama has spoken out against the immorality of putting poor countries in paralyzing debt to richer ones. And he proposes that the European immigration crises would be best helped by boosting the economies of the countries in Africa and Eastern Europe those people are fleeing.

The Dalai Lama realizes there inevitably will be resistance to such innovative thinking. When he told a visiting Russian filmmaker that the empty vastness of Siberia could absorb many Chinese, the reaction was, "No, no, no," he told me with a laugh.

Receptiveness to such new ideas will mean letting go of old ways of thinking. He gave as an example how in the traditional Hindu funeral the body is cremated on a wooden pyre. He lauded the creative thinking of his late friend Baba Amte, who started a new practice with his own final wishes: Bury the body in a cloth without a coffin, and plant a tree to grow there.

"Eventually the body dissolves into the earth and feeds the tree," the Dalai Lama said approvingly. "No damage to the environment, not using trees for burning, but rather grow a tree. I say, very good."

He applauds such new ways of thinking. "My body belongs to

the twentieth century," the Dalai Lama said. "But I try to have my mind be in the twenty-first."

However we manage to create a positive change, one mark of success comes when that new way of doing things becomes a norm, taken for granted—as has happened, for instance, with outlawing slavery or child labor. What at first seems a distant, even unreachable goal can become a given.

The Dalai Lama's vision of a world radically different from the one we know today can seem impossibly idealistic. Yet, as Baba Amte once put it, "No one has the right to arrange a funeral for the future."

A Theory of Change

About thirty thousand people live in Ain El-Sira, a huge slum in Cairo. Most of them inhabit makeshift dwellings, some just large crate-like rooms patched together from plywood. Those patchwork homes are likely to hold a family in just a room or two.

The inhabitants of Ain El-Sira lucky enough to find work typically labor away in the lowliest, least secure jobs. The vast majority are illiterate, and about half the people dwelling in those makeshift homes have a serious health problem.

Such are the data collected by a professor at the American University in Cairo. Such sad demographics could well have been collected from the poorest parts of most any city throughout much of the world.

But this study caught the attention of a student at that same university, Samar Soltan. She zeroed in on the fact that two-thirds of people in that dirt-poor area had virtually no marketable skills. When they did find work, they often still did not get a living wage.

So Soltan teamed with another student, Bassma Hassan, to set up a job-training facility for slum-dwelling women. Using T-shirts to demonstrate basic skills like basting seams and sewing, they taught not just how to work in the textile trade but also basic workers' rights—knowledge hard to come by in the political atmosphere of that country.

The two college women had been given a grant of $5,000 for the project when they were chosen as Dalai Lama Fellows, a program in ethical leadership. Soltan and Hassan had been picked for this program by their college, the American University in Cairo.

That school, along with the Tata Institute of Social Sciences in Mumbai, and the Ashesi University near Accra, Ghana, join colleges in America in being able to nominate students as fellows. Of the sixty-five fellows so far, twenty-five have come from countries outside the United States.

The Dalai Lama, who lent his name and early support to the fellows project, hoped these young leaders would focus their efforts on the problems of the world's poor, in Africa, the Arab world, and beyond. He urged them to move from the feeling of compassion to action on the ground. And they have.

Titus K. Chirchir was one of nine children born to a family of subsistence farmers in a small village in the Rift Valley of Kenya. Over the seventeen years he lived there, Titus saw rivers start to run dry and the greenness of the surrounding country turn brown. A population explosion in his area, Tiboiywo, led to more and more jobless and landless villagers who, in desperation, felled trees in nearby forests to open new land for farms.

While they benefited in the short term, the long-term consequences of their deforestation included the drying of rivers and land, species loss, and lower crop yields for everyone. The government's response was to evict people. But that, Titus saw, increased anger and agitation—and violence. Evicted farmers torched forests in retaliation.

So Titus, who despite the obscurity of his origins managed to attend Amherst College, returned as a Dalai Lama Fellow to Tiboiywo. He developed a plan to show farmers methods of agroforestry, planting trees to sprout alongside their crops. When those trees reach sufficient height, they will be distributed widely to farmers in Tiboiywo, to reforest the land.

Titus finds inspiration in this favorite quote attributed to Albert Einstein: "The world is a dangerous place to live; not because of the people who are evil, but because of the people who don't do anything about it."

In the sense that a "leader" influences or guides people toward a shared goal, leadership is widely distributed—everyone has some sphere of influence, as the Dalai Lama Fellows attest. Whether within our family, among friends, on social media, in an organization, or in society as a whole, we are all leaders in one way or another, if only from time to time.

Each of us can play a part in this network of influence and impact. The Dalai Lama's analysis shows that the changes we need are systemic, at a level governments cannot or do not deal with.

All of us together can make a shift. We are everywhere.

The map for a better world the Dalai Lama envisions does not depend on any particular person or office but on all of us, each doing our part in a larger orchestration of collective energies.

During the darkest hours of World War II, I told the Dalai Lama, there was a young American scientist who was recruited into the Manhattan Project to work on developing the atom bomb but who immediately after the war's end joined those nuclear physicists who renounced working on weapons. He was one of the first American scientists who, during the Cold War, entered into dialogues with his Russian counterparts on how to avoid nuclear conflict.

The Dalai Lama applauded that change of heart from hunkered-down hostility to person-to-person engagement. Those dialogues, and the relationships formed between scientists across a political divide, were among the very first human threads in a weave that finally ended the Cold War.

Consider how societies change. "Society" is but the aggregate of us all. In the Dalai Lama's view, society, government, or corporations do not really exist apart from the cumulative efforts of individuals. A government, he said, has "no brain, no mouth—just offices and some papers. So a government, like a corporation, is really just individuals," and, of course, the interactions between them, as well as their common purpose.

The Dalai Lama's theory of change puts less faith in the power of rulers to make lasting change in such systems than in the power of the people. That transition will come not from government fiats but from people starting changes for the better, on their own, and from others spontaneously supporting them.

While he envisions a century more just and peaceful than the last, he emphasized that this will not come to pass by wishing it so. It will take a people's movement for change.

"Sometimes we feel all the world's problems are huge," the Dalai Lama observed. "But who creates these problems? Humanity is only a collection of individuals, so change must come from each of us. I myself am also one of the seven billion human beings, so I have both moral responsibility and the opportunity to make a contribution, which starts at the mental level with fewer destructive emotions—more constructive ones.

"Then share with friends, anyone we can. Change spreads that way. Ultimately each individual has responsibility. That's the only way to bring about this change."

Wishful thinking is not enough. "Change only comes through action."

If we think, Oh, I can't do anything, he continued, nothing will happen—the world will just stay the same. "We can't blame our leaders if a whole society just talks about 'me, me, me.' And we can't depend on some totalitarian leader to demand we become more compassionate—that's hypocrisy. Impossible! Impossible!

"All these changes must come voluntarily, by people who realize their true value," he added. It comes down to each person mobilizing and then joining together. "The individual is very, very important, but the real effect comes from a mass movement."

He gave as an example the movement within science to study contemplative practice and how that started with individual scientists who, through personal friendships and discussions at conferences, had formed an active network. Isolated and on their own, the scientists were nowhere near as influential as the network as a whole.

"No single person can change the world. Jesus Christ tried and didn't succeed entirely. Now we are in a modern era, with democracy, so it's really the voice of the people together, the collective, that will make a difference."

If the trajectory of human history has a positive vector, imagine what we might accomplish. It's up to us.

Plant the Seeds for a Better World

But what of the discouragement many feel, I asked the Dalai Lama, realizing they may not see results from their best efforts? Why do anything?

His answer had an unexpected twist: "That is selfish. That very attitude signifies a lack of compassion." We need to act with the view "not in my generation, but in the next generation. We have to think long term."

It will take a few generations to change society, he said. "Maybe in twenty or thirty years we will start to have a better society."

Back in 1774, Captain James Cook was sailing the South Pacific for the second time when, on an island to the northeast of Australia, he came upon a variety of tree that amazed him with how straight and high it grew. He thought these trees could provide the perfect wood for ship masts, a prized commodity in his day—and one that might save the lives of crews stranded by storms that had destroyed their ship's masts.

As the story goes, Captain Cook gathered seeds of the Norfolk Island pine (so named for the island near New Caledonia where Cook first found it) and, as he landed on other islands around the Pacific, planted them there, thinking that in decades to come they might become life-saving masts.

The Dalai Lama beamed as he was told this bit of history. It fits his view that we should plant the seeds of a better world, even if we will not see the fruits.

When a group of environmental scientists and activists was discouraged by the difficulties of getting the public to pay attention to threats to the planet, the Dalai Lama advised them, "Sometimes you see people start something important and work hard, and if it doesn't materialize right away, they lose interest." But, the Dalai Lama noted, these bigger, important goals are almost impossible to achieve immediately. "We're talking about humanity, and over time humanity can change."

Such shifts are gradual. "But someone must begin. Our generation must start these important efforts, even if the results don't materialize in our lifetimes. That's okay. It's our responsibility to begin to shape the world for the better, even though at present it is only a dream. Yet through education and through awareness, we must inspire the younger generation."

As he advised students at MIT, "This generation has a responsibility to reshape the world. We have the capacity to think several centuries into the future."

And, he added, they should not be daunted by the goal. "If we make an effort, it may be possible to achieve. Even if it seems hopeless now, never give up. Offer a positive vision, with enthusiasm and joy, and an optimistic outlook."

The Dalai Lama said that when it comes to the spread of the programs he promotes, "I am not expecting to see a result. It may take twenty or thirty years or more—I tell students in their twenties they may live to see results. But we all should act now, even if we will never see the fruition of our efforts."

Think for the long run, for today's children or their children. We don't have to leave for them the world as we found it.

CHAPTER TWELVE

Act Now

In February 1993, a group of seven Nobel Peace Laureates gathered in Thailand to protest the continuing house arrest in nearby Burma of Aung San Suu Kyi. Although she had won that very Nobel Prize two years before, she was still being kept a virtual prisoner in her house by the Burmese government.

For the Dalai Lama, his twenty-seven-hour visit was one more stage in a campaign he had been waging on her behalf for decades. Some of his efforts were private: He wrote personal letters to Aung San Suu Kyi, praising her fortitude and staunchly principled position—a determined passive resistance and search for dialogue with her opponents—and offering his encouragement and support.

Part had been public: At meetings of Nobel Peace Laureates, an empty chair was left for her, as a symbolic reminder. And the Dalai Lama often spoke up to make appeals for her release.

"Like my own people in neighboring Tibet," he said in one such statement, back in 2000, "you suffer under an oppressive regime beyond the reach of international relief. We can only achieve a lasting resolution of our struggle by employing nonviolent means. That does not make it easier. It requires immense determination, for nonviolent protest by its nature depends on patience."

When Aung San Suu Kyi was finally released, she joyously met with the Dalai Lama in Europe, as they have several times since. But for the Dalai Lama, the determined spirit of that campaign continues—now on behalf of his fellow Nobel Laureate Liu Xiaobo, a human-rights activist imprisoned by the People's Republic of China for speaking out to protest single-party rule and to call for reforms.

For now that laureate's chair remains empty—for Liu Xiaobo.

The Dalai Lama's efforts for these two exemplify what he invites us all to do, each in our own way: Act now, and persist. Act even if the cause seems hopeless—and never give up.

His vision, as we've seen, suggests the "what" and "how": Begin by taking more control of our destructive emotions rather than acting from them; act on our concern for the well-being of others, from a sense of the oneness of humanity.

He sees compassion expressed in many ways, like taking moral responsibility not just for those in need but also, for instance, in exposing and holding accountable cronies who corrupt governments, or reinventing our material world so it no longer endangers life on our planet.

His core counsel: Cultivate a warm heart; foster human values. He suggests that whatever we do after that will have a positive consequence—but there's no "must" or "have to" in his advice. Rather than lecture us about what specific steps we should take, he leaves the details to each of us.

Even as he urges us toward good works, he sees they should be voluntary, motivated from a genuine sense of compassion.

The Dalai Lama's vision for shifting our social reality originates from a point oddly overlooked in most pictures of the human future: inside each of us.

He reminds us this better future begins with our own mind. "If you want to change the world," he says, first try to improve—change within yourself. "That will help change your family. From there it just gets bigger and bigger."

We can accelerate the transformation of our society, the Dalai Lama tells us, by transforming ourselves. This begins with shifting the emotional center to become better vessels for compassion—and continues over generations by revamping education to include tools for this inner shift.

Start with yourself, but don't stop there. Act for others, with positivity.

Take Dekila Chungyalpa. She spent her childhood in the natural beauty of the lower Himalayas, in Sikkim, but at fifteen had been brought to New York City to go to school by an aunt who was working at the United Nations. In Sikkim, a compassionate view toward all life comes embedded in the culture.

"Sikkim is very green, with lots of wilderness," Dekila recalls. "I'd always looked to nature for a place that was healing, and other than Central Park I didn't have a place to go. It was very shocking."

She spent lots of time in Central Park, her refuge. "My attitude from childhood toward wilderness has always been to long for it when I'm not in it."

Feeling very connected to nature, she joined Greenpeace while in high school and started a letter-writing campaign in her school to protest the killing of whales—her first taste of activism, at fifteen.

On her return to her family home, she joined a group fighting a proposed hydroelectric dam. It was the first stirring of an environmental movement in Sikkim.

"The dam would displace many indigenous people and be very damaging to the local ecosystem, causing huge deforestation," she says. "And it would have flooded a renowned *chorten* and part of a sacred mountain."

Returning to the States to attend college in Ohio, Dekila designed a major for herself in international environmental politics. At her college, she created their first student recycling program, Greenhouse, in which volunteers went from dorm to dorm, collecting recyclables. "It was my first experience managing an environmental project."

Her taste for activism increased from there. Following graduation from college, she went to Nepal and worked for the World Wildlife Fund, studying ways to stop the poaching of wildlife in nature preserves. The prevailing view among WWF workers was that the local people were the source of the problem. But Dekila had another insight.

"All the guides were from the local area and most of them knew the forests, wildlife patterns, and ecology better than anyone else. In the most practical terms, it was such a waste of resources and allies to alienate them. But, more importantly, if we are not working together with local communities to protect wildlife and manage natural resources, who will continue the work when we leave?"

She saw that "if you want to protect the environment, it's people you have to focus on."

In graduate school at American University, she concentrated on development policy and the environment. Rejoining WWF, she applied that knowledge to influence institutions like the World Bank to make their practices more environmentally sound, and then she headed the Greater Mekong program, which negotiated agreements not to dam that river's main stem, as we saw in Chapter Nine.

In a slight detour, Dekila helped create environmental guidelines for Buddhist monasteries and nunneries headed by the Seventeenth Karmapa. That naturally led to her launching a pilot program at

the World Wildlife Fund: Sacred Earth, which works with religious leaders on environmental causes.

When I last spoke with her, Dekila was at the Yale School of
Forestry and Environmental Studies, having received the McClus-
key Fellowship (previous winners include Nobel winners Wangari
Maathai, a Kenyan activist for women's rights and for the environ-
ment, and R. K. Pachauri, head of the Intergovernmental Panel on
Climate Change). She still heads Sacred Earth.

At a Mind and Life meeting on the environment, she explained
the secret of her activist trajectory when she told the Dalai Lama, "If
we have a long-term goal and we see that we're advancing toward
it, even if it is one tiny step at a time, it makes a big difference. If it
is a short-term goal, and we're just doing it to stop something, or
we're protesting from anger, then it never goes anywhere. So finding that joy has been my solution.

"Almost every activist I know is actually an optimist at heart:
You really have to believe that the society will be better off," Dekila
added. "I think there is a natural ebullience, an enthusiasm that
comes from inside. We're convinced, no matter what the odds are,
that we will win."

Take It to Scale

The Dalai Lama recalls being the guest of a women's college in
Bombay, where he stayed in a room overlooking a shantytown. The
day was roasting and humid, and despite the air-conditioning, the
rooms were still very warm. "I complained a little that it was too
noisy, and maybe too hot.

"Then I thought, these people in the slums are the same human
beings, experience the same, have the same desire" to be happy. As

he reflected on the shantytown dwellers, he thought, We're here for just a few days, but these denizens of the slums are here for their entire lives.

During a meeting with some of the students, he wondered if they had any plan to help the shanty dwellers, saying that, if so, he wanted to make a donation. Perhaps, he proposed, they might "start some sort of social work with those in the slums in your area.

"Don't take for granted that this is just their way of life," he added. "Don't think that way. You can think how to improve things, how to change this. Otherwise, you see, the children born in slum areas grow up playing in places that are quite dirty, and eventually they may feel that this is due to their karma, or that this is just how things are, that it's quite normal. That's wrong!"

Sensing that the young women seemed eager to help, he encouraged them to start an educational program for those children by tutoring them and helping them gain the self-confidence to overcome their deprived background.

When one of the students told him she wanted to act on that, the Dalai Lama, pleased, did not stop there.

He advised her, "There are slums throughout Bombay and many other places. You can start in your area for these poor people, and then maybe your friends will get interested and you can develop an NGO to do this work more widely. Then you might meet at the national level with other NGOs with the same interest and share your experiences."

In short, go to scale, spreading the good you do as far as possible. If we embark on some good work, he encourages us to do it as well as we can, and with maximal impact.

"Tell ten people, then ten more, and ten more. That way you can reach ten thousand, one hundred thousand."

At another college, the Dalai Lama was asked how just one person could make much difference. Throughout history, he answered, it has always been the actions of one person that culminated in change: Jesus, Buddha, Gandhi, all were "just one person" who made a huge difference.

"When we consider the enormity of the challenges, we may feel like giving up," the Dalai Lama acknowledged. "But we can each start with ourselves, wherever we are. Something as simple as turning off the light when we leave a room matters.

"Everything we do has some effect—even a simple act," the Dalai Lama said. "Although it might seem insignificant, when we multiply it by billions of others who might do the same thing, we can have an enormous impact."

When a group presented him with their plans for a school curriculum aimed at cultivating compassion in children—one directly inspired by his vision—they said it would be piloted in a local school.

The Dalai Lama, without a moment's hesitation, said to them not to think of just that one school, one city, or even one country— make it global. There are seven billion people on the planet. Make it available to all of the children.

Think big.

The Human Connection

The Reverend Bill Crews runs a host of humanitarian projects in Sydney, Australia, ranging from soup kitchens and shelters for the homeless to clinics for free health and dental care, as well as offering tutors in remedial reading for poor schoolchildren.

When the Dalai Lama visited Sydney, his rapport with Crews, whom he admires, was obvious. He likes when people actually *do* something to ease human suffering. And so the Dalai Lama himself put on an apron over his monk's robes and joined Bill Crews serving food.

"What matters is not what you believe, but what you do," he says.

"The pathway from thought to action is through making a commitment to other people," the Dalai Lama was told at an MIT conference by Marshall Ganz, who studies—and has participated in—social action from the civil rights movement and Cesar Chavez's campaign for farm workers' rights to today's environmental crisis.

Ganz, based at Harvard's JFK School of Government, added, "The human connection is key. We struggle together, not as isolated individuals. We work with one another, commit to one another, act with one another."

"That's right!" the Dalai Lama agreed.

"Nonviolence works," Ganz went on, "because it requires the cooperation of many, many people," who take moral responsibility together. It's our ability to say no together, "just like Gandhi. But we will only succeed if we act together."

After Ganz spoke, the Dalai Lama heard from Rebecca Henderson, who teaches about innovation and the environment (and also a course on "reimagining capitalism") at Harvard Business School.

She told him about a local mothers' movement to fight global warming. "All the mothers I talk to are distressed about warming," Henderson said. "But they feel they can't do much just sitting in their house alone."

So a handful of mothers gathered and decided on a specific target: to get their neighbors to choose an option, offered by the local utility, of getting their power mainly from green sources. "It started with a few mothers in a living room, and now there are thousands across the country," Henderson said.

Then Ganz told of a twenty-one-year-old Latina housewife in Chicago who became an activist because children in her neighborhood were being hurt by asthma caused by particulate-choked air from two coal-burning electric plants nearby. The movement she sparked resulted in the closing of those plants.

Compassionate acts are contagious. Thomas Jefferson called this "moral elevation," the inspiration we feel to help others when we witness an act of kindness. Psychologists have verified such inspira-. tion contagion in studies, but we all know the feeling.

The Dalai Lama was perhaps moved by such contagion at that MIT conference. He joined in with enthusiasm, saying these tales reminded him of a meeting he had once in Delhi with a group concerned about the growing numbers of homeless poor in that city. "I told them," he recalled, "now may be the time for a mass demonstration to make the problem known."

And, with brio, he added that he then told them, "If you organize it, I will join you—shouting, shouting, for the well-being of humanity."

That burst of enthusiasm may have just been the Dalai Lama's way of encouraging the cause. To my knowledge he has rarely, if ever, been in the front lines that way. His own range of activities, though worldwide, is constrained by schedules, security, the rules of monkhood, protocol, and the like.

But he supports all who are moved to act for a larger benefit, especially when that motive comes from a deeply felt compassion. "Altruism," he told the MIT group, "must be translated into action."

There are countless ways to follow this dictum. The father of a family in Brooklyn, for instance, told me that he and his wife are looking for a place—say, a soup kitchen—where they can bring their young daughters regularly to help those in need. We want, he said, "to show them that charity should be part of life," and to teach them the "wise-selfish" truth that "altruism feels good."

And, to be sure, there are myriad organizations helping the world in a multitude of ways. Joining with any of those efforts—even through a donation—adds your personal force to this greater good.

That's why there is a website that mirrors this book, inviting anyone who feels aligned with the Dalai Lama's vision to join together and name the good they do or aim for and, en masse, show the world the promise of a force for good: www.joinaforce4good .org.

My wife, Tara Bennett-Goleman, who had the idea for that Web platform, asked the Dalai Lama if he thought this effort could really make a difference in the world. "Certainly!" was his instant response.

"I think this is not a question of how difficult it might be" to create a force for good that stands in opposition to negative forces everywhere, he added. It might be difficult to achieve, but, he said, "We have to make the attempt.

"The world's population is increasing, resources are more and more limited, the disasters from global warming are increasing. So the twenty-first century will not be a happy one unless we make the effort now."

Think, Plan, Act

"I really thank you for this uplifting work," the Dalai Lama told a Vancouver woman who had developed a school program on educating the heart. Half in jest, he added, "My job is just talk—blah, blah, blah."

And then, shifting to a quiet, sincere tone, "You are really implementing. Thank you."

The Dalai Lama encourages each of us to take action to change the world for the better, wherever we are, with whatever means we have.

The Dalai Lama believes far more in the power of individuals to gather strength together than in top-down changes, whether from an organization, government, or dictator. As he said, "You can't force people to be compassionate."

Don't wait for society to change. Start now, wherever you are, the Dalai Lama says: "Everyone can find a context where they make a difference. The human community is nothing but individuals combined."

Strategy implements vision. The Dalai Lama's vision offers us a rich spectrum of possibilities. If we are inspired by it, we can translate that vision into practical strategies in our own ways to suit our times, our place, and its particular needs.

As Richard Moore—who was blinded at age ten but went on to form a group helping impoverished children in countries around the world—says, "Focus on what we can do—not what we can't do."

Some of us have inside access, such as to business or government. Others connect to the worldwide family of non-governmental organizations focused on given issues or problems. Then there is the path of using laws and courts as levers for change.

And any of us can become grassroots activists, working outside the centers of power. Then there are the countless ways we can help the people in our lives, our city or town, our neighborhoods. Giving money to the downtrodden helps, the Dalai Lama says, but he also urges people to take more-concrete action and, as he told that university student, to organize so their efforts spread. "When you see something wrong, if you have some sort of concern for their well-being, then take responsibility—act on this enthusiasm," he says. If you remain indifferent, nothing will happen to help.

As he says, when intelligence operates in the service of greed and hatred, we become dangerous to ourselves, to others, and to the planet. But if that intelligence serves the aims of compassion, the good we can do together has countless possibilities.

Over the years, the Dalai Lama has become ever more interested in meeting with fresh younger faces, like college students—people who can carry this vision forward into our future. As the Dalai Lama told an overflowing gym-turned-auditorium at Macalester College in St. Paul, Minnesota, "That's why I'm here."

"When I talk about these things to young students, I say you will see this—I will not," the Dalai Lama told me. "So think, plan, act. This is the way to create the latter part of the twenty-first century so it can be a happier world—if we start the effort now."

Today's young, he says, are the genuine citizens of the twenty-first century and so will shape its course. To be sure, the troubles of the last century have spilled over into the first decade or two of this one. But their causes lie in the past. There are still decades left in this century to redirect the trajectory of our future.

"For myself, I'm not concerned about dying," he added at age seventy-nine. "I may live to eighty-nine or even ninety-nine, then gone. But those generations who are now in their teens, twenties, or thirties I think will see a different world by the time they reach fifty or sixty. It can be done, so we need to make the effort."

The crucial point: Seize the opportunity now.

"Many people are just complaining," the Dalai Lama declared, about what's wrong with the world but not making any effort to change it. "That's due to a lack of awareness and of a vision. So this book can be helpful by making clear the possibilities. Then we have no regret."

Neither he nor I, we reflected, might see the fruition of this map for the future. But still we agreed to work together on this book, acting now for a better world.

Acknowledgments

My gratitude goes first to the Dalai Lama, whose message to the world I have attempted to share here. He has always inspired me, since our first meeting in the 1980s and in our encounters over the years.

Most of this book is based on several hours of interviews he granted, mainly in Pomaia and Livorno, Italy, but also in Rochester, Minnesota, and Princeton, New Jersey. For decades his message has guided me personally, and I am delighted at the opportunity to share it with a wider audience.

I've based the vision recounted here on a mix of those interviews as well as on what he has said in his worldwide lectures and in his writings, and also drawn on others' accounts of him. Throughout I have also added my own observations, thoughts, and perspectives, which I trust the reader will distinguish from the Dalai Lama's own articulation of his vision. I apologize for any errors or misrepresentations, which are inadvertent, and rejoice in any ways my efforts are of benefit to readers.

I am grateful for the help of many people in writing this book.

First to Thupten Jinpa, who brought this project to me and initially shaped the chapter outline and tone. He has been a vital source of feedback throughout.

Huge gratitude also to Jeremy Russell, who generously hunted through and shared his notes and blogs on the Dalai Lama's travels (some of which have been incorporated verbatim into this text) and who took great pains, even searching archives, to answer my questions, no matter how trivial.

To the Private Office of the Dalai Lama, especially Tenzin Taklha and Chhime Rigzing, who facilitated my meetings with the Dalai Lama, and to Kaydor Aukthong, the representative in Washington, D.C., of the Tibetan government-in-exile, who was so helpful in arranging interviews in the United States.

I owe a deep bow to Ngari Rinpoche, who has helped this project in many ways, and to Geshe Tenzin Sherab and Geshe Tashi Tsering, who accompanied the Dalai Lama during our interviews in Italy. My thanks to the kind staff at Institute Lama Tzong Khapa in Pomaia, Italy, particularly the charming director Filippo Scianna, who were remarkable in helping my wife and me with logistics, smoothing the way for our interviews with the Dalai Lama. Rip Gellein provided essential housing.

In the writing itself many others have helped: Richard Davidson for advice on research, Paul Ekman for the same as well as briefing me on his many meetings with his good friend, the Dalai Lama. And there were many others, including Josh Baran, Diana Chapman Walsh, Dr. Paul Mueller, Larry Brilliant, Trinette Wellesley-Wesley, Sonam Wangchuk, to name but a few of all those who helped me with insights or pieces of this story.

My thanks to Jonathan Rose for a careful reading and useful critique of an early draft, and for his insightful ideas and research (and prose), some of which have been included in this book. I drew generously on the presentations to the Dalai Lama of my colleagues in several Mind and Life meetings.

This telling of the Dalai Lama's vision features people and projects who exemplify the force for good the Dalai Lama pictures—some directly guided by the Dalai Lama's vision, others aligned with that mission on their own. Thanks here to Eve Ekman, Melody Hobson, Richard Layard and Mark Williamson, Kim Reichl-Schoenert, Gregory Norris, A. T. Ariyaratne, Linda Lantieri, Dekila Chungyalpa, Sam Intrator, and Marty Krasney, each of whom helped me tell their inspiring stories. And the same to the teachers, Emily Endris, Robbie Murphy, Jennifer Erikson, and Joanne Martin, who kindly let me observe their classes.

Special thanks go to Amy Cohen for sharing her insights into the intellectual journey of her late husband Francisco Varela, and his remarkable friendship with the Dalai Lama. Likewise to Victor Chan, founder of the Dalai Lama Center in Vancouver, and to Arthur Zajonc, president of the Mind and Life Institute, and his talented staff.

As always, my thinking was helped by the insights of my wife, Tara Bennett-Goleman, and the text improved by her sharp-eyed reading of the final draft. And I'm particularly thankful for her most essential loving support throughout the writing of this book and in bringing this entire project to the world. She had the inspired insight that this book should have a mirroring Web platform, which she founded, that can extend the call to join a force for good beyond the circle of those who read this book.

Thanks also to Jessica Brackman, who partnered early with Tara to find the best home for the vision's Web platform and has been a thoughtful collaborator from the start. And to those who advised and facilitated the Web campaign: Jeanluc Castagner, Robyn

Brentano, and Diana Calpthorpe Rose of the Garrison Institute, which has partnered in steering the Web campaign; Mollie Rodriguez of the Gere Foundation; MJ Viederman of the Mind and Life Institute.

Gratitude also to those at Melcher Media for executing that Web campaign: Lauren Nathan, Shannon Funuko, and Andrew Kennedy. Charles Melcher has been most generous in handling all this at cost. My thanks go to the social media team at MORE Partnerships, Jacob Marshall and Brian Patrick, and to the webmeisters at Crossbeat, Becky Wang and David Justus.

An especially deep appreciation goes to those whose support has made the Web platform possible: Connie and Barry Hershey, Don Morrison, Tara Melwani, and Pierre and Pam Omidyar.

After book-related expenses, all royalties will go to nonprofit organizations, mainly the Mind and Life Institute and the Dalai Lama Trust, to support their good work. I am working pro bono, writing this as a labor of love, an offering to the Dalai Lama

Notes

6 **I remember, for example . . . an unexpected gesture at such an event:**
Peacemaking: The Power of Nonviolence (San Francisco, California,
June 9–11, 1997). At the end of every occasion with the Dalai Lama for
which there is an entry fee, the organizers routinely announce a full
disclosure of how much money was taken in, what the expenses were,
and what will happen with any remainder. He takes no fees for his
speeches and teachings; those organizing his engagements meet the expenses. If there is a surplus of funds at the end of an event, he asks that
it be divided: 40 percent to the Dalai Lama Trust for charitable pur-
poses, 30 percent to the local organizing group for charitable use, and
30 percent for local or national charitable causes. With a major portion
of the Nobel award, the Dalai Lama established the Foundation for
Universal Responsibility in New Delhi. Headed by Rajiv Mehrotra, the

foundation sponsors a yearly teaching for Indians, which the Dalai
Lama gives in New Delhi, and other events in support of his ethical initiatives within India. Only months before our meeting for this book,
the Dalai Lama visited a colony in Delhi for those with leprosy, where
he promised he would donate several thousand dollars over the next
five years—depending on how much came into his charitable trust
from book royalties (including this one): http://www.dalailama.com
/news/post/1095-dalai-lama-pledges-support-to-leprosy-centers-in
-capital-and-visits-lady-shri-ram-college.

7 **That was years ago . . . (as he has done with his share of the proceeds
from this book):** For this book, Daniel Goleman gave half the royalties
to the Dalai Lama, who has designated the Mind and Life Institute as
the main beneficiary, with a smaller part to the Dalai Lama Trust, his
charitable organization. Daniel Goleman, who has written this book
pro bono, will donate his portion of royalties to a range of charities
from what remains after covering expenses such as travel, transcripts,
and the like.

7 **The next morning the Dalai Lama . . . last until 7:00 A.M. or so (with a
break for breakfast and the BBC):** Despite his constant travels around
the world, and in defiance of jet lag and, presumably, careening bio-
rhythms, the Dalai Lama follows the identical daily schedule, with very
few exceptions.

7 **Meanwhile, his private secretary . . . had often been reluctant to cover
him:** In those days, the Dalai Lama traveled with little fanfare. Josh
Baran, at the time a Hollywood publicist who sometimes did pro bono
work for the Tibetan cause, had tried in previous years to interest various journalists in interviewing the Dalai Lama—with few takers. But
that night a reporter from CBS called Baran at 3:00 A.M. Where in the
world, CBS wanted to know, was the Dalai Lama? The Dalai Lama
was in Newport Beach, California, Baran told CBS. Baran, one of the
few in the world of journalism who knew that answer, hopped in his
car to drive the hour or so south to Newport Beach, as soon as he heard
about the Nobel. He knew the Dalai Lama had just finished a three-
day meeting on compassionate action and was about to start a two-day
dialogue with neuroscientists. Arriving sometime around dawn, he of-

fered his services to Tenzin Geyche Tethong, then the Dalai Lama's personal secretary, and became the organizer of an instant press conference.

8 **I happened to be present for . . . psychotherapists and social activists on compassionate action:** The Dalai Lama, et al. *Worlds in Harmony: Dialogues on Compassionate Action.* Berkeley, Calif.: Parallax Press, 1992. In the early 1980s, Robert Thurman, then a professor at Amherst College, introduced me to the Dalai Lama, who expressed his desire to meet with scientists. That eventually led to the Newport Beach meeting, one of a dozen or so such events I've organized or moderated since.

8 **He had been to many such meetings . . . a yeti who was catching marmots:** The Dalai Lama and Daniel Goleman. *Destructive Emotions: How Can We Overcome Them?* New York: Bantam Books, 2003.

11 **how to fill his ritual role:** The Potala Palace was built by the fifth Dalai Lama in the seventeenth century. Before that, the Dalai Lamas were based at Drepung Monastery outside Lhasa.

12 **autonomy, not independence:** The Dalai Lama's statement was made to the European Parliament in Strasbourg, France, in June 1988.

16 **a better future worldwide:** I intentionally use the term "transformative" rather than the more familiar "transformational" leader. As originally intended by the late historian James MacGregor Burns (who coined the term "transformational leader"), that idea applied to leaders with a world-changing vision. But in common use today, the notion has become diminished, applying instead to leaders who increase people's motivation, job performance, and the like—but offer nothing like a vision that might change the world. And neither term applies to those whom Burns, in contrast, dubbed "transactional" leaders, who are adept at getting things done (LBJ was a prime example of such leadership).

18 **doom-and-gloom messages:** Shellenberger, Michael, and Ted Nordhaus. "The Death of Environmentalism." *Geopolitics, History, and International Relations,* 2009, pp. 121–163.

18 **"seeing things invisible" to other people:** This paraphrases Jonathan Swift, the eighteenth-century British essayist best known for his satirical "A Modest Proposal," from his *Thoughts on Various Subjects from Miscellanies.*

PART TWO:

Looking Inward

CHAPTER TWO: Emotional Hygiene

25 **lengthy scientific career:** Early in Paul Ekman's career, he traveled to New Guinea to study remote Stone Age tribes who had had virtually no contact with the modern world; he wanted to see if basic emotions were expressed the same everywhere and by everybody (he found they are). Another of Ekman's landmark research accomplishments was a complete map of how the twenty or thirty key facial muscles behave when expressing a given emotion: how the frontalis muscle in the forehead tightens while we worry, for instance, or what each of a key half dozen muscles does during happiness or disgust. The map has such precision that automated versions of it are used in research to measure people's emotions, and derivatives of his research are at the heart of computerized programs that give even cartoon figures the right facial expressions (see https://www.paulekman.com/facs/). Ekman first met the Dalai Lama at the 2000 Mind and Life meeting on "destructive emotions," which I moderated, and has since spent many hours in dialogue with him. In 2004 Ekman retired from his post as a professor in psychiatry at the University of California at San Francisco and has continued to be active in the field.

26 **read other people's emotions:** Another app would monitor people's faces while they watched ads on the Web, to tell ad makers which are most compelling. Khatchadourian, Raffi. "We Know How You Feel." *The New Yorker,* January 19, 2015, pp. 50–59.

27 **"faced a lot of problems":** The Dalai Lama was addressing the meeting on Ecology, Ethics, and Interdependence, which I co-organized with John Dunne of Emory University. This twenty-third Mind and Life meeting was held at the Dalai Lama's residence in Dharamsala, India, in 2011. The proceedings of that meeting are being prepared for publication.

27 **"I don't feel much disturbance":** The Dalai Lama, et al. *Worlds in Harmony,* p. 7.

27 **one hallmark of well-being:** Davidson, Richard J. "Well-Being and Affective Style: Neural Substrates and Biobehavioral Correlates." *Philosophical Transactions of the Royal Society B,* 2004, pp. 359, 1449.

28 **healthy place ... destructive side:** This was the focus of the 2000 Mind and Life meeting, which I related in *Destructive Emotions: How Can We Overcome Them?* The phrase "destructive emotions" was the emphatic choice of the Dalai Lama for the topic of the meeting with scientists and for the subsequent book. Though no one in the book business liked the title that much, it raised a crucial point: that every emotion has its place and purpose, but when they capture us in ways that are harmful to ourselves or to those around us, they become destructive. At least that was the rule of thumb proposed by psychologists to demarcate "constructive" and "destructive." The Tibetan perspective was more subtle, seeing emotions as "destructive" when they upset our inner equilibrium and distorted our perception.

29 **"go the wrong way":** The Dalai Lama at the Mind and Life meeting on Ecology, Ethics, and Interdependence.

29 **"or as a friend":** The Dalai Lama spoke in Matera, Italy, on June 25, 2012, as reported by Jeremy Russell (www.dalailama.com). Modern psychology would add the distinction that episodes of anger can be highly appropriate, mobilizing us to deal with an obstacle to our goal. On the other hand, sustained anger and hostility, many studies have found, damage our health, as the Dalai Lama says.

30 **the founder of cognitive therapy:** The Dalai Lama met Dr. Aaron Beck in Gothenburg, Sweden, in 1993, at a world congress on cognitive therapy. Their meeting of minds was strong and warm; when I spoke to the Dalai Lama for this book, he was happy to hear that Dr. Beck was still alive at ninety-three, and soon after he visited Dr. Beck in his home in Philadelphia.

31 **"can ruin lives":** The Dalai Lama and Alexander Norman. *Beyond Religion: Ethics for a Whole World.* New York: Houghton Mifflin Harcourt, 2011, p. 126.

31 **"our own destructive tendencies":** The Dalai Lama and Alexander Norman. *Beyond Religion,* p. 127.

31 **Kevin Ochsner:** Ochsner, Kevin, et al. "Rethinking Feelings: An fMRI

Study of the Cognitive Regulation of Emotion." *Journal of Cognitive Neuroscience,* Vol. 14, 2002, pp. 1215–1229.

32 **reasoning with himself about his negative:** Kevin Ochsner et al. "Rethinking Feelings."

32 **"mindfulness-based cognitive therapy":** Combining mindfulness with cognitive therapy has proved a fruitful tool for reshaping such emotional habits. Research shows this mix helps lessen the frequency and intensity of negative emotions, from the everyday variety to hard-to-treat depression. The first book on this integration for a general audience was written by my wife (Bennett-Goleman, Tara. *Emotional Alchemy.* New York: Harmony Books, 2001). At about the same time, a research group at the University of Oxford published a book about their successful method for treating severe depression (Teasdale, John, et al. *Mindfulness-Based Cognitive Therapy for Depression.* New York: Guilford Press, 2001). There has been an explosion of such books, methods, and teachers since.

33 **a kind of mental radar:** The steps in this chain, roughly speaking, start with our first sensory impression—say, a sound. A next step includes our interpretation of the meaning of that sound, and then the emotions it brings, and finally our overt response. For someone with post-traumatic stress disorder, e.g., any sound reminiscent of the original trauma can unleash a flood of what was felt then. And any of us can have strong emotional habits that work in the same way.

34 **"The one I feed":** I took this version of the tale, which has often been retold (and likely is apocryphal), from Bennett-Goleman, Tara. *Emotional Alchemy,* p. 12.

34 **a psychologist at the University of California:** From Mind and Life XXII, "Neuroplasticity: The Neuronal Substrates of Learning and Transformation," October 18–22, 2004, Dharamsala, India. This meeting was reported on by Sharon Begley (*Train Your Mind, Change Your Brain.* New York: Ballantine Books, 2007). Phillip Shaver directs the Adult Attachment Laboratory at the University of California at Davis.

34 **flavor close adult relationships:** Begley, Sharon. *Train Your Mind.*

35 **"intolerance and lack of compassion":** Phillip Shaver in Begley, Sharon. *Train Your Mind,* p. 202.

35 **lessening destructive emotions:** The Dalai Lama, et al. *Worlds in Harmony.*

36 **take more active charge of our own minds:** Of course, not everyone will want to take charge of the mind in this way, being content with—or just used to—the familiar wash of anger, jealousy, and so on that may provide a partial sense of comfort or personal safety. The Dalai Lama, though, encourages us to shift our emotional economy toward a more positive range of emotions—which takes both effort and motivation. Still, the Dalai Lama invites only those who find this of interest to pursue this path.

36 **chart the way toward self-mastery:** The "map" takes two forms. One focuses on the terrain of our emotions and is under way. The larger effort, a map of the entire mind—which includes emotions—would, as the Dalai Lama envisions it, integrate ancient Indian psychological maps with modern data. This effort, far more ambitious, has just begun (http://www.mindandlife.org/research-and-initiatives-category /mapping-the-mind/).

38 **"emotional script in my life":** The Dalai Lama and Daniel Goleman. *Destructive Emotions,* p. 151.

39 **a transformative experience:** I've described Paul Ekman's life-changing encounter with the Dalai Lama in *Destructive Emotions.*

39 **generating two books:** The Dalai Lama and Paul Ekman. *Emotional Awareness: Overcoming the Obstacles to Psychological Balance and Compassion.* New York: Holt, 2009. Ekman, Paul. *Moving Toward Global Compassion.* San Francisco: Paul Ekman Group, 2014.

39 **from Tibetan contemplative traditions and modern psychology:** Alan Wallace continues to instruct the CEB course for training teachers, with Eve Ekman (see http://www.cultivatingemotionalbalance.org/).

39 **"the compassion he so strongly feels":** Ekman, Paul. "Why I Don't Call the Dalai Lama 'Your Holiness.'" Unpublished reflections, San Francisco, 2013.

40 **anger, fear, disgust, enjoyment, and sadness:** Paul Ekman confirmed that these five are agreed on by a majority of emotion researchers by surveying 248 who had published at least four peer-reviewed articles on emotion in the last four years before 2014.

40 **recent book on meditation:** Harris, Dan. *10% Happier.* New York: HarperCollins, 2014.

40 **"forecloses the possibility that they may change":** The Dalai Lama and

Alexander Norman. *Beyond Religion,* p. 62. The Dalai Lama has been a staunch supporter of Amnesty International's campaign against the death penalty.

42 **much time reflecting on their lives:** But the third trainer, an American ordained as a nun in the Tibetan tradition, was not surprised by the men's openness. She has been working in prisons for more than a decade.

CHAPTER THREE: The Kindness Revolution

44 **"I call him my hero":** Williams, Kimberly. "Dalai Lama's Challenge: A 21st Century of Peace and Compassion." *Emory Report,* October 9, 2013.

45 **caught up in the midst of war:** http://www.childrenincrossfire.org/home.

45 **Moore's close friend:** I'm indebted to Victor Chan for his moving retelling of Richard Moore's tale in his book with the Dalai Lama, *The Wisdom of Compassion.* New York: Riverhead Books, 2012.

45 **"but not your vision":** Moore, Richard. *Can I Give Him My Eyes?* North York, U.K.: Magna Large Print, 2011.

47 **no absolute foundation for ethics:** There remains a rather abstract struggle among modern philosophers of ethics between a moral absolutism and a subjective relativity. The Western approach to ethics is a vast and complicated field (see, for example, MacIntyre, Alasdair. *A Short History of Ethics: A History of Moral Philosophy from the Homeric Age to the Twentieth Century.* Notre Dame, Ind.: University of Notre Dame Press, 1998). One approach that aligns with the Dalai Lama's argues that when we are "wide awake" and so least distorted in our thinking and perceptions, our ethical judgments shift in the direction of compassion. See Davis, Jacob. "Acting Wide Awake: Attention and the Ethics of Emotion." Ph.D. dissertation, City University of New York, February 2014.

48 **"to alleviate the suffering of others":** The Dalai Lama and Alexander Norman. *Beyond Religion,* p. 53.

48 **"for the entire working class on the planet":** While that works as an example of the nonreligious espousing compassion, genuine Marxists too could do better: Global compassion goes beyond feelings for any partic-

ular group—it would include capitalists, those not working, and any-one else, for that matter.

48 **but also implying inclusive:** As the Dalai Lama explains, his use of "sec-ular" implies both religious believers of all faiths and those who hold to no faith. This usage is common in India but sometimes confusing in other parts of the English-speaking world, where "secular" implies "nonreligious."

50 **hardly ever touched, let alone held:** He heard this from the late neuro-scientist Bob Livingston, one of his early tutors in neuroscience. See also Field, Tiffany. *Touch.* Cambridge, Mass.: The MIT Press, 2001. Sadly, these conditions are common among orphaned infants in crowded, un-derstaffed facilities in some countries.

50 **grow up to be more tense and aggressive:** The chimp studies were done by Harry Harlow. Anna Freud was perhaps the first to document the ill effects of separation from parents on the young; the line of research was developed by the British psychiatrist John Bowlby, the developmental psychologist Mary Ainsworth, and continues to this day. See, e.g., Cas-sidy, Jude, and Phillip Shaver, eds. *Handbook of Attachment: Theory, Re-search and Clinical Applications, Second Edition.* New York: Guilford Press, 2010.

51 **while they sit in their mothers' laps:** Hamlin, J. Kiley, et al. "Three-month-olds Show a Negativity Bias in Their Social Evaluations." *De-velopmental Science,* 13, 6, 2010, pp. 923–929; Hamlin, J. Kiley, and Karen Wynn. "Young Infants Prefer Prosocial to Antisocial Others." *Cognitive Development,* 26, 1, 2011, pp. 30–39; Hamlin, J. Kiley, Karen Wynn, and Paul Bloom. "Social Evaluation by Preverbal Infants." *Na-ture,* 450, November 22, 2007. doi:10.1038/nature06288.

51 **try to help the other child in some way:** Zahn-Waxler, Carolyn, et al. "Development of Concern for Others." *Developmental Psychology,* Vol. 28, January 1992, pp. 126–136.

52 **evolution was built around cooperation and altruism:** See, e.g., Warneken, Felix, and Michael Tomasello. "Altruistic Helping in Human Infants and Chimpanzees." *Science,* Vol. 311, No. 5765, 2006, pp. 1301–1303. Also, Goetz, Jennifer L., et al. "Compassion: An Evolu-tionary Analysis and Empirical Review." *Psychological Bulletin,* Vol. 136, No. 3, 2010, pp. 351–374.

52 **"a biological feature of our species":** See Jerome Kagan in Harrington, Anne, and Arthur Zajonc, eds. *The Dalai Lama at MIT.* Cambridge, Mass.: Harvard University Press, 2006. Also, Sober, Eliot, and David Sloan Wilson. *Unto Others: The Evolution and Psychology of Unselfish Behavior.* Cambridge, Mass.: Harvard University Press, 1998.

53 **"guides us toward positive emotions":** The Dalai Lama and Alexander Norman. *Beyond Religion,* p. 47. This line of argument was the topic of a Mind and Life dialogue I moderated in 1990. Goleman, Daniel. *Healing Emotions.* Boston: Shambhala, 1997.

53 **erode both cardiovascular health:** Gallo, Linda, and Karen Matthews. "Understanding the Association Between Socioeconomic Status and Physical Health: Do Negative Emotions Play a Role?" *Psychological Bulletin,* Vol. 129, No. 1, 2003, pp. 10–51.

53 **risk of heart disease:** Fredrickson, Barbara. "Cultivating Positive Emotions to Optimize Health and Well-being." *Prevention and Treatment,* Vol. 3, No. 1, 2000. Published online: http://dx.doi.org/10.1037/1522 -3736.3.1.31a. The research on health and emotions continues to uphold these basic hypotheses; see Uskul, Ayse, and A. D. Horn. "Emotions and Health." *International Encyclopaedia of Social and Behavioral Sciences* (J. Wright, ed.). London: Elsevier, 2015.

53 **a group that cares about one another's well-being:** The Dalai Lama has heard this data on the detrimental impacts of loneliness from many scientists. For a recent summary that connects this to compassion, see Seppala, Emma, et al. "Social Connection and Compassion: Important Predictors of Health and Well-being." *Social Research,* Vol. 80, No. 2, 2013, pp. 411–430.

54 **"Loving is of even greater importance than being loved":** The Dalai Lama and Alexander Norman. *Beyond Religion,* p. 45.

54 **buzzes when we focus on ourselves and our problems:** Lutz, Antoine, et al. "Regulation of the Neural Circuitry of Emotion by Compassion Meditation: Effects of Meditative Expertise," PLoS ONE 3(3): e1897. doi:10.1371/journal.pone.0001897.

56 **"a sense of purpose and meaning in life":** The Dalai Lama and Alexander Norman. *Beyond Religion,* p. 45.

56 **" 'Self-compassion' ":** The Dalai Lama was addressing a conference in 1989; see *Worlds in Harmony.* Since that time, the word has

entered English, and there are programs of psychological research on the topic of self-compassion. See, e.g., Neff, Kristin. "Self-Compassion: An Alternative Conceptualization of a Healthy Attitude Toward Oneself." *Self and Identity,* Vol. 2, 2003, pp. 85–101. The term seems to have been adopted as a reaction against the failed concept of "self-esteem," not because the Dalai Lama suggested it.

56 **"no differences, no distinctions":** Iyer, Pico. *The Open Road: The Global Journey of the Fourteenth Dalai Lama.* New York: Vintage, 2008, p. 91.

58 **"we are all equal in terms of our basic humanity":** The Dalai Lama. *Ethics for the New Millennium.* New York: Riverhead Books, 2001, pp. 28–29.

58 **the Dalai Lama often speaks about:** See, e.g., the Dalai Lama's commentary on Shantideva's *Bodhicaryavatara,* published by Shambhala in 1994: *A Flash of Lightning in the Dark of Night.* The Dalai Lama's vision has been heavily influenced by Shantideva, though he frames it in modern terms with a more universal appeal.

58 **comment on from his own spiritual perspective:** The Dalai Lama. *The Good Heart: A Buddhist Perspective on the Teachings of Jesus.* Somerville, Mass.: Wisdom Publications, 1996.

59 **tolerance, patience, and understanding:** The first text by Shantideva is the *Compendium of All Practices;* the second, *A Guide to the Bodhisattva's Way of Life.* As recounted in *The Good Heart,* pp. 48–49.

59 **based on genetic closeness or surface similarity:** In his book *Moving Toward Global Compassion,* Paul Ekman explores what science needs to learn about compassion, raising around two hundred research questions, including many that would help in the design of evidence-based methods for cultivating global compassion—which, he notes, is one of the hardest kinds to cultivate.

60 **"plans to cultivate warmheartedness and compassion":** The Dalai Lama was addressing the Mind and Life meeting on Ecology, Ethics, and Interdependence.

60 **no religion required:** Still, the Dalai Lama says that among the religious, compassion based on reason and science can be reinforced by faith—they are synergistic.

CHAPTER FOUR: Partnering with Science

62 **a method for cultivating a compassionate attitude:** Weng, Helen Y., et al. "Compassion Training Alters Altruism and Neural Responses to Suffering." *Psychological Science,* Vol. 24, No. 7, 2013, pp. 1171–1180.

63 **and finally for everyone on the planet:** Phrases like these are commonly used in compassion or "loving-kindness" cultivation methods. See, e.g., Jinpa, Thupten. *A Fearless Heart: How the Courage to Be Compassionate Can Transform Our Lives.* New York: Hudson Street Press, 2015.

64 **"spread them very widely":** Goleman, Daniel. *Destructive Emotions,* p. xiv.

64 **being tested at a preschool there:** Flook, Lisa, et al. "Promoting Prosocial Behavior and Self-Regulatory Skills in Preschool Children Through a Mindfulness-Based Kindness Curriculum." *Developmental Psychology,* advance online publication, November 10, 2014, http://dx .doi.org/10.1037/a0038256. See also http://www.investigatinghealthy minds.org/pdfs/Kindness%20Curriculum%20Study.pdf.

66 **than can any religious faith:** The Dalai Lama. *The Universe in a Single Atom.* New York: Harmony, 2006. Another area of collaboration he envisions research on is contemplative practices and their behavioral and neural impacts.

66 **acting both as science adviser and tutor:** Around 1987, Bob Livingston tailor-made a primer on brain science and biology for the Dalai Lama, who by 1989 was telling a group that science had found "we need affection for our brains to develop properly. This shows that our very nature is involved with affection, love, and compassion." The Dalai Lama, et al. *Worlds in Harmony,* p. 19.

67 **the "ancient Indian psychology" to which the Dalai Lama refers:** I spent fifteen months in India as a Harvard pre-doctoral traveling fellow. The main text I studied was by Buddhaghosa (Ven. Nanamoli, translator. *Visuddhimagga: The Path of Purification.* Berkeley, Calif.: Shambhala, 1976). My copy had been printed in Varanasi, India, by Motilal Banarsidass, a venerable Indian scholarly publisher.

67 **the ups and downs of our inner life:** I was on a Social Science Research Council post-doctoral fellowship and spent half my time in Sri Lanka,

studying with Venerable Nyanaponika Mahathera, and the other half
in Dharamsala, studying at the Library of Tibetan Works and Archives. I summarized parts of this ancient science of the mind in *The
Meditative Mind* (New York: Tarcher/Penguin, 1988).

68 **in the presence of buoyancy and pliancy:** In the "law of opposites," positive states neutralize negative ones. Irritation, for instance, creates a
breeding ground for anger. Its opposite: equanimity. And if we can
apply this antidote when our irritability arises, we can extinguish the
mental sparks that might otherwise ignite a blazing anger. This partial
list of opposites is from my book *The Meditative Mind,* and I offer it
here just to give a rough idea of how one set of mental states opposes
another. For more scholarly accounts of this list of wholesome and unwholesome mental factors from *Abhidhamma* (which is the Pali word;
"Abhidharma" in Sanskrit means literally "manifest knowledge")
sources, see Bodhi, Bhikku. *A Comprehensive Manual of Abhidhamma.*
Kandy, Sri Lanka: Buddhist Publication Society, 2003. Also see Asanga
(Sara Boin-Webb, English translator). *Abhidharmasamuccaya.* Fremont,
Calif.: Asian Humanities Press, 2001.

68 **inclusion in that curriculum:** Lobsang Tenzin Negi directs the initiative. http://www.tibet.emory.edu/.

69 **founded by Varela and businessman Adam Engle:** The third founding
partner, Adam Engle, was the organization's first CEO. I am a board
member and have moderated three of the Mind and Life science dialogues with the Dalai Lama. The current chair of the Mind and Life
board is Thupten Jinpa; Arthur Zajonc is current president. See www
.mindandlife.org.

69 **led a research group at the Centre National de la Recherche Scienti-
fique:** This is France's main national center for scientific research.
While Francisco Varela published more than one hundred scientific ar-
ticles and many academic books, two of his particularly seminal publi-
cations are: Maturana, Humberto, and Francisco Varela. *The Tree of
Knowledge: The Biological Roots of Human Understanding.* Boston:
Shambhala, 1992; and Varela, Francisco, Evan Thompson, and Eleanor
Rosch. *The Embodied Mind: Cognitive Science and Human Experience.*
Cambridge, Mass.: The MIT Press, 1991.

70 **at which Varela was one of the presenters:** Francisco Varela did not

take part in the second Mind and Life meeting, on neuroscience, during which the Dalai Lama learned he had received the Nobel Peace Prize. But in addition to presenting at the third, on destructive emotions, he organized the fourth, on sleeping, dreaming, and dying, and presented at others.

70 **"begin to talk to each other"**: Unpublished conversation between Francisco Varela and Anne Harrington. Paris, France, March 12, 1998.

71 **the *only* data gathered in neuroscience**: Varela, Francisco, Evan Thompson, and Eleanor Rosch. *The Embodied Mind.*

71 **licking and grooming her babies**: The presentation of Michael Meaney's results was at the Mind and Life meeting on neuroplasticity, which was reported in Sharon Begley's book *Train Your Mind, Change Your Brain.*

72 **akin to those of the stressed animals**: Michael Meaney's groups confirmed this hunch in 2009, finding alterations in the DNA of suicide victims who had been abused in childhood. McGowan, Patrick, et al. "Epigenetic Regulation of the Glucocorticoid Receptor in Human Brain Associates with Childhood Abuse." *Nature Neuroscience,* Vol. 12, 2009, pp. 342–348.

73 **"I'd be a farmer"**: The Dalai Lama went on to add that he might even have been drafted into the PLA, the People's Liberation Army, since his hometown area is now technically within China, though culturally Tibetan. His interest in philosophy, consciousness, the mind, and so on, he added, is largely due to his monastic education.

74 **literally off psychiatry's charts**: Goleman, Daniel. "The Dalai Lama Has Ideas for Neuroscience." *The New York Times,* Week in Review, October 8, 1989, p. 1.

74 **from the medical clinic to the office and classroom**: Kabat-Zinn, Jon, and Richard J. Davidson (eds.). *The Mind's Own Physician: A Scientific Dialogue with the Dalai Lama on the Healing Power of Meditation.* Oakland, Calif.: New Harbinger Books, 2011. Kabat-Zinn, Jon. *Full Catastrophe Living: Using the Wisdom of Your Body and Mind to Face Stress, Pain, and Illness.* New York: Bantam Books, revised edition, 2013.

76 **suitable for anyone**: For Compassion Cultivation Training, see Thupten Jinpa's *A Fearless Heart.* The Library of Tibetan Classics: http://www

.tibetanclassics.org/en/our-projects/library-of-tibetan-classics-lotc. Thupten Jinpa holds an advanced monastic degree in Buddhist philosophy as well as a doctorate in religious studies from Cambridge University. That deep-breathing technique for calming down, for example, adapts a Tibetan practice, a way to calm and focus before beginning a meditation session.

76 **Stanford's Center for Compassion and Altruism Research and Education:** Directed and founded by Dr. James Doty in 2009. http://ccare .stanford.edu/ccare/.

76 **their spouses reported them to be less angry:** Ruchelli, G., et al. "Compassion Meditation Training for People Living with Chronic Pain and Their Significant Others: A Pilot Study and Mixed-methods Analysis" (abstract). *The Journal of Pain,* Vol. 15, No. 4, supplement, 2014. Jazaieri, H., et al. "A Randomized Controlled Trial of Compassion Cultivation Training: Effects on Mindfulness, Affect, and Emotion Regulation." *Motivation and Emotion,* 2013. Advance online publication. doi: 10.1007/s11031-013-9368-z. These studies did not measure if the compassion exercise actually increased altruist acts.

76 **strengthening their connections with family and friends:** Fredrickson, Barbara, et al. "Open Hearts Build Lives: Positive Emotions, Induced Through Loving-kindness Meditation, Build Consequential Personal Resources." *Journal of Personality and Social Psychology,* Vol. 95, 2008, pp. 1045–1062.

76 **in the face of stress:** Pace, Thaddeus W. W., et al. "Effect of Compassion Meditation on Neuroendocrine, Innate Immune and Behavioral Responses to Psychosocial Stress." *Psychoneuroendocrinology,* Vol. 34, 2009, pp. 87–98. That pilot study, which was based on correlations, is currently being followed up with a longitudinal design to better assess the longer-term impacts of cultivating compassion.

76 **lowered levels of stress hormones:** Pace, Thaddeus W. W., et al. Op cit. Pace, Thaddeus W. W. "Engagement with Cognitively-Based Compassion Training Is Associated with Reduced Salivary C-reactive Protein from Before to After Training in Foster Care Program Adolescents." *Psychoneuroendocrinology,* Vol. 38, No. 2, 2012, pp. 294–299.

77 **enhanced the activity of different neural systems:** Klimecki, Olga, et al.

"Differential Pattern of Functional Brain Plasticity After Compassion and Empathy Training." *Social Cognitive and Affective Neuroscience Advance Access,* May 9, 2013, doi:10.1093/scan/nst060. Taking advantage of this finding, Singer's group has embarked on an ambitious research project, where one hundred volunteers are being trained in three ways. For three months they practice presence, using a breath meditation and body scan; for another three they practice cognitive empathy, understanding the views of another person (via a dyadic meditation); in the third they cultivate compassion and caring. http://www.resource -project.org/en/home.html.

77 **for feeling pain and anguish:** Klimecki, Olga, et al. Op cit.

77 **Cultivating Emotional Balance program at their hospital:** Eve Ekman's work as a medical social worker, with, e.g., staff in emergency rooms, inspired her to become a post-doctoral fellow at the University of California's medical school in San Francisco. There she plans to adapt CEB in shortened formats more readily used in medical settings.

78 **builds resiliency instead of burnout:** Klimecki, Olga, et al. "Functional Neural Plasticity and Associated Changes in Positive Affect After Compassion Training." *Cerebral Cortex,* published online June 5, 2013, doi: 10.1093/cercor/bhs142.

78 **burnout inoculation:** On the other hand, while short-term training in compassion enhanced empathy with the suffering, it had its limits. If the person in need was also rude, the compassion training did not result in helping. Condon, Paul. "Cultivating Compassion: The Effects of Compassion- and Mindfulness-based Meditation on Pro-social Mental States and Behavior." Ph.D. dissertation, Northeastern University, 2014. Early results on the positive effects of cultivating compassion are encouraging. But, as Paul Ekman reminds us, science has just begun to understand the best ways to enhance compassion—and the global variety seems the biggest challenge.

79 **"The pain will have won":** As reported by Daniel Siegel.

PART THREE:

Looking Outward

CHAPTER FIVE: A Muscular Compassion

85 **his T-shirts fray from use:** The flip-flops and fraying T-shirt were noted by Thomas Laird, co-author with the Dalai Lama of *The Story of Tibet: Conversations with the Dalai Lama* (New York: Grove Press, 2007).

85 **a million-dollar landscaping job:** See, e.g.: http://www.washingtonpost .com/news/morning-mix/wp/2014/03/28/how-the-bishop-of-bling-spent -43-million-renovating-this-house/; http://www.reuters.com/article /2014/03/26/us-vatican-germany-idUSBREA2P0SJ20140326; http://en.wikipedia.org/wiki/Franz-Peter_Tebartz-van_Elst; http:// ncronline.org/blogs/francis-chronicles/pope-francis-i-would-love -church-poor.

86 **"no ethics is disastrous":** "Bangalore, Karnataka, India 6 January 2014." Blog by Jeremy Russell at www.dalailama.org.

86 **"We must act":** The first time I heard this from the Dalai Lama— which he often repeats—was at the 1989 *Harmonia Mundi* meeting. The Dalai Lama, et al. *Worlds in Harmony,* p. 96.

87 **"more likely to hit the target directly!":** The Dalai Lama, et al. *Worlds in Harmony,* p. 113.

88 **upsetting emotions like anger:** The Dalai Lama and Paul Ekman. *Emotional Awareness.* Lazarus, Richard. *Stress and Emotion: A New Synthesis.* New York: Springer, 2006.

88 **"of practical benefit":** From the Dalai Lama's foreword. Kochhar, Sangeeta. *My Life, My Words: Remembering Mahatma Gandhi.* New Delhi: Natraj, 2007.

89 **"the strength to face challenges":** The Dalai Lama at the meeting on Ecology, Ethics, and Interdependence.

89 **"deterrent to wrong motives":** The Dalai Lama at the meeting on Ecology, Ethics, and Interdependence.

91 **"they were setting them up":** John C. Coffee, professor of securities law

at Columbia University, was quoted by Stewart, James B. "Barclays Suit Sheds Light on Trading in the Shadows." *The New York Times,* July 4, 2014, p. B1.

91 **a deep ethical flaw in the culture of the financial industry:** Among the sins some of the world's largest banks have committed in those years and since, a financial journalist writes, are: "Money laundering, market rigging, tax dodging, selling faulty financial products, trampling homeowner rights and rampant risk-taking." Eavis, Peter. "Regulators Size Up Wall Street, with Worry." *The New York Times,* March 12, 2014. http://dealbook.nytimes.com/2014/03/12/questions-are-asked-of-rot-in -banking-culture/?_php=true&_type=blogs&_r=0.

92 **measures of engagement:** Kraus, Michael, and Dacher Keltner. "Signs of Socioeconomic Status." *Psychological Science,* Vol. 20, No. 1, 2009, pp. 99–106.

92 **In the Netherlands:** van Kleef, Gerben A., et al. "Power, Distress, and Compassion." *Psychological Science,* Vol. 19, No. 12, 2008, pp. 1315–1322. While this finding shows the effect in Europe too, we do not know if collectivist cultures such as those in East Asia would also have this empathy gap. That's an empirical question. But the social inequities that gap seems to foster are found worldwide.

94 **generations yet unborn:** Larry Brilliant formulated this well, as I quoted him in my book *Focus* (New York: HarperCollins, 2013, p. 256).

94 **"is going to be of any use to him":** Parel, Anthony J. (ed.). *Gandhi, Freedom, and Self-Rule.* Lanham, Md.: Lexington Books, 2000, p. 15.

95 **"without doing harm":** The Dalai Lama's remarks in New Delhi on September 13, 2012, as reported by Jeremy Russell at www.dalailama .com.

95 **an automaker:** Norris, Floyd. "History Gives Other Cases of G.M.'s Behavior." *The New York Times,* March 27, 2014, p. B1.

98 **the damage individual greed might do:** Elinor Ostrom received a Nobel Prize in economics for documenting how shared resources have been regulated. Ostrom, Elinor. *Governing the Commons: The Evolution of Institutions for Collective Action.* New York: Cambridge University Press, 1990.

98 **"One of the most important things":** The Dalai Lama wrote this in his foreword to Kochhar, *My Life, My Words: Remembering Mahatma Gandhi.*

CHAPTER SIX: Economics as if People Mattered

101 **inequality seems built into the free-market economy:** Piketty, Thomas. *Capital in the Twenty-First Century.* Boston: Harvard University Press, 2014. This technical critique seems to support the notion put forward by Marx that capitalism makes owners (whether of investments or businesses) richer at the expense of workers—those who own little or nothing; the wealthy get richer, the poor even poorer. Economists like Piketty who share this school of thought see this trend as an indictment of a too laissez-faire attitude and envision as correctives governing markets in ways that protect the poor and discourage crony capitalism, for instance.

102 **creating opportunity for individuals:** Brooks, Arthur C. "Capitalism and the Dalai Lama," *The New York Times,* April 17, 2014, http://www .ny-times.com/2014/04/18/opinion/capitalism-and-the-dalai-lama .html. Cynics might see this embrace of compassion by conservatives as mere "spin," associating with an appealing idea to further a political agenda. The proof, as the Dalai Lama might say, will be in actions, not words.

103 **in the world around us:** Layard, Richard, and David M. Clark. *Thrive: The Power of Evidence-Based Psychological Therapies.* London: Allen Lane, 2014. The "revolution" Layard would like to see is the establishment of a church-like organization where people who share the goal of helping people lead happy lives could meet and work together—an expression of applied kindness. Lord Layard was a founder of Action for Happiness, a movement whose members pledge to create more happiness and alleviate misery. As of 2014, the organization had upward of thirty thousand members in one hundred countries.

104 **the financial collapse of 2008:** For the insights of behavioral economics and psychology on this paradox, see, e.g, Kahneman, Daniel. *Thinking, Fast and Slow.* New York: Farrar, Straus and Giroux, 2013. Kahneman, a psychologist, won a Nobel Prize in economics.

105 **dollar a day or less fell by 80 percent:** Sala-i-Martin, Xavier, and Maxim Pinkovskiy. "Parametric Estimations of the World Distribution of Income." Vox, January 22, 2010. http://www.voxeu.org/article/parametric -estimations-world-distribution-income.

105 **on the lower half of the income ladder:** Oxfam. "Wealth: Having It All and Wanting More." Report issued at the World Economic Forum, Davos, Switzerland, January 19, 2015.

107 **"but not for the mind":** The Dalai Lama at the Mind and Life meeting on Ecology, Ethics, and Interdependence.

108 **warned against using it to gauge people's welfare:** Simon Kuznets developed GDP in 1934 for the U.S. Congress, as a tool to steer the economy out of the Great Depression.

108 **life satisfaction in their official statistics:** Layard bases the rationale for assessing well-being on the work of psychologist Edward Diener. "Subjective Well-Being: The Science of Happiness and a Proposal for a National Index." *American Psychologist,* Vol. 55, No. 1, 2000, pp. 34–43. Also see Dolan, Paul, et al. "Measuring Subjective Well-being for Public Policy." United Kingdom Office for National Statistics, February 2011. http://eprints.lse.ac.uk/35420/1/measuring-subjective-wellbeing -for-public-policy.pdf.

109 **rather than simply by financial gain:** Layard, Richard. *Happiness: Lessons from a New Science.* New York: Penguin, 2006.

109 **health and education:** Layard, Richard, and David M. Clark. *Thrive.*

110 **with no particular religious interest:** Action for Happiness can be found at http://www.actionforhappiness.org/.

111 **"This is my life: no life":** Jasmine Hodge-Lake's story came to me in an e-mail from her to Mark Williamson, which he forwarded on to me.

113 **"Our purpose is to make the world a better place":** Ted Barber quoted by Wulkan, Hannah. "Easthampton-Based Business Aims to Provide Marginalized People with Gainful Employment." *Daily Hampshire Gazette,* June 23, 2014, p. C1.

113 **profits, people, and planet:** The accounting framework of a "triple bottom line" adds a company's social and ecological impacts to the standard profit-or-loss math of the bottom line. Along with reporting revenues and costs, the business also evaluates the social and environmental impacts of its operations.

114 **instead of from petroleum:** Cardwell, Diane. "At Patagonia, the Bottom Line Includes the Earth." *The New York Times,* July 30, 2014, p. B1.

115 **giving them steady incomes:** Consider the arc of history at Unilever,

with its roots in Unie, a margarine conglomerate in the Netherlands. As the grandniece of one of that Dutch company's founders told me, at the start of the twentieth century Margarine Unie was a bully, ruthlessly taking over competitors in this new business niche (the formula for margarine, a lower-cost butter substitute made from palm oil, was then a fairly recent discovery). In the 1930s, Margarine Unie merged with another intensive palm-oil user, the British soap maker Lever Brothers, to form Unilever. Fast-forward to the start of the twenty-first century, when Unilever was about to acquire Ben & Jerry's ice cream. An insider's word has it that one of those at the top hoped compassionate DNA from Ben & Jerry's idealism would infect the rest of the company. And, lo and behold, a decade later the new CEO, Paul Polman, announced a major business goal to source raw materials from a half million Third World small farmers.

116 **other tech firms to emulate:** When I last looked at the Salesforce website, more than $65 million had been donated to charities, 22,000 nonprofits and colleges had gotten free or discounted computer services, and every employee got six paid days off a year to volunteer for community service—around 620,000 hours of volunteering. http://www.salesforcefoundation.org/about-us/.

116 **We all could emulate to some extent:** Of course, unlike most of us, the Dalai Lama, as a monk, has spare personal needs, all of which are covered by his host, the government of India. Even so, he immediately gives away any money given to him.

CHAPTER SEVEN: Care for Those in Need

118 **heard throughout much of France:** http://en.wikipedia.org/wiki/Abb%C3%A9_Pierre.

119 **the Emmaus houses for the homeless:** http://emmaus-international.org/.

120 **analyzed by psychologist James Flynn:** Goleman, Daniel. "An Emerging Theory on Blacks' I.Q. Scores." *The New York Times,* April 10, 1988. Nisbett, Richard E., et al. "Intelligence: New Findings and Theoretical Developments." *American Psychologist,* Vol. 67, No. 2, 2012, pp. 130–159.

122 **"an inspiration to us all":** From the Dalai Lama's foreword. Kainthla, Anita. *Baba Amte: A Biography.* New Delhi: Viva Books Private Limited, 2006.

122 **"Charity destroys, work builds":** Baba Amte: http://www.anandwan.in /about-anandwan/baba-amte.html.

122 **Over five thousand residents:** http://en.wikipedia.org/wiki/Anandwan.

128 **the "marshmallow test":** Mischel, Walter. *The Marshmallow Test: Mastering Self-Control.* New York: Little, Brown, 2014.

129 **the wealth of the family they grew up in:** Moffitt, Terrie E., et al. "A Gradient of Childhood Self-control Predicts Health, Wealth, and Public Safety." *PNAS,* Vol. 108, No. 7, 2011, pp. 2693–2698.

129 **particularly those who are disadvantaged:** Heckman, J. J. "Skill Formation and the Economics of Investing in Disadvantaged Children." *Science,* Vol. 312, 2006, pp. 1900–1902.

129 **do well in a tough course:** Yeager, David Scott, and Carol Dweck. "Mindsets That Promote Resilience: When Students Believe That Personal Characteristics Can Be Developed." *Educational Psychologist,* Vol. 47, 2012, pp. 302–314.

129 **predict success:** Duckworth, Angela, et al. "Grit: Perseverance and Passion for Long-term Goals." *Journal of Personality and Social Psychology,* Vol. 92, No. 6, 2007, pp. 1087–1101.

130 **change circumstances for the better:** Deci, Edward, and Richard Ryan. *Intrinsic Motivation and Self-Determination in Human Behavior.* New York: Plenum, 1985.

130 **"hungry and spiritually starving millions":** Parel. *Gandhi, Freedom, and Self-Rule,* p. 15. The emblematic image of Gandhi at the spinning wheel was a symbol of *swaraj*—taking your destiny in your own hands. The spinning wheel, which made yarn from raw wool or cotton, offered a bit of livelihood to India's poverty-stricken rural masses, many of whom had lost jobs as the Indian textile industry foundered in the face of cheaper textiles from British factories. After Gandhi, the rough-hewn *khadi* garments made from that hand-spun fabric took on a new appeal, becoming the uniform of the Congress Party, which ruled India for decades after independence.

130 **tiny tunnels in coal mines:** Kailash Satyarthi's organization, Bachpan Bachao Andolan, does not oppose children working after school with

their parents to help support their family but rather takes on abusive labor practices where children are forced to work rather than attend school. The group has succeeded in an international agreement called GoodWeave, which certifies that rugs are made without such child labor (and so opposes a common practice in many parts of the rug-producing world). Its raids on businesses have freed tens of thousands of children from indentured labor.

132 **"responsibility and leadership"**: The Dalai Lama speaking in London, June 19, 2012, as reported by Jeremy Russell at www.dalailama.com. Among the women leaders the Dalai Lama has personally met and admired, he listed Aung San Suu Kyi, with whom he had been recently in Europe, and Shirin Ebadi, a Nobel Peace Prize winner for her efforts on behalf of women's rights in Iran. He added to the list the late Indira Gandhi, whom he regarded as an able leader; the late Israeli prime minister Golda Meir; and Mary Robinson, formerly president of Ireland, who went on to become the UN High Commissioner for Human Rights and since then has led a range of humanitarian causes.

132 **more strongly in women than in men**: See, e.g., Schulte-Rüther, Martin, et al. "Gender Differences in Brain Networks Supporting Empathy." *Neuroimage,* Vol. 42, No. 1, 2008, pp. 393–403.

132 **than men do**: But when it comes to compassionate action, the research findings are mixed, with no clear female advantage (though see Singer, Tania, et al. "Empathic Neural Responses Are Modulated by the Perceived Fairness of Others." *Nature,* Vol. 439, 2006, pp. 466–469). Matthieu Ricard, reviewing the scientific findings, concluded that men are more likely to act to help another in risky emergency situations, while women are more nurturing in general than are men (Ricard, Matthieu. *Altruism: The Power of Compassion to Change Yourself and the World.* New York: Little, Brown, 2015). Tania Singer, who heads a division of four hundred people at the Max Planck Institute's center for social neuroscience, argues for more women leaders from another angle: Women represent half those on the planet!

133 **more naturally to women**: Social scientists who study gender differences report that any specific behavior can be found in both genders but that the proportions differ. Typically, the distribution for any behavior takes the form of largely overlapping bell curves for men and women.

For compassionate leadership, presumably, this would mean that such a style was more common among women, although a smaller number of men exhibited it too.

133 **replaced its kerosene lamps with solar ones:** Brara, Sarita. "Lead Kindly Light." *The Hindu,* October 30, 2012, http://www.thehindu.com /features/metroplus/society/lead-kindly-light/article4044171.ece.

134 **Roy told the Dalai Lama:** Bunker Roy presented to the Dalai Lama at the Mind and Life meeting on Altruism and Compassion in Economic Systems: A Dialogue at the Interface of Neuroscience, Economics, and Contemplative Science, Zurich, 2010.

135 **at a Mind and Life meeting in Zurich:** Altruism and Compassion in Economic Systems.

CHAPTER EIGHT: Heal the Earth

137 **head of the systems dynamics group at that university:** John Sterman spoke to the Dalai Lama at a meeting on Change-Makers for a Better World, convened by the Dalai Lama Center for Ethics and Transformative Values at MIT, October 2014, http://thecenter.mit.edu/media /videos/.

138 **now teaches at the University of Arizona:** The Dalai Lama has had briefings on our eco-crisis many times, perhaps in most detail at a Mind and Life meeting on Ecology, Ethics, and Interdependence. Diana Liverman presented at that meeting.

139 **the Great Acceleration, which began in the 1950s:** Steffen, Will, et al. "The Anthropocene: Are Humans Now Overwhelming the Great Forces of Nature?" *Ambio,* Vol. 36, No. 8, December 2007, pp. 614–621.

140 **"without so much environmental damage":** The Dalai Lama made these remarks to the Australian Tibet Council in June 2007.

141 **"we must do so before it is too late":** The Dalai Lama. "An Ethical Approach to Environmental Protection." June 5, 1986, statement in recognition of World Environment Day.

141 **told the Dalai Lama at a meeting on the environment:** Dekila Chungyalpa at the meeting on Ecology, Ethics, and Interdependence.

142 **"they take place more stealthily":** The Dalai Lama, in a letter to one hundred mayors around the world who joined in an effort by the orga-

nization Avaaz, committing their cities to 100 percent clean energy by
2050. September 2014.

142 **cyanide over circuit boards to recover gold:** Carroll, Chris. "India's Poor
Risk Health to Mine Electronic 'E-Waste.'" *National Geographic,*
June 28, 2014, http://news.nationalgeographic.com/news/2014/06
/140628-electronics-waste-india-pictures-recycling-environment
-world/.

143 **to the contaminated water released:** See www.goodguide.com for ratings
of consumer products; for cell phones: http://www.goodguide.com
/categories/332304-cell-phones. For the personal-care category,
http://www.ewg.org/skindeep/?gclid=CjwKEAjwjd2pBRDB4o_
ymcieoAQSJABm4egor3LAls7fKwsVP4-fJOlmemDM_
0T07TadFRaM5GwrtRoClmPw_wcB ranks cosmetics according to the
toxicity of their ingredients. I go into more detail on ecological transparency in *Ecological Intelligence: How Knowing the Hidden Impacts of What
We Buy Can Change Everything* (New York: Broadway Books, 2009).

143 **dangerous for laborers and local communities alike:** Sibaud, Philippe.
"Short Circuit: The Lifecycle of Our Electronic Gadgets and the True
Cost to Earth." London: Gaia Foundation, 2013.

144 **Social Hotspots Database:** http://socialhotspot.org.

145 **more efficient cooking stoves to families in Ghana:** On Gregory Norris's recommendation, I chose www.climatecare.org as a reliable source
of my carbon offsets. The cooking stoves in Ghana are but one example
of a wide suite of carbon-reducing endeavors supported by my offset
purchase.

146 **switched off the light:** Iyer, Pico. *The Open Road.*

147 **and so keeps us going:** www.handprinter.org. Gregory Norris also presented to the Dalai Lama at the meeting on Ecology, Ethics, and Interdependence.

147 **who smelt coltan into tantalum:** See http://www.enoughproject.org/files
/minetomobile.pdf. On the other hand, many companies in the industry
are trying to police their supply chain; see http://www.microsoft.com/en
/mobile/about-us/people-and-planet/supply-chain/supply-chain/.

147 **they should be in school:** http://socialhotspot.org/.

148 **lower their impacts:** The handprinter learning community operates
through the Sustainability and Health Initiative for NetPositive Enter-

prise (SHINE). See http://www.chgeharvard.org/category/corporate
-sustainability-and-health-shine-0.

149 **a total savings of six hundred dollars:** The program asks those who get
the blankets to share with the school $45, which buys two more blan-
kets at wholesale from Owens Corning; these are then donated to the
same project at two other schools—plus net $4,500 for the school itself.
After five rounds, the thirty-two schools that participated would collect
a total of $140,000.

149 **the root system of mushrooms:** http://www.ted.com/talks/eben_bayer
_are_mushrooms_the_new_plastic.

152 **suggested systems thinking:** As I've argued in a book with Peter Senge,
education should add three kinds of "focus": helping children
strengthen attention and self-regulation skills like cognitive control; enhancing caring and compassion; and imparting an understanding of the
systems we inhabit, from relationships to how human systems degrade
the global systems that support life on the planet. Goleman, Daniel, and
Peter Senge. *The Triple Focus: A New Approach to Education.*
Northampton, Mass.: More ThanSoundMedia, 2014.

152 **"They are our real hope":** The Dalai Lama at the meeting on Ecology,
Ethics, and Interdependence.

CHAPTER NINE: A Century of Dialogue

156 **"a century of dialogue":** The Dalai Lama, speaking to leaders of youth
organizations in Manchester, England, June 16, 2012, www.dalailama
.com.

156 **"the best levers":** Dekila Chungyalpa, at the twenty-third Mind and
Life meeting, 2011.

157 **"your health is my health":** http://www.examiner.com/review/the-dalai
-lama-shares-his-vision-compassion-without-borders-at-sdsu.

158 **rather than focusing on our differences:** See the Dalai Lama's books *Beyond Religion* (with Alexander Norman) and *Toward a True Kinship of
All Faiths* (New York: Random House, 2011).

160 **with responses from a quarter of a million people:** Pettigrew, Thomas,
and Linda Tropp. "A Meta-analytic Test of Intergroup Contact The-

ory." *Journal of Personality and Social Psychology,* Vol. 90, No. 5, 2006, pp. 751–783.

161 **"showing concern about others brings benefit to us":** The Dalai Lama, et al. *Worlds in Harmony,* pp. 18–19.

162 **protect his people and their cultural heritage:** In 2001, the Dalai Lama introduced a system for electing the Tibetan people's political leader for their government-in-exile. The Dalai Lama then semi-retired, though he still had a nominal leadership role. In 2011, he fully abdicated, ending the age-old tradition of the Dalai Lama institution's temporal leadership.

164 **"in our day-to-day life":** From the Dalai Lama's foreword. Desai, Narayan. *My Life Is My Message.* Hyderabad: Orient BlackSwan, 2009.

164 **"may not be the best solution in the long run":** The Dalai Lama's statement on the first anniversary of September 11, 2001; remarks at the National Cathedral, Washington, D.C.

167 **"when people manipulate religion":** The Dalai Lama at the meeting on Ecology, Ethics, and Interdependence. In this respect, the Dalai Lama observes, there is more honesty in the stance of atheists and the antireligious. At least they are open about their lack of belief and negativity toward religion.

167 **restrain yourself from harming anyone:** The Dalai Lama addressing local Muslims in Leh, Ladakh, India, July 16, 2014, www.dalailama.com.

168 **are disastrous:** The Dalai Lama's statement on the first anniversary of the September 11, 2001, attacks.

169 **"ended up being much more beneficial":** Dekila Chungyalpa at the Ecology, Ethics, and Interdependence meeting.

170 **"a simple necessity":** The Dalai Lama, May 17, 2012, Maribor, Slovenia.

172 **According to Ayer's biography:** Rogers, Ben. *A. J. Ayer: A Life.* London: Chatto & Windus, 1999. The story is told on p. 344.

173 **from kindergarten up through high school:** Carlsson-Paige, Nancy, and Linda Lantieri. "A Changing Vision for Education." *Educating Citizens for Global Awareness* (Nel Noddings, ed.). New York: Teachers College Press, 2005.

174 **enhance acceptance and appreciate diversity:** The peaceable classroom

curriculum was developed by Educators for Social Responsibility, Metro Area, now called the Morningside Center for Teaching Social Responsibility.

175 **a new sheepskin coat:** Raymond's story was told to me by Linda Lantieri and appears in her book (Lantieri, Linda, and Janet Patti. *Waging Peace in Our Schools.* Boston: Beacon Press, 1996, p. 62).

CHAPTER TEN: Educate the Heart

179 **her concentration level:** The device represents a new generation of biosensors; this one derives a metric for concentration from a single EEG sensor worn on the forehead.

180 **crucial for the readiness to learn:** Ochsner, Kevin N., and James J. Gross. "The Cognitive Control of Emotion." *Trends in Cognitive Science,* Vol. 9, No. 5, 2005, pp. 242–249.

182 **"So how can we bring balance to this":** The Dalai Lama made this remark at the Ecology, Ethics, and Interdependence meeting.

184 **two books with the Dalai Lama:** The Dalai Lama and Victor Chan. *The Wisdom of Forgiveness.* New York: Riverhead Books, 2005. Dalai Lama and Victor Chan, *The Wisdom of Compassion.*

184 **90 percent of schools in British Columbia had such programs:** These include Roots of Empathy, a program that aims to boost empathy and kindness, which is taught throughout the province's schools. Friends of Life extends that to listening and open communication and is taught by around six thousand teachers; more than three thousand teach MindUp, which cultivates attention skills like mindfulness.

184 **in short, emotional hygiene and compassion:** See www.casel.org.

185 **and being attentive:** http://dalailamacenter.org/about/heart-mind.

185 **and offer activities beyond the school day:** See Best Practices at www.casel.org.

185 **their cardiovascular health improves:** Oberle, Eva, et al. "The Role of Supportive Adults in Promoting Positive Development in Middle Childhood: A Population-based Study." *Canadian Journal of School Psychology,* published online June 22, 2014. Schreier, Hannah M. C., et al.

"Effect of Volunteering on Risk Factors for Cardiovascular Disease in Adolescents: A Randomized Control Trial." *JAMA Pediatrics,* published online February 25, 2013.

186 **among the students who needed help most:** Durlak, Joseph A., et al. "The Impact of Enhancing Students' Social and Emotional Learning: A Meta-analysis of School-based Universal Interventions." *Child Development,* Vol. 82, No. 1, 2011, pp. 474–501.

187 **Call to Care:** Makransky, John, and Brooke Dodson-Lavelle. "Embodying Care: Three Practices That Help Us Receive, Develop, and Extend Care." http://www.mindandlife.org/research-and-initiatives/embodying -care/.

189 **give SEL a strengthened knowledge base:** Goleman, Daniel. "The Future of Social and Emotional Learning." *Handbook of Social and Emotional Learning: Research and Practice* (Joseph A. Durlak, ed.). New York: The Guilford Press, 2015.

PART FOUR:

Looking Back, Looking Ahead

CHAPTER ELEVEN: The Long View

193 **"When I was born in 1935":** The Dalai Lama speaking in Milan, June 26, 2012, www.dalailama.com.

195 **"may yet come to pass":** Morris, Ian. "War, What Is It Good For? Just Look Around You." *New Scientist,* April 19, 2014, p. 31. Morris, Ian. *War! What Is It Good For?* New York: Farrar, Straus and Giroux, 2014. Pinker, Steven. *The Better Angels of Our Nature.* New York: Penguin, 2012.

195 **"as they do now":** The Dalai Lama was speaking at the Nobel Laureates' Peace Summit in Italy, as reported on www.dalailama.com, December 14, 2014.

195 **"to create a happier world":** Dalai Lama at Matera, Italy, June 25, 2012. See www.dalailama.com.

197 **"of true benefit to people both in Tibet and abroad":** The Dalai

Lama's statement on the first anniversary of the September 11, 2001, attacks.

198 **far greater than the aggression actually acted out:** This mental exercise was proposed to the Dalai Lama by the Harvard professor Jerome Kagan. See Harrington, Anne, and Arthur Zajonc, eds. *The Dalai Lama at MIT.*

198 **or to alert us to potential threats:** Goleman, Daniel. "Down with Reptilian News!" *Columbia Journalism Review,* Vol. 28, No. 3, September/October 1989, p. 60.

199 **may take this charge to heart:** There are some notable exceptions, like *Yes!* magazine, which reports on solutions rather than just problems, and the website Upworthy, which is among an increasing number of compassion-, solution-, and positivity-oriented media. And given the emergence of alternative pipelines for information, like social media, there are other ways to raise the visibility of the forces for good in our world. Within mainstream media, a model for the solutions-oriented coverage the Dalai Lama encourages might be Justin Gillis ("Restored Forests Breathe Life into Efforts Against Climate Change." *The New York Times,* December 23, 2014, page 1).

201 **and plant a tree to grow there:** When Baba Amte died, his body was buried next to a bamboo grove. As his son, Dr. Vikas Amte, explained, Baba Amte "wanted every particle of his body to be useful to humanity. He felt his burial would add to the organic content in soil, whereas the usual cremation rites would pollute river waters." Dr. Vikas Amte, quoted in "Baba Amte Bidden Adieu with Full Honours." *IBN Live,* February 11, 2008. http://ibnlive.in.com/news/baba-amte-bidden-adieu -with-full-honours/58614-1.html.

202 **"funeral for the future":** http://www.anandwan.in/about-anandwan /baba-amte.html.

202 **at the American University in Cairo:** El-Saadani, Somaya M. (Associate Professor of Demographics and Biostatistics). "Characteristics of a Poor Urban Setting in Egypt: Ein El-Sira," January 2008.

203 **being able to nominate students as fellows:** See http://www .dalailamafellows.org/.

204 **who renounced working on weapons:** The scientist was Alvin Weinberg (my uncle), who became the director of Oak Ridge National Laboratory, a center of the "atoms for peace" initiatives that developed, for example, nuclear medicine. Weinberg's insistence on finding safer designs for nuclear reactors and warning of the dangers of storing nuclear waste resulted in his being fired by the Nixon administration. He then founded the Institute for Energy Analysis in 1974, one of the first scientific centers to study the relationship between energy production and global warming.

206 **"that will make a difference":** The Dalai Lama said this at the Mind and Life meeting on Ecology, Ethics, and Interdependence. Still, he recognizes that such efforts are a luxury for the very poor, who struggle to survive day to day. As Elke Weber, a cognitive scientist, told him at that meeting, "If our immediate needs are taken care of, we can afford the luxury of being concerned about the future."

207 **they might become life-saving masts:** Unfortunately, the Norfolk pines did not prove to have the strength required for masts. A later plan to use Norfolk pines for plywood was vetoed as not sustainable, though they are still used by island artists and for wood turning.

207 **"over time humanity can change":** The Dalai Lama was speaking at the Mind and Life meeting on Ecology, Ethics, and Interdependence.

CHAPTER TWELVE: Act Now

210 **"depends on patience":** The Dalai Lama's statement on behalf of Aung San Suu Kyi, May 8, 2000.

211 **"bigger and bigger":** The Dalai Lama, et al. *Worlds in Harmony,* p. 125.

213 **"that joy has been my solution":** Dekila Chungyalpa at the Mind and Life meeting on Ecology, Ethics, and Interdependence.

215 **"we can have an enormous impact":** The Dalai Lama, et al. *Worlds in Harmony,* p. 125.

216 **to today's environmental crisis:** Marshall Ganz participated in Change-Makers for a Better World, organized by Tenzin Priyadarshi and his

Dalai Lama Center for Ethics and Transformative Values at MIT, October 31, 2014.

217 **we all know the feeling:** Schnall, Simone, et al. "Elevation Leads to Altruistic Behavior." *Psychological Science,* Vol. 20, No. 20, 2010, pp. 1–6.

219 **"community is nothing but individuals combined":** The Dalai Lama, et al. *Worlds in Harmony,* p. 125.

ABOUT THE AUTHOR

Daniel Goleman, a former science journalist for the *New York Times*, is the author of many books, including the international bestseller *Emotional Intelligence*. He co-founded the Collaborative for Academic, Social and Emotional Learning at the Yale University Child Studies Center (now at the University of Illinois at Chicago). He lives in Massachusetts.

@DanielGolemanEI
danielgoleman.info

ABOUT THE TYPE

This book was set in Granjon, a modern recutting of a typeface produced under the direction of George W. Jones (1860–1942), who based Granjon's design upon the letterforms of Claude Garamond (1480–1561). The name was given to the typeface as a tribute to the typographic designer Robert Granjon (1513–89).